BIOMEDICAL ETHICS

Opposing Viewpoints®

OTHER BOOKS OF RELATED INTEREST

OPPOSING VIEWPOINTS SERIES

Abortion
AIDS
Alcohol
Chemical Dependency
Constructing a Life Philosophy
Death & Dying
Euthanasia
Genetic Engineering
Health and Fitness
Health Care in America
Mental Illness
Science & Religion
Suicide
Tobacco and Smoking

CURRENT CONTROVERSIES SERIES

The Abortion Controversy
Alcoholism
Assisted Suicide
The Disabled
Ethics
Genetics and Intelligence
Reproductive Technologies
Smoking
Teen Addiction

AT ISSUE SERIES

Cloning
Physician-Assisted Suicide
Smoking
The Spread of AIDS

BIOMEDICAL ETHICS
Opposing Viewpoints®

David L. Bender, *Publisher*
Bruno Leone, *Executive Editor*
Brenda Stalcup, *Managing Editor*
Scott Barbour, *Senior Editor*
Tamara L. Roleff, *Book Editor*

OPPOSING
VIEWPOINTS®
SERIES

Greenhaven Press, Inc., San Diego, California

Cover photo: Photodisc

Library of Congress Cataloging-in-Publication Data

Biomedical ethics : opposing viewpoints / Tamara L. Roleff, book editor.
    p.   cm. — (Opposing viewpoints series)
    Includes bibliographical references and index.
    ISBN 1-56510-792-6 (pbk. : alk. paper). —
ISBN 1-56510-793-4 (lib. : alk. paper)
    1. Medical ethics. 2. Genetic engineering—Moral and ethical as-
pects. I. Roleff, Tamara L., 1959–   . II. Series: Opposing viewpoints
series (Unnumbered)
R724.B492 1998
174'.2—dc21   97-51374
                                                          CIP

Greenhaven Press, Inc., P.O. Box 289009
San Diego, CA 92198-9009

"CONGRESS SHALL MAKE NO LAW...ABRIDGING THE FREEDOM OF SPEECH, OR OF THE PRESS."

First Amendment to the U.S. Constitution

The basic foundation of our democracy is the First Amendment guarantee of freedom of expression. The Opposing Viewpoints Series is dedicated to the concept of this basic freedom and the idea that it is more important to practice it than to enshrine it.

CONTENTS

WHY CONSIDER OPPOSING VIEWPOINTS?

"The only way in which a human being can make some approach to knowing the whole of a subject is by hearing what can be said about it by persons of every variety of opinion and studying all modes in which it can be looked at by every character of mind. No wise man ever acquired his wisdom in any mode but this."

John Stuart Mill

In our media-intensive culture it is not difficult to find differing opinions. Thousands of newspapers and magazines and dozens of radio and television talk shows resound with differing points of view. The difficulty lies in deciding which opinion to agree with and which "experts" seem the most credible. The more inundated we become with differing opinions and claims, the more essential it is to hone critical reading and thinking skills to evaluate these ideas. Opposing Viewpoints books address this problem directly by presenting stimulating debates that can be used to enhance and teach these skills. The varied opinions contained in each book examine many different aspects of a single issue. While examining these conveniently edited opposing views, readers can develop critical thinking skills such as the ability to compare and contrast authors' credibility, facts, argumentation styles, use of persuasive techniques, and other stylistic tools. In short, the Opposing Viewpoints Series is an ideal way to attain the higher-level thinking and reading skills so essential in a culture of diverse and contradictory opinions.

In addition to providing a tool for critical thinking, Opposing Viewpoints books challenge readers to question their own strongly held opinions and assumptions. Most people form their opinions on the basis of upbringing, peer pressure, and personal, cultural, or professional bias. By reading carefully balanced opposing views, readers must directly confront new ideas as well as the opinions of those with whom they disagree. This is not to simplistically argue that everyone who reads opposing views will—or should—change his or her opinion. Instead, the series enhances readers' understanding of their own views by encouraging confrontation with opposing ideas. Careful examination of others' views can lead to the readers' understanding of the logical inconsistencies in their own opinions, perspective on why they hold an opinion, and the consideration of the possibility that their opinion requires further evaluation.

EVALUATING OTHER OPINIONS

To ensure that this type of examination occurs, Opposing Viewpoints books present all types of opinions. Prominent spokespeople on different sides of each issue as well as well-known professionals from many disciplines challenge the reader. An additional goal of the series is to provide a forum for other, less known, or even unpopular viewpoints. The opinion of an ordinary person who has had to make the decision to cut off life support from a terminally ill relative, for example, may be just as valuable and provide just as much insight as a medical ethicist's professional opinion. The editors have two additional purposes in including these less known views. One, the editors encourage readers to respect others' opinions—even when not enhanced by professional credibility. It is only by reading or listening to and objectively evaluating others' ideas that one can determine whether they are worthy of consideration. Two, the inclusion of such viewpoints encourages the important critical thinking skill of objectively evaluating an author's credentials and bias. This evaluation will illuminate an author's reasons for taking a particular stance on an issue and will aid in readers' evaluation of the author's ideas.

As series editors of the Opposing Viewpoints Series, it is our hope that these books will give readers a deeper understanding of the issues debated and an appreciation of the complexity of even seemingly simple issues when good and honest people disagree. This awareness is particularly important in a democratic society such as ours in which people enter into public debate to determine the common good. Those with whom one disagrees should not be regarded as enemies but rather as people whose views deserve careful examination and may shed light on one's own.

Thomas Jefferson once said that "difference of opinion leads to inquiry, and inquiry to truth." Jefferson, a broadly educated man, argued that "if a nation expects to be ignorant and free . . . it expects what never was and never will be." As individuals and as a nation, it is imperative that we consider the opinions of others and examine them with skill and discernment. The Opposing Viewpoints Series is intended to help readers achieve this goal.

David L. Bender & Bruno Leone,
Series Editors

INTRODUCTION

"The way bioethics works is that all the questions of right and wrong aren't always all up for grabs at the same time."
—Arthur Caplan, New York Times Magazine,
December 15, 1996.

Much of the world was in shock when Ian Wilmut and his colleagues announced in February 1997 that they had taken a cell from a ewe's udder and cloned a sheep named Dolly. After reviewing the issue, the National Bioethics Advisory Commission recommended a five-year moratorium on human cloning in the United States to allow further study of cloning technology and ethics. A few months later, in December 1997, Wilmut's lab in Scotland announced that they had cloned two more sheep, Molly and Polly, this time with human blood-clotting proteins in their milk. The proteins will be extracted from the milk and used to treat human hemophilia. Wilmut's experiment was repeated in January 1998 when researchers in Texas announced they had cloned calves whose milk produced the human serum albumin, a protein that is critical for burn patients and those suffering from liver disease. Wilmut and other researchers hope the cloned sheep and cows will become "living pharmaceutical factories" for blood proteins. Cloned animals with the human proteins are more desirable than animals that have the proteins added to their cells at a later time, scientists maintain, because the cloned animals produce the human proteins more consistently.

Further news revealed that cloning research has risen to a more disturbing level. In January 1998 physicist Richard Seed of Chicago announced that he intended to clone a human being by mid-1999. All he needs to successfully clone a human, he maintains, is $2 million, a suitable laboratory, and willing DNA donors. He expects that up to 10,000 infertile couples will use his services.

The prospect of an eccentric scientist attempting to clone humans is exactly what many bioethicists and researchers feared. In fact, some claim that in vitro fertilization (IVF)—the fertilization of an egg outside the human body—was just the first step to some serious ethical dilemmas, including eugenics, in which an embryo's genes are manipulated to produce a child with the desired eye or hair color or with enhanced physical prowess or intelligence. Another fear is that a human will be cloned to provide organs for transplants for its genetic twin, if needed.

A *Los Angeles Times* editorial echoed the beliefs of many ethicists, scientists, and policy makers when it stated "such doomsday scenarios are bunk." Critics assert that human cloning is simply not an ethical or practical solution to infertility under any circumstances. They point out that it took 276 attempts to finally clone the sheep embryo that became Dolly. Some of Wilmut's 276 cloned embryos were born seriously deformed or died shortly after birth. Most people would find the risk to or use of that many human embryos unacceptable, they maintain, and therefore human research is not a possibility.

Others believe that, practical drawbacks aside, biomedical research should continue unrestrained. At a senate hearing on cloning, Tom Harkin, a senator from Iowa, argued that those who want to stop research on human cloning should "take your ranks alongside Pope Paul V, who in 1616 tried to stop Galileo" from publishing his theory that the earth orbited the sun. Others assert that science should proceed as far as it wants, and if something offends public sensibilities, then laws can be passed to prohibit certain procedures, if necessary. However, it appears that near-universal revulsion of human cloning among scientists, researchers, and the public will prevent the cloning of humans for eugenics or for their organs.

The ethical dilemmas presented in the arguments over human cloning are equally present in all the issues covered in *Biomedical Ethics: Opposing Viewpoints*. This book explores the relationship between ethics and medical science in the following chapters: Is Human Cloning Ethical? What Ethics Should Guide Organ Donations? Are Reproductive Technologies Ethical? What Ethics Should Guide Genetic Research? The authors in this anthology examine the advancements in medical science that have benefited many people but have also raised troubling questions over whether science has gone too far.

CHAPTER 1

IS HUMAN CLONING ETHICAL?

CHAPTER PREFACE

The February 1997 announcement that a sheep named Dolly had been born from a cloned adult mammary cell touched off a fierce scientific debate about the ethics of cloning. While frogs had been cloned from tadpoles since 1952, mice from embryos since 1970, and sheep and cattle from embryos since 1979, never before had a mammal been cloned from a somatic cell.

To create Dolly, Ian Wilmut, Keith Campbell, and their colleagues at the Roslin Institute in Scotland used a process called nuclear transfer. They removed the nucleus from a mammary cell and placed it into an egg cell which had had its DNA removed. After starving the egg cell of nutrients, the nucleus and donor cell were fused with an electrical charge and the egg was implanted into a surrogate sheep. Most scientists considered Dolly's birth a giant breakthrough in biomedical research.

Dolly's creators see cloning as an easier way to produce sheep, cows, and other animals with desired genetic traits. In December 1997, for example, the same scientists announced that they cloned two sheep with a human blood-clotting protein that can be used to treat human hemophilia. These animals can then be bred to produce a larger herd with the protein.

Scientists and ethicists who support Wilmut and Campbell maintain that their work has exciting implications for biomedical research. For example, Colin Stewart, director of a cancer research laboratory in Frederick, Maryland, speculates that if nerve cells can be cloned, it may be possible to someday regenerate damaged nerve cells in a human.

Many scientists and bioethicists regard Dolly's birth and the technology that produced it with alarm. They especially fear these techniques will be applied to humans, perhaps used to clone humans for spare parts or replace a dead or dying child with its genetic equivalent. Others maintain that cloning violates the sanctity of life by placing creation in the hands of humans, rather than God, and therefore should be banned.

Although scientists argue that these techniques could not be applied to humans yet, debate over whether human cloning research should be explored continues. The National Bioethics Advisory Commission, asked by Bill Clinton to study the ethical and legal implications of human cloning, recommended a three- to five-year moratorium on human cloning research to give the public time to debate and examine the issues involved. The authors in the following chapter explore the merits of human cloning and whether the risks involved outweigh the benefits.

"*As is nearly always the case with scientific advances, the likely potential benefits vastly outweigh the possible risks.*"

THE BENEFITS OF CLONING OUTWEIGH THE RISKS

Richard T. Hull

In the following viewpoint, Richard T. Hull contends that the cloning of a sheep in Scotland is an extraordinary scientific advance that should be pursued. Although not enough is known yet about cloning to try it on humans, Hull asserts that many of people's fears about human cloning are unfounded. Moreover, the development and future use of cloning technology could have enormous benefits for humans. Hull, a philosophy professor at the State University of New York in Buffalo, has written numerous articles on medical ethics, reproduction, and genetics.

As you read, consider the following questions:

1. How does Hull respond to the argument that cloning will weaken human diversity?
2. Why will narcissists and egomaniacs be disappointed with cloning, according to the author?
3. In Hull's opinion, how should people with religious scruples respond to the cloning debate?

Reprinted from "No Fear," by Richard T. Hull, *Free Inquiry*, Summer 1997, by permission of the Council for Democratic and Secular Humanists.

My typical reaction to noteworthy scientific advances is amazement and joy: amazement at the complexity of scientific knowledge and its rate of expansion, joy at living in a time when there is so much promise offered by science for having a major impact on human destiny. As a humanist, I see the ability of my species to manage its own evolution to be one of its most wonderful emerging properties, an ability that distinguishes humans from every other species. So I am deeply suspicious of attempts to impose bans on specific efforts to extend to humans new technologies achieved in animal models.

THE POWER OF SCIENCE

The modern biological journey we are on, viewed unclouded by irrational fears and sweeping theological generalizations, is truly extraordinary. The cloning of a female sheep in Scotland stands as testimony to the power of the scientific method. Again and again, things we seem to know are overturned by the scientific testing of those knowledge claims. The cloning of Dolly from nucleus material taken from a cell of her progenitor's udder and inserted into an unfertilized egg (sans nucleus) was stunning. It refuted the widely held belief that the specialization of cells that goes on through the development and maintenance of an organism is an irreversible, linear process.

Such a belief underlies the distinction many held between a fertilized ovum and a body cell. People found it tempting to call the former an individual human being, the latter merely an individual human cell because of the supposed difference in potential. But now we know that most of our cells have the potential, if situated and manipulated appropriately, to generate an individual human being. We have yet to hear from the theologians on this point, but my guess is that the status of the fertilized ovum in such circles is going to have to be fundamentally rethought as a result of this advance. Once again, when science and faith have been put to the test, beliefs generated by faith have not survived. The production of Dolly is on a par with Galileo pointing his telescope at the moon and seeing mountains and craters.

Nor do I view kindly the efforts of the Clinton administration to block the extension of this technology to humans. I hope the intent was a temporary moratorium to permit the President's Commission on Bioethics time to assemble the testimony of a variety of experts and commentators to quiet the fears fanned by the media's sensationalism. But I fear that the result may be a chilling effect on our most advanced researchers in this field.

The similar knee-jerk reaction of the British government in ending the grant to Dr. Ian Wilmut under which Dolly was brought about was alarming. It is implausible to say that the aims of the grant have been completed when the experiment produced but a single sheep out of several hundred attempts. Such a success is but a first indicator of possibilities, not the perfection of a technology. Withdrawal of funding in the face of the initial reports of the media must give any scientist in this field serious doubts about continuing investigations, even on the remaining questions to be answered in animal models.

UNDETERRED INQUIRY

Those remaining questions, of course, should be answered before proceeding to human applications. They include the question of whether the DNA of an adult animal's cells has "aged." We know that errors of transcription in the DNA of specialized body cells accumulate as those cells divide and are replaced during the animal's life. Such mutations come from environmental factors (radiation, exposure to chemicals) that produce genetic breakage and from errors caused by imperfect replication. And there seems to be a theoretical limit in humans of about 50 cell divisions, after which division of a line of cells ceases and the cells simply age and die. The question these facts pose, then, is whether the DNA of Dolly's progenitor cell, taken from a six-year-old adult ewe's udder, carries with it such signs of aging. We simply don't know whether Dolly was born "six years old" or whether she faces the prospect of a life as lengthy as that of a sheep produced sexually. And we don't know whether Dolly will contract earlier the kinds of cancers and other age-related diseases that sheep produced sexually will.

Moreover, Dolly was the only ewe born of several hundred attempts at the same procedure. Why the procedure worked in roughly 0.3% of the cases and none of the others needs to be understood. The technology of cloning must be improved before it is commercially viable in animal husbandry, let alone appropriate to try in humans.

So while I think the technology should continue to be developed, it would not be appropriate to try it yet on a human. No serious scientist would attempt to do so without the above risks being substantially reduced and without the success rate substantially improved.

Should such matters be controlled by governmental panels? Governmental panels are poor substitutes for the good sense and open communications of scientists working towards the same goal. What possible expertise does a congressman or senator have that is relevant to the question of whether the technology is good enough to try on a human? Such "solons"—wise lawgivers—are not dedicated to the rational advance of scientific questions—at least, not as their prime mission. They are, for the most part, motivated to reflect the interests of the strongest contributors among the groups they represent. And the presidency is also subject to pressures of media sensationalism, special interest groups, and polls.

FALSE ALARMS

Contrast the humanistic view of cloning with some of the more irrational concerns raised about Dolly and the prospect of cloning humans.

Handicapped infants will surely be the unavoidable result of early cloning attempts. If the standard of producing no damaged, handicapped infants were the litmus test of a method of human reproduction, the species should have stopped sexual reproduction long ago since it is the chief source of such unfortunates!

Cloning humans will contravene nature's wisdom in constantly mixing the human gene pool. The claim here is that having children genetically identical with their parents and grandparents and great-grandparents will eventually weaken human diversity and deny future generations the benefits of what in the plant world is called "hybrid vigor." I have mentioned the two questions that are related to the genetic health and longevity of cloned individuals, and they must surely be answered before we proceed to introduce the technology into human reproduction. But just as the presence of carrots in the human diet doesn't mean we will necessarily all turn yellow from overindulgence in carotene-bearing foods, so the presence of cloning in medicine's arsenal doesn't mean that at some future date all humans will be clones of past generations. As an expensive medical therapy, cloning will have a small number of takers. And the worry associated with its development is no greater than the worries associated with the development of in vitro fertilization, or artificial inseminations, and probably considerably less than those associated with surrogacy.

NO EXACT COPIES

Egomaniacal individuals will have themselves cloned to achieve a kind of immortality. We already know enough about the interaction between heredity and environment to know that it's impossible to reproduce all the influences that go into the making of an individual. Big egos may seize upon cloning as a kind of narcissistic self-recreation just as individuals now seize upon sexual reproduction as a kind of narcissistic self-recreation. When people do have children for narcissistic reasons, they are usually disappointed that the children don't turn out as their parents did. Because of the essentially unreproducible nature of environmental influences, cloning won't be any more successful at producing copies of their progenitors than sexual reproduction is. Yet another disappointment for big egos!

Reprinted with permission of Don Addis.

Cloning will be used to create embryos that can be frozen, then thawed and gestated as organ farms for their progenitors to harvest when facing major organ failure. This interesting worry—interesting because it may have some basis—deserves serious reflection. Given the way the fact of cloning transforms the question of the special status of the fertilized ovum, we may be on the verge of rethinking the whole question of what abortion is. If even the most conservative positions must now reopen the question of when the individual human begins, we may come to see harvesting fetal organs to be more like taking specialized cells from a culture than like taking organs from a baby.

MASTERING THE GENETIC CODE
But the more interesting possibility is that the development of cloning technology will be accompanied by mastery of the genetic code by which genes are turned on or off to sequence specialization. It may be possible in the future to clone individual organs without having to employ the medium of the fetus. Such a process should be faster than a nine-month gestation, and the availability of artificial womb technology (or some equivalent

suitable for organ cloning) would make possible enormously important advances in organ transplantation that would be free of the complications of immune system suppression necessary for transplanting genetically non-identical organs. So while there are potential moral problems and temptations along the way, we should not recoil from them. As is nearly always the case with scientific advances, the likely potential benefits vastly outweigh the possible risks.

Those with religious scruples concerning cloning and other future biomedical technologies need not employ them. Plenty of existing children need adoption; a more rational routine retrieval practice for transplantable organs would increase the supply; real wombs, whether owned or rented, will continue to provide an ample supply of human babies. Those of us who see the future of humankind in evolving greater and greater control over our destinies, who see human strivings and human achievements as the source of humanity's value, say this: cancel the executive orders, unchain our science, minimize its regulation, and let us rejoice in its fruits.

"The significant risks to the fetus and physical well-being of a child created by . . . cloning outweigh arguably beneficial uses of the technique."

THE RISKS OF HUMAN CLONING OUTWEIGH THE BENEFITS

National Bioethics Advisory Commission

The National Bioethics Advisory Commission (NBAC) was established by Bill Clinton in 1995 to provide advice and make recommendations on such bioethical issues as using human research subjects and what limits to place on genetic engineering. When Scottish scientists announced in February 1997 that they had cloned an adult sheep, Clinton directed the NBAC to prepare a report on the legal and ethical issues involved in cloning. In the following viewpoint excerpted from its report, the NBAC contends any possible benefits of cloning are outweighed by the risks involved. The NBAC maintains, however, that if human cloning does proceed, cloned people should be granted the same rights and moral status as any other human.

As you read, consider the following questions:

1. What are some of the risks involved in human somatic cell nuclear transfer cloning, according to the commission?
2. In the opinion of the NBAC, what is problematic about arguments claiming that human cloning experiments are beneficial to the resulting child?
3. What does it mean to objectify a person, according to the commission? Why might this happen to a clone?

Reprinted from Cloning Human Beings: Report and Recommendations of the National Bioethics Advisory Commission, Rockville, Maryland, June 1997.

There is one basis of opposition to somatic cell nuclear transfer cloning on which almost everyone can agree. [A somatic cell is any cell of the embryo, fetus, child, or adult which contains a full complement of two sets of chromosomes; in contrast with a germ cell, i.e., an egg or a sperm, which contains only one set of chromosomes. During somatic cell nuclear transfer cloning, the nucleus—which contains a full set of chromosomes—is removed from the somatic cell and transferred to an egg cell which has had its nucleus removed.] There is virtually universal concern regarding the current safety of attempting to use this technique in human beings. Even if there were a compelling case in favor of creating a child in this manner, it would have to yield to one fundamental principle of both medical ethics and political philosophy—the injunction, as it is stated in the Hippocratic canon, to "first, do no harm." In addition, the avoidance of physical and psychological harm was established as a standard for research in the Nuremberg Code, 1946-49. At this time, the significant risks to the fetus and physical well-being of a child created by somatic cell nuclear transplantation cloning outweigh arguably beneficial uses of the technique.

It is important to recognize that the technique that produced Dolly the sheep was successful in only 1 of 277 attempts. If attempted in humans, it would pose the risk of hormonal manipulation in the egg donor; multiple miscarriages in the birth mother; and possibly severe developmental abnormalities in any resulting child. Clearly the burden of proof to justify such an experimental and potentially dangerous technique falls on those who would carry out the experiment. Standard practice in biomedical science and clinical care would never allow the use of a medical drug or device on a human being on the basis of such a preliminary study and without much additional animal research. Moreover, when risks are taken with an innovative therapy, the justification lies in the prospect of treating an illness in a patient, whereas, here no patient is at risk until the innovation is employed. Thus, no conscientious physician or Institutional Review Board should approve attempts to use somatic cell nuclear transfer to create a child at this time. For these reasons, prohibitions are warranted on all attempts to produce children through nuclear transfer from a somatic cell at this time.

A DIFFERENCE OF OPINION

Even on this point, however, NBAC [National Bioethics Advisory Committee] has noted some difference of opinion. Some argue, for example, that prospective parents are already allowed to con-

ceive, or to carry a conception to term, when there is a significant risk—or even certainty—that the child will suffer from a
serious genetic disease. Even when others think such conduct is
morally wrong, the parents' right to reproductive freedom takes
precedence. Since many of the risks believed to be associated
with somatic cell nuclear transfer may be no greater than those
associated with genetic disorders, some contend that such
cloning should be subject to no more restriction than other
forms of reproduction.

And, as in any new and experimental clinical procedure,
harms cannot be accurately determined until trials are conducted in humans. Law professor John Robertson noted before
NBAC on March 13, 1997 that:

> [The] first transfer [into a uterus] of a human [embryo] clone
> [will occur] before we know whether it will succeed. . . . [Some
> have argued therefore] that the first transfers are somehow un-
> ethical . . . experimentation on the resulting child, because one
> does not know what is going to happen, and one is . . . possibly
> leading to a child who could be disabled and have developmen-
> tal difficulties. . . . [But the] child who would result would not
> have existed but for the procedure at issue, and [if] the intent
> there is actually to benefit that child by bringing it into being
> . . . [this] should be classified as experimentation for [the
> child's] benefit and thus it would fall within recognized excep-
> tions. . . . We have a very different set of rules for experimenta-
> tion intended to benefit [the experimental subject].

But the argument that somatic cell nuclear transfer cloning
experiments are "beneficial" to the resulting child rest on the
notion that it is a "benefit" to be brought into the world as
compared to being left unconceived and unborn. This metaphysical argument, in which one is forced to compare existence
with non-existence, is problematic. Not only does it require us
to compare something unknowable—non-existence—with
something else, it also can lead to absurd conclusions if taken to
its logical extreme. For example, it would support the argument
that there is no degree of pain and suffering that cannot be inflicted on a child, provided that the alternative is never to have
been conceived. Even the originator of this line of analysis re-
jects this conclusion.

In addition, it is true that the actual risks of physical harm to
the child born through somatic cell nuclear transfer cannot be
known with certainty unless and until research is conducted on
human beings. It is likewise true that if we insisted on absolute
guarantees of no risk before we permitted any new medical inter-

vention to be attempted in humans, this would severely hamper if not halt completely the introduction of new therapeutic interventions, including new methods of responding to infertility. The assertion that we should regard attempts at human cloning as "experimentation for [the child's] benefit" is not persuasive. . . .

CLONING AND INDIVIDUALITY

The concept of creating a genetic twin, although separated in time, is one aspect of somatic cell nuclear transfer cloning that most find both troubling and fascinating. The phenomenon of identical twins has intrigued human cultures across the globe, and throughout history. It is easy to understand why identical twins hold such fascination. Common experience demonstrates how distinctly different twins are, both in personality and in personhood. At the same time, observers cannot help but imbue identical bodies with some expectation that identical persons occupy those bodies, since body and personality remain intertwined in human intuition. With the prospect of somatic cell nuclear transfer cloning comes a scientifically inaccurate but nonetheless instinctive fear of multitudes of identical bodies, each housing personalities that are somehow less than distinct, less unique, and less autonomous than usual.

Is there a moral or human right to a unique identity, and if so would it be violated by this manner of human cloning? For such somatic cell nuclear transfer cloning to violate a right to a unique identity, the relevant sense of identity would have to be genetic identity, that is a right to a unique unrepeated genome. Even with the same genes, two individuals—for example homozygous twins—are distinct and not identical, so what is intended must be the various properties and characteristics that make each individual qualitatively unique and different than others. Does having the same genome as another person undermine that unique qualitative identity?

IGNORANCE AND KNOWLEDGE

Along these lines of inquiry some question whether reproduction using somatic cell nuclear transfer would violate what philosopher Hans Jonas called a right to ignorance, or what philosopher Joel Feinberg called a right to an open future, or what Martha Nussbaum called the quality of "separateness." Jonas argued that human cloning, in which there is a substantial time gap between the beginning of the lives of the earlier and later twin, is fundamentally different from the simultaneous beginning of the lives of homozygous twins that occur in nature.

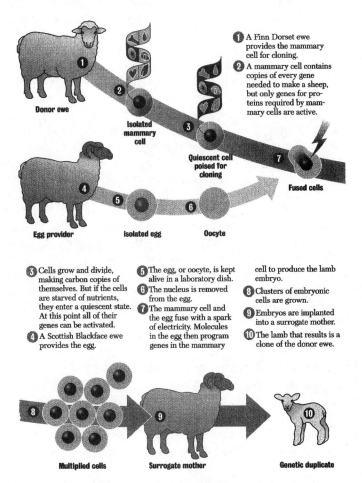

1. A Finn Dorset ewe provides the mammary cell for cloning.
2. A mammary cell contains copies of every gene needed to make a sheep, but only genes for proteins required by mammary cells are active.

Donor ewe

Isolated mammary cell

Quiescent cell poised for cloning

Fused cells

Egg provider

Isolated egg

Oocyte

3. Cells grow and divide, making carbon copies of themselves. But if the cells are starved of nutrients, they enter a quiescent state. At this point all of their genes can be activated.
4. A Scottish Blackface ewe provides the egg.
5. The egg, or oocyte, is kept alive in a laboratory dish.
6. The nucleus is removed from the egg.
7. The mammary cell and the egg fuse with a spark of electricity. Molecules in the egg then program genes in the mammary cell to produce the lamb embryo.
8. Clusters of embryonic cells are grown.
9. Embryos are implanted into a surrogate mother.
10. The lamb that results is a clone of the donor ewe.

Multiplied cells

Surrogate mother

Genetic duplicate

Although contemporaneous twins begin their lives with the same genetic inheritance, they also begin their lives or biographies at the same time, in ignorance of what the twin who shares the same genome will by his or her choices make of his or her life. To whatever extent one's genome determines one's future, each life begins ignorant of what that determination will be, and so remains as free to choose a future as are individuals who do not have a twin. In this line of reasoning, ignorance of the effect of one's genome on one's future is necessary for the spontaneous, free, and authentic construction of a life and self.

A later twin created by cloning, Jonas argues, knows, or at least believes he or she knows, too much about him or herself. For there is already in the world another person, one's earlier twin, who from the same genetic starting point has made the life choices that are still in the later twin's future. It will seem that one's life has already been lived and played out by another, that one's fate is already determined, and so the later twin will lose the spontaneity of authentically creating and becoming his or her own self. One will lose the sense of human possibility in freely creating one's own future. It is tyrannical, Jonas claims, for the earlier twin to try to determine another's fate in this way.

And even if it is a mistake to believe such crude genetic determinism according to which one's genes determine one's fate, what is important for one's experience of freedom and ability to create a life for oneself is whether one thinks one's future is open and undetermined, and so still to be largely determined by one's own choices. One might try to interpret Jonas' objection so as not to assume either genetic determinism, or a belief in it. A later twin might grant that he or she is not destined to follow in his or her earlier twin's footsteps, but that nevertheless the earlier twin's life would always haunt the later twin, standing as an undue influence on the latter's life, and shaping it in ways to which others' lives are not vulnerable. . . .

POTENTIAL HARMS TO IMPORTANT SOCIAL VALUES

Those with grave reservations about somatic cell nuclear transfer cloning ask us to imagine a world in which cloning human beings via somatic cell nuclear transfer were permitted and widely practiced. What kind of people, parents, and children would we become in such a world? Opponents fear that such cloning to create children may disrupt the interconnected web of social values, practices, and institutions that support the healthy growth of children. The use of such cloning techniques might encourage the undesirable attitude that children are to be valued according to how closely they meet parental expectations, rather than loved for their own sake. In this way of looking at families and parenting, certain values are at the heart of those relationships, values such as love, nurturing, loyalty, and steadfastness. In contrast, a world in which such cloning were widely practiced would give, the critics claim, implicit approval to vanity, narcissism, and avarice. To these critics, changes that undermine those deeply prized values should be avoided if possible. At a minimum, such undesirable changes should not be fostered by public policies. . . .

TREATING PEOPLE AS OBJECTS

Some opponents of somatic cell nuclear cloning fear that the resulting children will be treated as objects rather than as persons. This concern often underlies discussions of whether such cloning amounts to "making" rather than "begetting" children, or whether the child who is created in this manner will be viewed as less than a fully independent moral agent. In sum, will being cloned from the somatic cell of an existing person result in the child being regarded as less of a person whose humanity and dignity would not be fully respected?

One reason this discussion can be hard to capture and to articulate is that certain terms, such as "person," are used differently by different people. What is common to these various views, however, is a shared understanding that being a "person" is different from being the manipulated "object" of other people's desires and expectations. Writes legal scholar Margaret Radin,

> The person is a subject, a moral agent, autonomous and self-governing. An object is a non-person, not treated as a self-governing moral agent. . . . [By] "objectification of persons," we mean, roughly, "what Kant would not want us to do."

That is, to objectify a person is to act towards the person without regard for his or her own desires or well-being, as a thing to be valued according to externally imposed standards, and to control the person rather than to engage her or him in a mutually respectful relationship. Objectification, quite simply, is treating the child as an object—a creature less deserving of respect for his or her moral agency. Commodification is sometimes distinguished from objectification and concerns treating persons as commodities, including treating them as a thing that can be exchanged, bought or sold in the marketplace. To those who view the intentional choice by another of one's genetic makeup as a form of manipulation by others, somatic cell nuclear transfer cloning represents a form of objectification or commodification of the child.

Some may deny that objectification is any more a danger in somatic cell nuclear transfer cloning than in current practices such as genetic screening or, in the future perhaps, gene therapy. These procedures aim either to avoid having a child with a particular condition, or to compensate for a genetic abnormality. But to the extent that the technology is used to benefit the child by, for example, allowing early preventive measures with phenylketonuria, no objectification of the child takes place.

When such cloning is undertaken not for any purported benefit of the child himself or herself, but rather to satisfy the vanity of the nucleus donor, or even to serve the need of someone else, such as a dying child in need of a bone marrow donor, then some would argue that it goes yet another step toward diminishing the personhood of the child created in this fashion. The final insult, opponents argue, would come if the child created through somatic cell nuclear transfer is regarded as somehow less than fully equal to the other human beings, due to his or her diminished physical uniqueness and the diminished mystery surrounding some aspects of his or her future, physical development.

Eugenic Concerns

The desire to improve on nature is as old as humankind. It has been played out in agriculture through the breeding of special strains of domesticated animals and plants. With the development of the field of genetics over the past 100 years came the hope that the selection of advantageous inherited characteristics—called eugenics, from the Greek *eugenes* meaning wellborn or noble in heredity—could be as beneficial to humankind as selective breeding in agriculture.

The transfer of directed breeding practices from plants and animals to human beings is inherently problematic, however. To begin, eugenic proposals require that several dubious and offensive assumptions be made. First, that most, if not all people would mold their reproductive behavior to the eugenic plan; in a country that values reproductive freedom, this outcome would be unlikely absent compulsion. Second, that means exist for deciding which human traits and characteristics would be favored, an enterprise that rests on notions of selective human superiority that have long been linked with racist ideology.

Equally important, the whole enterprise of "improving" humankind by eugenic programs oversimplifies the role of genes in determining human traits and characteristics. Little is known about the correlation between genes and the sorts of complex, behavioral characteristics that are associated with successful and rewarding human lives; moreover, what little is known indicates that most such characteristics result from complicated interactions among a number of genes and the environment. While cows can be bred to produce more milk and sheep to have softer fleece, the idea of breeding humans to be superior would belong in the realm of science fiction even if one could conceive how to establish the metric of superiority, something that turns not only on the values and prejudices of those who construct the metric but also on the sort of a world they predict these specially bred persons would face.

Nonetheless, at the beginning of this century eugenic ideas were championed by scientific and political leaders and were very popular with the American public. It was not until they were practiced in such a grotesque fashion in Nazi Germany that their danger became apparent. Despite this sordid history and the very real limitations in what genetic selection could be expected to yield, the lure of "improvement" remains very real in the minds of some people. In some ways, creating people through somatic cell nuclear transfer offers eugenicists a much more powerful tool than any before. In selective breeding programs, such as the "germinal choice" method urged by the geneticist H.J. Muller a generation ago, the outcome depended on the usual "genetic lottery" that occurs each time a sperm fertilizes an egg, fusing their individual genetic heritages into a new individual. Cloning, by contrast, would allow the selection of a desired genetic prototype which would be replicated in each of the "offspring," at least on the level of the genetic material in the cell nucleus.

OBJECTIONS TO A EUGENICS PROGRAM

It might be enough to object to the institution of a program of human eugenic cloning—even a voluntary program—that it would rest on false scientific premises and hence be wasteful and misguided. But that argument might not be sufficient to deter those people who want to push the genetic traits of a population in a particular direction. While acknowledging that a particular set of genes can be expressed in a variety of ways and therefore that cloning (or any other form of eugenic selection) does not guarantee a particular phenotypic manifestation of the genes, they might still argue that certain genes provide a better starting point for the next generation than other genes.

The answer to any who would propose to exploit the science of cloning in this way is that the moral problems with a program of human eugenics go far beyond practical objections of infeasibility. Some objections are those that have already been discussed in connection with the possible desire of individuals to use somatic cell nuclear transfer that the creation of a child under such circumstances could result in the child being objectified, could seriously undermine the value that ought to attach to each individual as an end in themselves, and could foster inappropriate efforts to control the course of the child's life according to expectations based on the life of the person who was cloned.

In addition to such objections are those that arise specifically because what is at issue in eugenics is more than just an individual act, it is a collective program. Individual acts may be undertaken for singular and often unknown or even unknowable reasons, whereas a eugenics program would propagate dogma about the sorts of people who are desirable and those who are dispensable. That is a path that humanity has tread before, to its everlasting shame. And it is a path to whose return the science of cloning should never be allowed to give even the slightest support. . . .

Cloning Is Unethical

In summary, the Commission reached several conclusions in considering the appropriateness of public policies regarding the creation of children through somatic cell nuclear transfer. First and foremost, creating children in this manner is unethical at this time because available scientific evidence indicates that such techniques are not safe at this time. Even if concerns about safety are resolved, however, significant concerns remain about the negative impact of the use of such a technology on both individuals and society. Public opinion on this issue may remain divided. Some people believe that cloning through somatic cell nuclear transfer will always be unethical because it . . . will always risk causing psychological or other harms to the resulting child. In addition, although the Commission acknowledged that there are cases for which the use of such cloning might be considered desirable by some people, overall these cases were insufficiently compelling to justify proceeding with the use of such techniques. . . .

Finally, many scenarios of creating children through somatic cell nuclear transfer are based on the serious misconception that selecting a child's genetic makeup is equivalent to selecting the child's traits or accomplishments. A benefit of more widespread discussion of such cloning would be a clearer recognition that a person's traits and achievements depend heavily on education, training, and the social environment, as well as on genes. Should this type of cloning proceed, however, any children born as a result of this technique should be treated as having the same rights and moral status as any other human being.

| "There could be rare circumstances in the future where cloning technology would have medical benefits."

CLONING RESEARCH COULD BE BENEFICIAL TO HUMANS

Nature Genetics

The editors of *Nature Genetics*, a monthly magazine, maintain in the following viewpoint that although human cloning would be repugnant and inhuman, cloning research could result in medical technology that would be beneficial to humans. Moreover, the editors conclude, even if humans were cloned, they would merely look like each other, not be exact copies.

As you read, consider the following questions:

1. What was the reaction in Great Britain to the news that a sheep had been cloned, according to the author?
2. According to a poll cited by the editors of *Nature Genetics*, what percentage of Americans would clone themselves?
3. What could be some of the medical benefits of cloning research, in the editors' opinion?

Reprinted from the editorial "Clone Encounters," *Nature Genetics*, vol. 15, no. 4, April 1997, pp. 323–24, by permission of Nature America, Inc.

Film buffs attending *Alien 4: Resurrection*, which opens in 1997, will be able to marvel at the ingenuity of scientists and screenwriters alike as Ripley, the plucky heroine, who died at the end of *Alien³*, is miraculously revived by a process of 'tissue cloning'. But what was once merely a scriptwriter's convenient contrivance now has an uncanny shimmer of truth about it, thanks to the revolutionary work of Ian Wilmut and colleagues at Scotland's Roslin Institute, whose findings were published in the February 27, 1997, issue of *Nature*. Wilmut's team successfully created a lamb named Dolly by transferring the DNA of an adult mammary gland cell into an enucleated oocyte. Equally impressive in scientific terms, although rather overlooked in the stampeding media coverage, the Scottish team also reported three births from clones derived from fetal fibroblast cells [specialized cells, such as those in organs]. By manipulating the stage at which the donor and recipient cells were fused, Wilmut's team defied the conventional wisdom, based in part on work on amphibians in the early 1970s, that it would be impossible to re-programme a fully differentiated cell. If that wasn't enough, just one week after Dolly became the most famous sheep in history, Don Wolf and co-workers at the Oregon Regional Primate Research Center revealed that they had cloned rhesus monkeys from embryo cells (an achievement similar to that reported by Wilmut's group with sheep in 1996), which brought the spectre of applying cloning techniques to humans a little bit closer.

THE REACTION

The reaction to Dolly has spanned all facets of public opinion. In an extraordinarily ill-timed and ill-conceived decision, Britain's Ministry of Agriculture, which has funded Wilmut's work since the mid-1980s, said that it would terminate its support next year. "The commitment was never long-term," said a ministry spokesman. "Perhaps if the project is to progress, then it is up to industry to look at the commercial elements and fund it that way." Presumably, this is exactly what PPL Therapeutics, which holds a licence for the cloning work, will do. In the United States, President Bill Clinton, who will receive a report on cloning from his National Bioethics Advisory Commission in June 1997 [the commission recommended a three- to five-year moratorium on human cloning research], banned all government funding for human cloning research, and urged privately funded foundations and industry to follow suit (an act one correspondent to the *New York Times* likened to "living at the time of Galileo's breakthrough and . . . banning the telescope").

CLONING COULD HELP WITH TRANSPLANTS

With cloning, it may be possible to add human genes encoding a clotting factor, hormone, or other useful protein to thousands of cells in culture rather than inject such genes into a much smaller number of fertilized eggs. This would enable researchers to assess the results in vitro and select only the most promising candidates, such as cells with particularly high expression of desired protein, to clone into individual animals.

If successful, this approach also could be applied to generating transgenic pigs and other animals bearing human surface antigens on their tissues to make them more acceptable by the immune systems of organ transplant recipients.

Joan Stephenson, *JAMA*, April 12, 1997.

Public opinion on human cloning is highly sceptical, although, in one poll, 7 per cent of Americans said they would clone themselves if given the chance. Many scientists, including the Roslin researchers, have used terms such as "offensive" and "repugnant" in reference to human cloning. However, while the ethical and technical barriers to cloning may prove insurmountable, two issues are worth keeping in mind. First, there could be rare circumstances in the future where cloning technology would have medical benefits. Harold Varmus, the director of the National Institutes of Health, recently told a congressional committee that infertility might be one such example. Second, a clone would indisputably *not* be identical to the person it was derived from. One scientist amused a congressional hearing by noting that although a hypothetical clone of the actor Mel Gibson would look just like him, it is Gibson's "charm and personality" that make him who he is. A transplanted nucleus would develop in a different cytoplasmic milieu, the fetus in a different womb, the embryo (and child) in a unique environment. "This triumph of genetic engineering," writes David Berreby of Dolly, "might well mark the defeat of the idea that genes determine who and what we are." Applying the recently reported cloning successes will help create improved transgenic animals for biotechnology and reduce the numbers of animals necessary for medical studies. Noting the technical as well as ethical complexities, Wilmut (an agnostic) says that "to contemplate using our present technique on humans would be quite inhuman". He is absolutely right, but it is important that society not prematurely deny itself the potentially profound insights into mammalian development and medical benefits that Dolly heralds.

| "There is no reason . . . to start the
more ethically problematic research
into human cloning."

CLONING RESEARCH WOULD NOT BENEFIT HUMANS

Kevin T. Fitzgerald

Kevin T. Fitzgerald argues in the following viewpoint that human cloning research should be banned as it would be of no benefit. Human cloning is too risky for its human subjects; it will not replace a dead or dying child, nor will it ease the pressure of reproductive choices, he contends. Furthermore, Fitzgerald asserts that cloning humans for their organs is manipulative and diminishes the value of a human being. Fitzgerald is a research professor in molecular genetics at Loyola University's Cardinal Bernardin Cancer Center in Chicago.

As you read, consider the following questions:
1. According to Fitzgerald, what are some of the possible benefits of cloning research?
2. In the author's opinion, what may change people's minds about the desirability of human cloning research?
3. Why is human cloning research too risky, in Fitzgerald's view?

Reprinted from "Little Lamb, Who Made Thee?" by Kevin T. Fitzgerald, *America*, March 29, 1997, by permission of the author.

The news that an adult sheep had been successfully cloned has created one common reaction: increasing anxiety about what our societies should and should not do in the face of the dizzying pace of scientific advances.

Even the scientific community itself was caught by surprise, because cloning an adult mammal was thought to be unattainable in the near future, if achievable at all. The surprise quickly changed to excitement as researchers considered the potential benefits this powerful new technology could bring.

SURPRISE AND EXCITEMENT

What caused such surprise and excitement? First, the *surprise*. The key breakthrough was the successful reactivation of *all* the genes required for the development of a new organism in a cell taken from adult tissue that had silenced many of these genes. Cells that perform the specialized tasks of a particular tissue or organ express only those genes necessary for the function of that tissue or organ—in this case sheep mammary tissue. But using one of these cells the researchers of the Roslin Institute in Edinburgh, Scotland, were able to stimulate the genes of this cell so that they could initiate the developmental process of creating a new individual animal.

Second, the *excitement*. By employing this technique, scientists may be able to clone endangered species in order to delay or prevent extinction, or study the processes of mammalian development to investigate the potential for organ regeneration and repair, or discover the mechanisms controlling mammalian gene activation so that genes inappropriately turned on or off in cancer may be reset to their normal levels of activity. Another possibility is the application of this technique to the cloning of humans. It is this startling possibility that has been the focus of much of the recent public discussion.

Now that the cloning of a mammalian adult has been achieved in one species, the consensus is that it could also be achieved in humans. But the vast majority of scientists, ethicists, theologians and politicians have publicly stated that there should be at least a moratorium on human cloning research, if not an outright ban. Public opinion polls have mirrored this response. Yet the more troubling question persists: Within a few years' time, will the medical and reproductive possibilities of human cloning be enticing enough to change public opinion and initiate research into the application of this technology to humans?

These fears are well founded. Research on human cloning would involve substantial risks to the health and welfare of the initial clones, because any research specific to human cloning would eventually have to be carried out on human beings. Moreover, there are the broader societal risks already raised in the public discussion surrounding this issue: the increasing objectification and devaluation of human life (e.g., children viewed as products rather than gifts), the pressure on women and couples to have their own genetically related children and the rebirth of eugenics programs seeking to create super- or sub-human populations. Considering the gravity of these risks, are there presently any compelling reasons for pursuing human cloning?

NO JUSTIFIABLE REASON FOR CLONING

Cloning a human being remains as far away in practice as it ever did. We can find no medically justifiable reason for any such attempts, assuming the technique could be made to work. . . . For the prevention of inherited diseases, existing techniques of in-vitro fertilisation and selective embryo transfer are or will become adequate. Cloning to provide "spare parts" is ethically unacceptable.

Lancet, March 8, 1997.

Several scenarios have been proposed as potentially justifying the use of cloning technology on humans. In general they fall into three categories: producing a clone in order to save the life of an individual who requires a transplant; making available another reproductive option for people who wish to have genetically related children but face physical or chronological obstacles preventing conception through intercourse alone; cloning a child who is dying from a tragic accident or a non-genetic disease in order to create another genetically identical child.

NO REASON FOR RESEARCH

A few general responses can be made to the above proposals. First, from a scientific perspective, solutions to these problems are already possible and are already the focus of current animal research. There is no reason, then, to start the more ethically problematic research into human cloning. Second, and more importantly, social and psychological problems cannot and should not be reduced to genetic or biological solutions. Human cloning will not replace a child, and it will not remove the existing pressures on people making reproductive choices. Finally, cloning a human being solely for the purpose of supplying organs or tissue makes it, at a minimum, a mere instrument for manipulation and negates the human identity of the clone.

But these discussions bring to the surface many of the deep-seated concepts and images people have about who we are and how we are to live together. Fortunately, the Judeo-Christian tradition can offer these discussions three important contributions. It brings careful and thoughtful convictions concerning the nature and purpose of human existence, a long history of practical care for the needs of the global human family and a strong appreciation for the contributions of science. Since scientific discoveries will continue to come at an increasingly rapid pace, these benefits are needed now more than ever, as are the cautions they contain.

| "Cloning . . . establishes an identity for the child which is . . . not freely owned by the child."

CLONING WOULD VIOLATE A PERSON'S INDIVIDUALITY

Allen Verhey

In the following viewpoint, Allen Verhey argues that to allow human cloning simply because it is possible diminishes family relationships by transforming them into contractual obligations. Furthermore, he contends, human cloning would strip the cloned child of whatever choice he or she had in establishing a personal identity. Cloned children could be seen by their parents as a product that could be discarded if it was imperfect, Verhey maintains, and not as a gift from God that should be cherished. Verhey is an ethicist and chairperson of the religion department at Hope College in Holland, Michigan.

As you read, consider the following questions:

1. What does Paul Ramsey think is the most persistent argument in favor of cloning, as cited by Verhey?
2. What is the happiness test for cloning, according to Ramsey?
3. Why would parents see their children as technical achievements instead of gifts from God, in the author's opinion?

Reprinted, by permission, from "Cloning and the Human Family: Theology After Dolly," by Allen Verhey, Christian Century, March 19–26, 1997. Copyright 1997, Christian Century Foundation.

S ome 30 years before the birth of Dolly, the cloned sheep, and
  sometime near the beginnings of bioethics, Nobel laureate
Joshua Lederberg wrote an article for the *American Naturalist*
(September-October 1966) commenting on the prospects for
cloning a human being. Frogs, toads, salamanders and fruit flies
had been cloned, and Lederberg was hospitable to the prospect
of cloning a human being. The article prompted a reply by several theologians, including Princeton's Paul Ramsey.

Some of the reasons Lederberg gave 30 years ago for cloning
a human being have been reiterated in recent weeks since we
first said Hello to Dolly: We might clone individuals of great intelligence or athletic ability or beauty as a service to society. We
might clone a sick child to provide that child a twin who could
supply materials for transplant. Or we might clone a child who
had accidentally suffered a severe brain injury, thereby giving
the parents an identical twin of the child for whom they will
shortly grieve. Lest we like sheep follow Dolly down this path,
we might revisit Ramsey's reply to Lederberg (later published in
Fabricated Man).

The Most Persistent Argument

Perhaps the most persistent argument in favor of cloning a human being is simply that some people will want to do it and
should be free to do so. To refuse them such freedom looks to
some people like an unwarranted intrusion into the privacy of
procreative decisions and a violation of reproductive rights and
freedoms. The argument makes some sense if freedom is regarded as a sufficient principle and if it is understood as the capacity of neutral agents to will whatever they will, uncon-
strained and uncoerced. Then reproduction is a right, and the
only "warranted" limit on that right is the requirement that it
be exercised by "consenting adults."

Ramsey, like a good Protestant, did not deny the moral signif-
icance of freedom. But he insisted that freedom is not a sufficient moral principle. "There are more ways to violate man-
womanhood than to violate the *freedom* of the parties," he said,
and "something voluntarily adopted can still be wrong." He insisted that people are always more than their rational autonomy,
and that we must regard and respect others always as *embodied*
and as *communal* beings, members of covenants and communities, some of which at least are not of their own choosing.

If freedom is regarded as a sufficient principle, then family
relationships are necessarily diminished, turned into merely
contractual relationships between autonomous individuals. If

one admits that freedom is insufficient for an account of the good life in a family—let alone for nurturing and sustaining it—then one may surely ask whether freedom is sufficient for considering new ways of becoming a family, including cloning.

A Right to a Unique Identity

The cloning of human beings . . . would be a profound threat to what might be called the right to our own identity. True, we are not just our genes; environment, history and cultural context matter. That's why no two people, not even identical twins, are exactly the same.

Still, engineering someone's entire genetic makeup would compromise his or her right to a unique identity.

Daniel Callahan, *New York Times*, February 27, 1997.

Moreover, Ramsey suggested, respect for freedom and for the struggle of the young for their own identity should itself caution us against cloning a human being. Cloning would manipulatively establish an identity for a child in the choice to have one: to design a human being—whether to be a good scientist or a good pianist—establishes an identity for the child which is not only not freely owned by the child but which does not invite anyone to nurture or even to engage the child's capacities for individual agency.

If, for example, one were to take seriously Joseph Fletcher's suggestion that we clone "top-grade soldiers," and if the procedure ended up producing a brilliant pacifist instead of a good soldier, then the procedure would be judged to have "failed." In such a procedure, the child's freedom will not be nurtured; it will be—and must be considered to be—a threat to the success of the reproductive procedures. The illustration need not be so fanciful; if one were to "replace" a dying child with its clone, the clone would have to live with the identity of the lost child and its "promise." A concern for freedom itself, then, should prohibit us from cloning a human being.

THE HAPPINESS TEST

A second kind of argument about cloning is quite candidly utilitarian: the test for cloning is simply whether it maximizes happiness. Ramsey, who was not a utilitarian, vigorously rejected the reduction of moral discernment to the calculation of consequences and the reduction of the good to the maximizing of happiness or preference satisfaction.

Relationships in a family are not simply contractual, nor are they instrumental relationships designed to achieve some extrinsic good. Maximizing happiness is not what family is all about. Again, if utility calculations are insufficient to account for the good life in a family—let alone to nurture and sustain it—then it may be asked whether they are sufficient to justify new ways of becoming a family, including cloning.

Moreover, calculations of utility often ignore what is for Ramsey a basic moral question, the question of distributive justice. It is not enough to count up the costs and benefits. It is necessary also to ask: Who bears the costs? Who stands to benefit? And is this distribution of costs and benefits fair? Ramsey consistently opposed the imposition of risks and harms upon those who could not voluntarily assume them, and who would not be able to share in any possible benefits. He tried to speak for the voiceless, for the "mishaps"; he urged protection of the weak, of embryos, even if such protection meant that a great number of others would not be benefited. Ramsey could be quite nonchalant about good consequences, at least compared to the seriousness with which he took the moral responsibility to protect and nurture "the least of these."

AN ENSOULED BODY

Even if we want to identify and weigh costs and benefits, Ramsey reminds us that these tasks are not simply technical assessments; they inevitably express and form our profoundest convictions concerning our relationships with our bodies, with nature and with children. And on these matters, too, Ramsey's reply to Lederberg is instructive.

Ramsey repudiated "the combination of *boundless determinism* with *boundless freedom*" in Lederberg's proposal. He refused to reduce "the person" to capacities for understanding and choice, to something altogether different from the body, something over and over against the body. And he refused to reduce the body to a mere object to be measured, mastered and manipulated for the sake of "personal" choices. He insisted instead on our embodiment and claimed again and again that the person is "an embodied soul or an ensouled body."

Because the sexual person is "the body of his soul as well as the soul of his body," procreation (and intercourse) may not be reduced either to mere physiology or to simple consent to a technology. Because of our embodiment Ramsey refused to reduce baby-making (or love-making) to a technical accomplishment or to a matter of contract.

Our culture has sat at the feet of Francis Bacon. We take knowledge to be power over nature, and we assume that it leads (almost) inevitably to human well-being. Ramsey was deeply suspicious of the Baconian vision. He sat, instead, at the feet of C. S. Lewis. Ramsey saw that technology always involves the power of some people over other people; it provides no remedy for greed, envy or pride, and can be co-opted into their service. Such an account of technology may have its epitome in cloning.

The relationship of parents and children may be at stake in our response to the proposal to clone a human being. Ramsey worried not only that "replication" or "'reproduction' (itself a metaphor of a machine civilization)" would depersonalize and disembody acts of begetting, but that technological reproduction—and especially cloning—would tempt us to view our children as human and technical achievements rather than as gifts of God.

If we see children as achievements, as products, then the "quality control" approach appropriate to technology will gradually limit our options to choosing either a perfect child or a dead child. Our capacity as parents to provide the sort of uncalculating care and nurture that evokes the trust of children will be diminished. If we would cherish children as begotten, not made, as gifts, not products, then we will not be hospitable to cloning.

| *"While it is possible to clone a body, it is impossible to clone a brain."*

CLONING WOULD NOT VIOLATE A PERSON'S INDIVIDUALITY

George Johnson

The fear that human cloning will cause people to lose their individuality is baseless, argues George Johnson in the following viewpoint. Environment is just as responsible for shaping personality as is genetics, he maintains. Variations in personal experiences would affect the brain of a human clone differently, he contends, resulting in a different individual. Johnson is a writer for the *New York Times*.

As you read, consider the following questions:

1. In Johnson's opinion, why does the idea of human cloning make people uneasy?
2. How is brain tissue different from other body tissues, according to the author?
3. According to Johnson, why would cloning a human brain still result in different individuals?

Explorers returning from distant lands tell of aborigines so afraid of cameras that they recoil from the sight of a lens as if they were looking down the barrel of a gun. Taking their picture, they fear, is the same as stealing their soul. You might as well just shoot them dead on the spot. Knowing that a photograph is only skin deep, people in the developed lands find such terror absurd. But the fear that one's very identity might be stolen, that one could cease to be an individual, runs deep even in places where cameras seem benign.

The queasiness many people feel over the news that a scientist in Scotland has made a carbon copy of a sheep comes down to this: if a cell can be taken from a human being and used to create a genetically identical double, then any of us could lose our uniqueness. One would no longer be a self.

There are plenty of other reasons to worry about this new divide the biologists have trampled across. Nightmare of the week goes to those who imagine docile flocks of enslaved clones raised for body parts.

THE MOST FUNDAMENTAL FEAR

But the most fundamental fear is that the soul will be taken by this penetrating new photography called cloning. And here, at least, the notion is just as superstitious as the aborigines'. There is one part of life biotechnology will never touch. While it is possible to clone a body, it is impossible to clone a brain.

That each creature from microbe to man is unique in all the world is amazing when you consider that every life form is assembled from the same identical building blocks. Every electron in the universe is indistinguishable, by definition. You can't tell one from the other by examining it for nicks and scratches. All protons and all neutrons are also precisely the same.

And when you put these three kinds of particles together to make atoms, there is still no individuality. Every carbon atom and every hydrogen atom is the same. When atoms are strung together into complex molecules—the enzymes and other proteins—this uniformity begins to break down. Minor variations occur.

But it is at the next step up the ladder that something strange and wonderful happens. There are so many ways molecules can be combined into the complex little machines called cells that no two of them can be exactly alike. Even cloned cells, with identical sets of genes, vary somewhat in shape or coloration. The variations are so subtle they can usually be ignored. But when cells are combined to form organisms, the differences become overwhelming. A threshold is crossed and individuality is born.

Two genetically identical twins inside a womb will unfold in slightly different ways. The shape of the kidneys or the curve of the skull won't be quite the same. The differences are small enough that an organ from one twin can probably be transplanted into the other. But with the organs called brains the differences become profound.

All a body's tissues—bone, skin, muscle, and so forth—are made by taking the same kind of cell and repeating it over and over again. But with brain tissue there is no such monotony.

A BRAIN CANNOT BE CLONED

Now the fear of the loss of your individuality is probably in the heads of most people, but be not afraid, all that can be cloned is your DNA. Not unless you were cloned at birth without your knowledge could you be strolling down the street and bump into someone who looks exactly like you at the present moment, possibly your clone in a far-fetched situation, but even your clone would not look exactly like you, because of the difference in age. If someone were to clone you, you would not see a mirror image of yourself in nine months. You might see exactly what you looked like as a newborn, but not at your actual age because we cannot accelerate growth to that extent. Even if that was possible, the clone might be in better shape from being nurtured in a lab, or you had a childhood injury that changed your appearance, plus the important role of environment. Smog could have stunted your growth, or sun exposure could have given you freckles, or moles, or even wrinkles.

But the one thing that makes you you is your brain. The simple reason why the entire you can't be cloned is that a brain can't be cloned.

Ryan Brown, *Ability*, vol. 97, no. III, 1997.

The precise layout of the cells, which neuron is connected to which, makes all the difference. Linked one with the other, through the junctions called synapses, neurons form the whorls of circuitry whose twists and turns make us who we are.

In the reigning metaphor, the genome, the coils of DNA that carry the genetic information, can be thought of as a computer directing the assembly of the embryo. Back-of-the-envelope calculations show how much information a human genome contains and how much information is required to specify the trillions of connections in a single brain.

The conclusion is inescapable: the problem of wiring up a brain is so complex that it is beyond the power of the genomic computer.

The best the genes can do is indicate the rough layout of the wiring, the general shape of the brain. Neurons, in this early stage, are thrown together more or less at random and then left to their own devices. After birth, experience makes and breaks connections, pruning the thicket into precise circuitry. From the very beginning, what's in the genes is different from what's in the brain. And the gulf continues to widen as the brain matures.

The genes still exert their influence—some of the brain's circuitry is hardwired from the start and immutable. People don't have to learn to want food or sex. But as the new connections form, the mind floating higher and higher above the genetic machinery like a helium balloon, people learn to circumvent the baser instincts in individual ways.

Even genetically identical twins, natural clones, are born with different neural tangles. Subtle variations in the way the connections were originally slapped together might make one twin particularly fascinated by twinkling lights, the other drawn to certain patterns of sounds.

Even if the twins were kept in the same room for days, these natural predilections would drive them each in different directions. Experience, pouring in through the senses, would cause unique circuitry to form. Once the twins left the room, the differences between them would increase. Send one twin around the block clockwise and the other counterclockwise and they would return with more divergent brains. For artificial clones the variations would accumulate even faster, for they would be born years apart, into different worlds.

Photography is only skin deep. Cloning is only gene deep. But what about the ultimate cloning—copying synapse by synapse a human brain?

If such a technological feat were ever possible, for one brief instant we might have two identical minds. But then suppose neuron No. 20478288 were to fire randomly in brain 1 and not in brain 2. The tiny spasm would set off a cascade that reshaped some circuitry, and there would be two individuals again.

We each carry in our heads complexity beyond imagining and beyond duplication. Even a hard-core materialist might agree that, in that sense, everyone has a soul.

PERIODICAL BIBLIOGRAPHY

The following articles have been selected to supplement the diverse views presented in this chapter. Addresses are provided for periodicals not indexed in the *Readers' Guide to Periodical Literature*, the *Alternative Press Index*, the *Social Sciences Index*, or the *Index to Legal Periodicals and Books*.

Jerry Adler	"Clone Hype," *Newsweek*, November 8, 1993.
Sharon Begley	"Little Lamb, Who Made Thee?" *Newsweek*, March 10, 1997.
Chris Bull	"Send in the Clones," *Advocate*, April 15, 1997.
Barry Came	"The Prospect of Evil," *Maclean's*, March 10, 1997.
Philip Elmer-Dewitt	"Cloning: Where Do We Draw the Line?" *Time*, November 8, 1993.
Free Inquiry	Special section on cloning humans, Summer 1997. Available from PO Box 664, Amherst, NY 14226-0664.
Christine Gorman	"To Ban or Not to Ban?" *Time*, June 16, 1997.
Hastings Center Report	Special section in response to the National Bioethics Advisory Commission's Report on human cloning, September/October 1997.
Kennedy Institute of Ethics Journal	Special issue on the ethics of cloning human embryos, September 1994. Available from 2715 N. Charles St., Baltimore, MD 21218-4319.
Daniel J. Kevles	"Study Cloning, Don't Ban It," *New York Times*, February 26, 1997.
Gina Kolata	"Ethics Panel Recommends a Ban on Human Cloning," *New York Times*, June 8, 1997.
R.C. Lewontin	"The Confusion over Cloning," *New York Review of Books*, October 23, 1997.
David Masci	"The Cloning Controversy," *CQ Researcher*, May 9, 1997. Available from 1414 22nd St. NW, Washington, DC 20037.
Stephen G. Post	"The Judeo-Christian Case Against Human Cloning," *America*, June 21, 1997.
Time	Special report on cloning, March 10, 1997.

CHAPTER 2

WHAT ETHICS SHOULD GUIDE ORGAN DONATIONS?

CHAPTER PREFACE

The number of people on the waiting list for organ transplants on any given day in 1996 ranged between 44,000 and 50,000, while approximately 70,000 Americans were registered for a transplant at some point during the year. Although 20,260 new organs were transplanted in 1996, only 5,411 people provided those organs. And the waiting list for organs never seems to diminish—about 4,300 people were added to the 1996 list, replacing the approximately 4,000 who died due to a lack of available organs.

Congress has attempted to alleviate the organ shortage with several acts. The Uniform Anatomical Gift Act of 1968 made it easy for people to donate their organs by simply signing organ donor cards. In 1986 Congress passed "routine enquiry" legislation, requiring hospitals that received Medicare and Medicaid funds to ask families of potential donors if they would allow their loved ones' organs to be harvested. Despite these measures, however, the number of organs donated has remained relatively level, or in some cases, has even declined, since the late 1980s.

Numerous solutions to ease the organ shortage have been proposed, but none has been adopted or is in widespread use. Some doctors, researchers, and ethicists believe that all that is needed is an intensive education program to inform the public of the need for organ donation. Others want to expand the pool of available organs by using organs obtained from pigs or primates, from executed prisoners, or from anencephalic babies (babies who are born with only a brain stem and die shortly after birth). Many advocate allowing organ donors or their families to be financially compensated for their donation. Some prefer presumed consent, in which hospitals would presume that a potential donor would be willing to have his or her organs donated. However, each proposal has as many opponents as advocates, and so changes have yet to be enacted. The authors of the viewpoints in the following chapter debate some of the ethical questions raised by these solutions.

"[Lifting] the current legal restriction on the purchase and sale of cadaveric organs ... would ... save thousands of lives."

SELLING ORGANS FOR TRANSPLANTS IS ETHICAL

Andy H. Barnett, Roger D. Blair, and David L. Kaserman

In the following viewpoint, Andy H. Barnett, Roger D. Blair, and David L. Kaserman contend that the shortage of organ donors is due to economics. A system in which the reward for organ donation is strictly altruistic will always result in a shortage of organs, they maintain. However, if the buying and selling of organs were legalized, they argue, donor organs would be plentiful and market prices for the organs would quickly stabilize. Barnett is the director of the Auburn Policy Research Center and associate professor of economics at Auburn University in Alabama. Blair is the Huber Hurst Professor of Business and Legal Studies at the University of Florida in Gainesville. Kaserman is the Torchmark Professor of Economics at Auburn University.

As you read, consider the following questions:

1. According to the authors, what would an organ market be like?
2. How would an organ market affect the quality of donated and transplanted organs, according to the authors?
3. What are the misperceptions of the ethical arguments opposing organ markets, in the authors' opinion?

Public awareness of the critical shortage of cadaveric human organs made available for transplantation was recently heightened by the unfortunate case of Mickey Mantle. Mr. Mantle's need for and relatively rapid receipt of a liver transplant brought widespread attention to the plight of thousands of other sufferers of heart, liver, lung, and kidney failure whose lives depend upon timely receipt of a suitable organ for transplantation. It also brought considerable suspicion and outright scorn regarding the integrity of the current system used to allocate these scarce organs among the growing pool of patients needing them. Disputes about allocation issues, however, tend to have the undesirable effect of diverting attention away from the more serious topic of devising public policies that will ultimately resolve the organ shortage. If the shortage problem is eliminated, allocation issues become moot.

Consequently, the principal message that should emerge from Mr. Mantle's case is not one involving the fairness of the system used to allocate those organs that are procured. Rather, it is that our current public policy has failed miserably to address the organ shortage. And that failure, in turn, has caused needless suffering and death. Rather than begrudging Mr. Mantle his transplant, we should seek out new public policies that will deliver the gift of life to others as well.

In this viewpoint, we propose an alternative public policy that, we believe, is capable of fully resolving the organ shortage. This policy relies upon the powerful incentives provided by free market forces to bring forth the additional supply of organs required to meet demand. . . . We consider both the economic and ethical arguments that have been raised in opposition to organ markets and find each of them to be demonstrably specious. As a result, we conclude that the current legal restriction on the purchase and sale of cadaveric organs should be lifted. This relatively simple alteration of our public policy would eliminate the organ shortage and, thereby, save thousands of lives each year.

THE CAUSE OF THE SHORTAGE

Thousands of critically ill patients presently wait for cadaveric organs that are desperately needed for transplantations, and many of these patients will die before a suitable organ becomes available. Numerous others will experience declining health, reduced quality of life, job loss, lower incomes, and depression while waiting, sometimes years, for the needed organs. And still other patients will never be placed on official waiting lists under the existing shortage conditions, because physical or behavioral traits make them relatively poor candidates for transplantation. Were it not for the shortage, however, many of these patients would be considered acceptable candidates for transplantation.

At the same time, however, many more organs are buried each year than the number of patients needing them. The sad fact is that only 15–25 percent of the cadaveric organs that could be donated are recovered. Thus, the current organ shortage and its associated costs are not mandated by nature but are the result of a failed public policy that refuses to recognize the intrinsic economic and human value of cadaveric organs.

A FAILED PUBLIC POLICY

The policy that yields this unfortunate result has been in place since kidney transplants first became feasible in the mid-1950s. It was eventually codified into law with the passage of the National Organ Transplant Act of 1984, sponsored by then-senator Albert Gore. This act makes the purchase or sale of human organs, even cadaveric organs, a felony. The official price of transplantable organs, then, is legally fixed at zero regardless of the relationship between demand and supply or the suffering and deaths that result. With the price fixed at zero, altruism is the sole motivating force for generating a supply of cadaveric organs under this policy. Importantly, this myopic policy has *never* yielded enough organs to satisfy demand, nor is there any reason to expect that it ever will.

The chronic failure to meet the annual demand for cadaveric organs has created a large and growing backlog of patients in need of transplantable organs. In 1987, there were 11,872 persons waiting for kidneys, 450 for livers, and 646 for hearts; by 1995 those numbers had grown to 29,238, 4,817, and 3,241, and there were 1,796 persons waiting for lungs. Moreover, this backlog (or waiting list) has recently begun to expand at an increasing rate as organ demand has continued to grow at an accelerated pace while organ supply has remained approximately constant. The resulting shortage is a tragedy.

Anyone who has studied basic economics could readily explain that the zero-price policy is the obvious cause of the current organ shortage: There are virtually no products, including cars, oranges, or other medical services, for which such a policy would not create a shortage. Consequently, responsibility for the unnecessary deaths and human suffering that are caused by this policy-created shortage falls squarely on the sponsors and supporters of the ill-conceived law that proscribes voluntary market exchange at a positive price. Similarly, any student of economics could suggest a straightforward policy to eliminate the shortage of transplantable organs: Allow the market price to rise to its equilibrium value. In other words, legalize the purchase and sale of cadaveric organs. Such a policy would vastly increase the number of organs made available for transplantation, thereby saving numerous lives. Both organ recipients and organ donors (or suppliers) would benefit from such free-market exchange.

THE ECONOMIC TRUTH

Proposals to adopt a market system of cadaveric organ procurement, however, have met strong opposition, particularly from physician and hospital groups. These groups have made both economic and ethical arguments in support of the current altruistic system and in opposition to a market system. In this viewpoint, we critically evaluate these arguments and find that each is specious on either theoretical or empirical grounds or both.

The question then arises: If the current organ procurement policy is so obviously flawed and the arguments against a market system are clearly mistaken, then why was the current system adopted and, more important, why has it persisted so long? The rather cynical but, we believe, correct answer lies in the policy's impact on profits to physicians and hospitals. The economic truth is that reliance on altruism at one stage of production can serve the purpose of greed at another. The supply restriction that accompanies a zero-price policy increases physicians' and hospitals' profits in much the same way that the politically motivated crude oil "shortage" of the early 1970s increased petroleum companies' profits to so-called obscene levels. A legal restriction on the purchase and sale of transplantable organs is economically equivalent to the formation and maintenance of a cartel in the provision of transplant services. The supply of transplant operations cannot expand if additional organs are not made available. Therefore the current policy and the shortage it creates enhance the overall profitability of transplant providers. Such profitability, in turn, ensures continuing political support for that policy. . . .

ORGAN MARKETS

Because the issue of markets for human organs is so emotionally charged and often misunderstood, let us be clear about what advocates of markets do, and do not, propose. They do not propose barkers hawking human organs on street corners. They do not envision transplant patients, or their agents, dickering for a heart or liver with families of the recently departed. They do not advocate a market for organs from living donors. Indeed, markets are seen as a device that could reduce the need for living donors by increasing the number of cadaveric organs collected. Proponents of markets do not advocate an auction in which desperate recipients bid against each other for life-sustaining organs. And most market advocates propose using the price system only for organ collection, not for distributing collected organs among potential recipients.

What is proposed is a system in which agents of for-profit firms offer a market-determined price for either premortem or postmortem agreements to allow the firm to collect organs for resale to transplant centers. For example, insurance companies could enter the organ procurement market by merging with existing organ procurement organizations. Then, organ procurement officers who presently negotiate with families of recently deceased individuals could offer payment in cash or burial expenses for the right to remove the needed organs. Such a system would be equivalent to providing the deceased with an *ex post* [retroactive] term life insurance policy with no premium. Alternatively, individuals may be offered a reduction in medical insurance rates in return for a premortem annually renewable agreement that allows their insurance company to collect and sell their organs in the event that they die during the policy year in a way that makes organ collection feasible. Firms that collect organs would then sell them to transplant centers that place orders for needed organs.

Compared to the current policy, markets for organ procurement dramatically change both the incentive of organ procurement personnel to ask for permission to remove organs and the incentive of potential donors to grant that permission when asked. Markets provide tangible rewards, that is, profits, to those who are successful at organ collection. Hence organ procurement firms have incentive to seek out potential donors and to structure requests and payment packages that are most likely to induce a positive response to the request for permission to collect the organs. Further, payment to organ donors provides a direct incentive, in addition to any altruistic inclination they may have, to grant permission. . . .

OPPOSITION TO AN ORGAN MARKET

Arguments opposing market-based organ procurement are most often based either upon impassioned claims regarding the moral or ethical superiority of altruism over market forces or upon mistaken impressions about how such a market would actually function. In addition, however, several economic arguments against the use of markets have also been offered. Both sets of arguments demand critical evaluation.

Economic Arguments. Several commentators have argued that payment to organ donors may reduce some individuals' desire to supply organs freely. That is, although some people who will not donate at a zero price might be willing to supply organs if they receive payment, others who might freely donate without compensation will refuse to supply organs if offered payment. If the number discouraged by compensation exceeds the number for whom payment is a positive inducement, then the total number of organs available for transplantation could conceivably fall when payment is offered.

Whether the introduction of positive prices will actually reduce organ supply by driving out altruistic donors is essentially an empirical issue. Unless one actually tries our proposed solution, the data will not be available to resolve the issue. We do know, however, that our current reliance upon altruism is misplaced since the quantities donated are consistently less than the quantities needed. In any event, we do not believe that the net effect will be a reduction in the number of organs available for transplant.

ORGAN DONATIONS WILL INCREASE

Two observations that appear beyond dispute suggest that the number of organs available under a market-based procurement system will not fall but will, instead, increase substantially. First, the number of organs demanded for transplantation is more a biological necessity than a decision based on price; hence the number of organs demanded is unlikely to fall substantially when organ prices rise above zero.

Second, in general, there is some price at which the quantity of transplantable organs demanded and the quantity supplied will be equal: the market equilibrium price. As we noted above, quantity supplied is substantially less than quantity demanded at the current zero price (that is, there is a large shortage). Because the demand for organs is insensitive to price movements, the quantity of organs demanded is unlikely to be substantially less at this equilibrium price than at the current zero price. If quantity demanded changes little with price and if there is a shortage at the current price of zero, the number of organs supplied must be greater at the equilibrium price than at a zero price. In short, simple economic reasoning strongly suggests that the number of organs supplied with market-based procurement will be greater than the number supplied under the altruistic system.

Will market procurement affect the quality of organs harvested? Substituting payment for altruism may reduce the share of organs obtained from comparatively higher-income individuals and increase the share obtained from lower-income individuals. If the quality of harvested organs is influenced by the general health of donors and if income and health are positively correlated, average organ quality may be adversely affected by market-based procurement. But if market-based procurement makes more organs available, as we believe it will, a decline in the quality of organs *collected* need not mean a decline in the average quality of organs *transplanted*. The current shortage forces surgeons to use substandard organs or to perform transplants despite a poor tissue match. For example, a recent policy change increases the maximum age of potential organ donors in order to increase the available supply. And many kidney transplant centers have also increased the number of transplants performed using living, unrelated donors. When more organs are available, higher standards can be set for transplantable organs. The average quality of transplanted organs then will be higher, not lower, with organ markets.

Ethical Arguments. Although opponents' ethical concerns about organ markets are seldom clearly stated, the primary issues are ensuring accessibility to organs by the poor, maintaining incentives to provide adequate care for critically ill patients, and promoting altruism in society. These ethical concerns, however, stem entirely from misinformation and faulty reasoning.

ORGAN TRANSPLANTS AND THE POOR

First, misperceptions about accessibility to organs are based on the premise that recipients will pay donors for organs and on the conjecture that organ prices will be high. At present, most of the costs of an organ transplant are borne by insurance companies and Medicare; otherwise, low-income patients would simply be unable to have transplants. In other words, under the current system, transplants are paid for by someone other than the organ recipient. This system of subsidizing transplant costs for relatively poor patients could easily be extended to cover the costs of organ procurement.

On a more technical note, the alleged inability of the poor to purchase organs is based on the unlikely premise that only a high price can induce an adequate supply of organs. This argument confuses anecdotal evidence regarding the current value, which is greatly inflated by the shortage, with a market equilibrium price. Because there is now a severe shortage, potential organ recipients may be willing to pay a very high price for a suitable organ to avoid extended waiting times. But if a relatively modest payment is all that is required to induce potential donors to contribute an adequate supply of organs, the market equilibrium price of organs will be low. Given this low price, the likelihood of third-party payment, and the expected increase in the number of organs collected, moving to a market-based organ procurement system will, in fact, increase the availability of organ transplants to the poor.

Mike Ramirez. Reprinted by permission of Copley News Service.

Moreover, there is some evidence that the current altruistic system discriminates against the poor. Claims of list-jumping by wealthy or influential recipients are widespread. The Mickey Mantle incident is a case in point. The 1984 National Organ Transplant Act, which created a nationwide computerized network for matching donors and recipients, has reduced opportunities for abuse, but some argue that a well-placed contribution to a medical facility can still influence the distribution of scarce organs. Where legalized trade of a valuable asset is prohibited, black market activity is likely, if not inevitable. A market-based policy that makes organs plentiful and relatively inexpensive will reduce such abuses and hence benefit poor patients.

How will the presence of organ markets affect the care of critically ill patients from whom organs could be harvested?

Some market opponents have argued that when cadaveric organs can be sold, physicians may have an incentive to withdraw care prematurely from critically ill potential organ donors. This concern is totally misplaced. First, it is based on the presumption that the market price of organs will be high enough to make premature termination of care tempting for attending physicians. As we explained above, however, market prices for organs will likely be low. When the procurement system produces an adequate supply at a comparatively low price, there is little incentive to allow patients to die so that their organs can be sold.

Second, and more important, the attending physician for a critically ill patient is not the seller of organs harvested from that patient. Indeed, in the market system we envision, participation in organ transplantation by medical personnel attending the donor could be and probably should be prohibited. In this event, attending physicians gain nothing from the donor's death. The market value of the organs of critically ill patients is assigned much like a bequest in a will. Someone will receive compensation from the patient's death, but not the attending physician. Thus concerns about premature termination of care under a market system are founded upon blatant misconceptions about how the system would operate in practice. . . .

PROSPECTS FOR REAL REFORM

The adage "If it ain't broke, don't fix it" clearly does not apply to our current cadaveric organ procurement policy. By any objective standard, it is a failed policy costing thousands of lives each year in addition to unnecessary suffering and financial loss. As longtime students of public policy issues, we have witnessed many other ill-conceived policies, yet we can safely say that we have never encountered a policy more at odds with the public interest than our current organ procurement system. In short, the present policy has two pronounced effects: It increases costs and it kills patients.

The issue of organ procurement is an emotional one, and discussing solutions objectively and analytically is difficult. But emotional issues do not require illogical solutions. Until the interested parties—physicians, hospitals, patients, and policy makers—can rationally consider alternative cadaveric organ procurement policies that rely on the powerful forces of the free market, the existing shortage will only worsen. While Mickey Mantle suffered scorn because he received an organ, thousands of other patients will suffer death because they do not receive an organ. It is these latter patients that deserve our attention.

"Making it acceptable for hospitals to purchase organs would immediately encourage the thugs already in the market to step up their work-rate."

SELLING ORGANS FOR TRANSPLANTS IS UNETHICAL

Alasdair Palmer

Alasdair Palmer is a columnist for the weekly British magazine the *Spectator*. In the following viewpoint, Palmer argues that legalizing the buying and selling of human organs for transplantation raises serious ethical questions. Buying organs exploits the desperately poor and would encourage criminals to kidnap victims to sell their organs, he maintains.

As you read, consider the following questions:

1. According to Palmer, what precipitated the Human Tissue Act of 1990 which outlawed the purchasing of human organs?
2. What are some of the risks associated with purchasing a kidney in India, according to Jonathan Odum, as cited by the author?
3. What policy has contributed to the shortage of organs, in Palmer's opinion?

Reprinted from "Rigging the Human Market," by Alasdair Palmer, *Spectator*, July 2, 1994, by permission of the *Spectator*, London.

In June 1994, Mr Stephen Hyett left hospital in Cambridge with a new kidney, liver, stomach, pancreas, duodenum and small bowel. He was lucky that the operation was such a success. He was even luckier that the appropriate organs were available. For many who need them, they are not—at least not through the normal channels. But there are others.

Consider this request, sent to *The Spectator* by Mr Chandrapandey, an Indian gentleman from Lucknow: 'With due regards I beg to state that I want to advertise to sell my fresh kidney at $150,000. I will pay you fifteen per cent of the receiving amount. I have chosen your magazine for its rich readers.'

Mr Chandrapandey was disappointed in his hopes of selling his kidney in this country for $150,000, and not just because he was wrong in his charming belief that 'for the British, $150,000 is not much'. Aware that payment, or facilitating payment, for human organs is a crime punishable by imprisonment in the United Kingdom, *The Spectator's* editor took the safe way out. He refused to run the advertisement.

Mr Chandrapandey was therefore forced back to the local market in human organs. And in India that market is flourishing. It has brought the price of kidneys down dramatically. In Bombay they can be purchased for considerably less than $150,000. Between £8,000 and £10,000 will buy you a new kidney, including the operation required to transplant it into your body.

OPERATIONS ON DEMAND

For those waiting on the long and continually growing list for kidney transplants in Britain, the option of an instant operation can be tempting. Anyone on the list knows that here demand exceeds supply by around four to one. Death on the NHS [National Health Service] waiting list is a regular occurrence. Whether you live or die can come down to a question of luck— and whether you can survive years undergoing the considerable pain and boredom of life on dialysis. Small wonder, then, that some find it impossible to resist the quick way out: a trip to Bombay to take advantage of the bargain prices and purchase a new kidney there.

It is a practice most common in the British Asian community, where there can be strong religious prohibitions against the use of kidneys from corpses. Dr Jonathan Odum, of New Cross Hospital in Wolverhampton, explained to me that a leading Wolverhampton Sikh started the trend amongst Wolverhampton Asians. The success of his Bombay operation encouraged others. 'We can't stop them going, however much we deplore the trade,' Dr

Odum told me. 'And we cannot refuse to treat them when they get back having had the transplant, when they need to continue courses of immuno-suppressant drugs or whatever.' Dr Odum was worried that he and his colleagues might be seen to be accessories to a crime by treating those who'd purchased kidneys in India. In fact, it turns out that legally they'd be more at risk if they refused treatment. 'But it is a dilemma. In effect, we're rewarding them for what they do,' he said gloomily.

THE BLACK MARKET TRADE IN KIDNEYS

The practice of purchasing kidneys—or any human organ—was outlawed in this country by the Human Tissue Act. That act was passed in haste in 1990, in the wake of a kidneys-for-cash scandal in London: Dr Raymond Crockett from the Humana Hospital arranged for Turks to come to London and have their kidneys out in return for a small fee. Dr Crockett lost his job and his licence, and the Human Tissue Act zipped through the Houses of Parliament in record time. What generated the hysteria, apart from the general revulsion against the traffic in human flesh, was that at least one of the Turks did not seem to appreciate that he was going into hospital to have his kidney removed.

The Humana Hospital scandal was, however, very tame stuff by comparison with what goes on routinely in India. Kidneys bought there come steeped in human misery, as Dr Odum reminds anyone who thinks of nipping off for a transplant. One Indian woman, for example, was forced by her brutish husband to give up one of her kidneys. She was given an alarm clock and a battery for her transistor radio for her pains. He received the money, which he proceeded to gamble away almost instantly. Anyone who investigates kidney transplantation in India comes back with dozens of stories like that. They don't move the blindly self-interested, but there are drawbacks to purchasing a kidney even for them. A study of 130 patients from the United Arab Emirates and Oman who had purchased new kidneys in India showed that four tested positive after the transplant for HIV (having tested negative before it); three were infected with hepatitis.

'But the trouble is,' sighs Dr Odum, 'none of the patients who has come back to this country has been infected. It makes it much more difficult to persuade people of the risks they are running.' Those risks are nonetheless very real. Blood is still not routinely tested for infections in many Indian hospitals, leaving aside the dubious qualifications of many of the surgeons.

The fact that people are willing to make the trip to Bombay and risk infection with the AIDS virus indicates how desperate the shortage of organs for transplantation has become in the United Kingdom. It is not just a question of kidneys. There aren't enough hearts, lungs or livers for those who need transplants either. All of which shows just how lucky Mr Stephen Hyett is. He was lucky that the operation worked. But he was even luckier that someone with his tissue type, and with all the relevant organs in good shape, died in the appropriate way and at the appropriate moment, with relatives who were prepared to authorise doctors to remove his insides. Most people who need livers, hearts and lungs, and many who need kidneys, are not so fortunate. They die before suitable replacements can be found.

NOT ENOUGH CORPSES

The basic problem, as any transplant surgeon will tell you, is not enough corpses. Corpses are the only source for lungs, hearts and livers, and for all but 8 per cent of kidneys. Road traffic accidents are one of the principal sources of corpses whose organs can be re-used: the victims are normally young and healthy, and die from head injuries which leave their organs intact. Legislation introducing compulsory seat-belts probably has done more to contribute to the organ shortage than anything else: countries like Austria and Belgium, which transplant kidneys at a rate more than twice that of the United Kingdom, also have more than twice as many fatal road accidents.

This is one NHS shortage which cannot be blamed on Mrs Virginia Bottomley, secretary of state for health. No amount of increased government spending is going to eliminate the waiting list for transplantable organs. Increasing road accidents would help, but even the most enthusiastic 'cutters' (apparently a term of endearment for transplant surgeons) will admit that it is not a feasible alternative. Changing the law to allow the use of organs unless an individual has specifically drawn up a document forbidding it whilst alive is one possibility, but not one that surgeons favour. Ignoring relatives' wishes is a recipe for a public relations disaster, even supposing there were no independent moral objections against changing the system of organ donation from a voluntary to an essentially coercive one. It's anyway unlikely that a switch of that kind would increase the supply significantly. At present, around 20 per cent of relatives refuse permission for the removal of organs from suitable victims. The majority of those are thought to be hard-core opponents of organ removal, who would stay that way however the law was changed.

Everyone wants the supply of transplantable organs increased.

Should families be financially compensated
for donating a relative's organ?

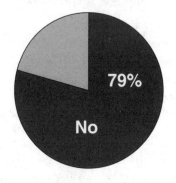

79%

No

Reasons why organ donation should not be compensated:

Organ donation should be an act of altruism	82 percent
Human body should not be treated as a commodity	70 percent
Would encourage families to withhold medical care	41 percent
Would not substantially increase the number of organ donations	28 percent

(Respondents could choose more than one answer.)

Glamour, February 1995.

No one, however, has any ideas which combine solving the shortage with being ethically acceptable. There are various technical suggestions relating to ventilating 'brain dead' bodies for longer in intensive-care units, and for improvements in the way that transplantable organs are co-ordinated with transplant surgeons. Those proposals might make a difference at the margins, but they aren't going to solve the problem. Michael Bewick, renal transplant surgeon at Dulwich Hospital, points to some of the more radical alternatives employed abroad. 'The Chinese use the organs of executed criminals,' he explained to me. 'It was the transplant surgeons who persuaded the Chinese authorities not to shoot criminals in the heart, but in the head. That way, the heart doesn't go to waste. I'm not personally in favour of capital punishment, but if you do have it, why let all those good organs simply be destroyed?' Mr Bewick points out that reusing their organs is a genuinely practical way in which a criminal can pay his debt to society. He mentioned the use of the guillotine in France to execute a murderer in 1958. 'Two leading French surgeons played poker for that man's kidneys. It was the pioneering days of renal transplants. You might not like the way they decided who would get them, but at least those organs weren't wasted.'

FINANCIAL INCENTIVES

Apart from corpses, the other source of kidneys is donation by live adults. Mr Bewick has some radical ideas here as well. Evolution has oversupplied humans with kidneys. We all have two, but each of us only needs one. Having the operation to remove one need not cause any health problems at all. 'There are thousands of usable kidneys out there, if only people could be persuaded to give them up,' he enthused. Money is the most effective incentive, and Mr Bewick suggests offering a financial reward for anyone willing to donate his kidney. He knows it can work. He has personal experience of it. He was the surgeon involved with Dr Crockett in the notorious kidneys-for-cash case in 1989.

Mr Bewick has always denied that in the Crockett case he knew that the men he operated on were being paid for their pains, but he was none the less censured by the General Medical Council for failing to find out, and banned from private practice for a year. But he has never been opposed to the principle of paying people in order to induce them to come forward and donate. 'Why should anyone be? At the moment, when a kidney is transplanted, the surgeon gets paid, the theatre staff get paid, the nurses get paid, and the hospital gets paid. The only person who doesn't get paid is the poor donor. But he's the one making the sacrifice. Is that a fair and humane way to treat him?'

Mr Bewick's view, though shared by some professors of medical ethics, has made him a pariah amongst transplant surgeons. Whilst his colleagues recognise his great contribution to the field, they are horrified by his ethics, or at least by his public avowal of them. The received wisdom, accepted by politicians of all persuasions, has been trenchantly expressed by Sir John Banham, Professor of Transplant Surgery at Oxford: selling organs is incompatible with human dignity. Mr Bewick, interestingly, takes the opposite view: not buying them is incompatible with it. 'The ban doesn't stop trading,' he told me. 'It merely drives it underground and makes exploitation more—not less—likely. People say it would mean the rich would exploit the poor. So what's new? That's capitalism! Or any other economic system, for that matter. We need government to control and organise payment, which would increase the supply and stop the worst of the exploitation.'

An Exploitative Market

Mr Bewick is convinced that the Human Tissue Act was not properly thought through. Repealing it, and establishing a controlled market in human organs, would, he argues, overcome the terrible shortages. He may be right that the absolute ban on payment has more sentimentality than sense behind it, but he has a wildly overoptimistic view of the ability of government to police an organ market successfully. 'Necessity makes a bad bargain,' wrote Sir Francis Bacon. No one is ever going to sell—as opposed to give—his kidney except through economic necessity. The fate of most of Bombay's organ donors is not an encouraging precedent. All the organ markets which exist seem to be hideously exploitative, if not straightforwardly brutal, and there is no particular reason to think that legalising it would magically enable governments to diminish the force, fraud, bullying and deception currently characteristic of the trade.

Reprinted by permission of Joel Pett.

And legalisation might have exactly the opposite effect. Making it acceptable for hospitals to purchase organs would immediately encourage the thugs already in the market to step up their work-rate. Criminal gangs are already known to have kidnapped children for their organs in Russia and South America.

Dr Jean-Claude Alt, one of the main campaigners against the trade, says brokers are regular visitors at one particular children's home in St Petersburg. They arrive saying they'll adopt any child, with any disability, no matter how severe—providing the child has no heart trouble. 'There's only one conclusion you can draw from that,' Dr Alt adds ominously. 'They want to transplant the child's heart.'. . . .

A campaign to increase live donors might help to reduce the waiting lists for kidneys, but without the introduction of financial incentives it won't eliminate them; and it cannot touch the shortage of other organs. The waiting lists, therefore, are here to stay. And so are the waiting-list deaths.

WHO TO TREAT?

The shortage leaves surgeons with the decision of who to treat. 'You can have a kidney which will fit either a man in his forties with a job and three children, or a retired single woman in her sixties without dependents. Strict medical criteria won't always make the choice for you,' explains Mr Christopher Rudge, a London surgeon. 'Deciding between them is a nightmare. It has got more difficult since the principles which formerly dictated distribution were abandoned.' It used to be the case, for instance, that younger patients automatically had priority over older ones. That has changed over the last ten years. Why? 'The surgeons themselves have got older,' suggested Mr Rudge. 'It may make us not quite so keen on an inflexible age cut-off.'

There are no official guidelines about how doctors should decide who shall live and who shall die, granted the suitability of a given organ for more than one patient. A nationally organised institution, the United Kingdom Transplant Association, acts efficiently as a clearing house for organs, helping to ensure that all that become available are effectively used. But surgeons have the final say on what they transplant to whom. 'There isn't always an objective way of making the decision', says Mr Robert Sells, who runs the renal unit in Liverpool. In the last analysis, he says, common sense is the best and only guide. But Mr Sells, like every other transplant surgeon, is unhappy with a situation in which it is not always possible to demonstrate clearly that scarce organs have been allocated fairly, or to justify decisions to those who lose from them.

PREFERENTIAL TREATMENT?

The mystery surrounding how those decisions are made encourages the suspicion that it all comes down to knowing the right people. The father of a friend of mine needed a heart transplant recently. The heart surgeon's first question, after deciding that the operation was necessary, was: 'You don't happen to know anyone on a medical committee, do you? . . . No? Pity.' The man died before a suitable heart could be found.

Surgeons reject absolutely that there is any preferential treatment available for anyone, no matter how well connected in the medical profession—although if there wasn't, surgeons would be the first group in human history not to look after their own. 'No, you don't understand,' Mr John Darke, a heart surgeon in Newcastle, told me. 'Transplant organs are very carefully controlled. It's a very small community. We'd know immediately if something unethical happened.' Perhaps. But the impossibility of explaining exactly how organs are allocated means that stories of that kind flourish. No one wants to codify how the decisions are made, for the simple reason that the most basic element in the relationship between doctor and patient—trust—will be destroyed if patients come to know that the doctors treating them have already mentally written them off as prospective recipients. The reaction to the doctors in Manchester who publicly announced in 1993 that they would not perform coronary bypass surgery on heavy smokers has demonstrated that.

It is precisely the conviction that they won't be treated if they wait on the list which leads people to look to the black market in organs. As waiting lists increase, the demand for black-market organs is going to go up. And so long as it happens outside the United Kingdom, there is nothing anyone here can do about it. Mr Chandrapandey failed to advertise his kidney in The Spectator. But it has probably been transplanted into a British citizen by now.

"Without compromising the
voluntary nature of organ donation,
[presumed consent] would increase
the rates of donation and possibly
expand the pool of potential donors."

CONSENT FOR ORGAN DONATION SHOULD BE PRESUMED

Linda C. Fentiman

In the following viewpoint, Linda C. Fentiman argues that the
need for organ donation is too great to depend on the current
system of altruistic donation. Fentiman contends that presumed
consent, which assumes that a potential organ donor would have
consented to donate his or her organs if asked, is the best
method of increasing the rate of donation and the pool of potential donors. Organ donation would remain a voluntary act, she
explains, because objectors would have many ways of opting out
of the program. Fentiman is a professor at Suffolk University Law
School in Boston.

As you read, consider the following questions:

1. Why is an expensive organ transplant a cost effective method
   of saving a person's life, in the author's opinion?
2. According to Fentiman, why has the Uniform Anatomical
   Gift Act had only a minimal effect in increasing the supply of
   organs available for transplant?
3. What are the six ways objectors to presumed consent organ
   donation could opt out of the program, according to the
   author?

The U.S. organ transplantation system is in crisis. At a time when transplant survival rates are at an all-time high, the waiting list for organs grows longer every day. More than 26,000 individuals are now on waiting lists to receive a kidney, and more than 2,900 are waiting for a heart transplant. In all, nearly 36,000 individuals are waiting for one or more vital organs, including livers, lungs, intestines, and pancreases. Since 1988, according to a 1993 General Accounting Office (GAO) report, more than 10,000 people have died while on a waiting list to receive an organ. Thousands more never even made it to a list.

For many persons, organ transplantation holds out the only hope of survival; for many others, it promises the only hope of survival with a good quality of life. Although initially expensive, the use of a transplant rather than drugs or artificial organs to prolong a life is ultimately cost-effective. The average kidney transplant procedure costs $80,000 for the surgery and first year's care (in 1990 dollars); thereafter, the annual cost of maintaining a transplant recipient on immunosuppressive drugs drops to $7,000. (More than 90 percent of kidney transplant recipients are still living two years after the operation.) In contrast, maintaining an individual on kidney dialysis, a much less successful, palliative technology employed while waiting for a kidney to become available, costs an average of $33,000 annually.

Tremendous pressure exists to reform the present organ transplantation system, which has been faulted for failing to tap the potential pool of transplantable organs as well as for failing to allocate fairly the organs that become available. Although legislation has been proposed to address the allocation issue, the underlying problem—the shortage of available organs—cannot be addressed until our society rethinks its approach to organ donation. This will require that we stop treating organ donation merely as an act of altruism and begin viewing it as a community obligation.

OBSTACLES TO DONATION

Since the late 1960s, when the development of immunosuppressive drugs made possible transplants from donors who were not biologically related to the recipient, academics and policymakers have collaborated on a number of mechanisms to encourage the donation of organs and tissues for transplant. These have achieved only limited success. The Uniform Anatomical Gift Act (UAGA), first proposed in 1968, has been adopted by every state and the District of Columbia. The UAGA's goal was to appeal to Americans' altruism and to make it easy to volunteer to donate one's organs and tissues by signing a donor card (usually when obtaining or renewing a driver's license). The card declares the individual's intent to donate his or her organs at the time of death. In theory, this would allow physicians to retrieve organs for transplant upon the individual's death without requiring the consent of the next of kin.

The UAGA has had only a minimal effect in increasing the supply of organs and tissues for donation. Although repeated polls show that a majority of people in the United States are willing to donate their organs upon death, and an even greater number indicate their willingness to donate the organs of a loved one, fewer than one-fifth actually sign donor cards. This may be for reasons as complex as the unwillingness to confront death or as simple as procrastination.

In addition, very few organ transplants are accomplished solely on the basis of a donor card. Often the card cannot be found upon a person's death. Even if it is, few physicians or nurses will retrieve organs for transplant without the consent of the donor's next of kin—despite the fact that the UAGA explicitly protects those who rely on a donor card from legal liability. Further, many health care providers are reluctant to approach grieving families with a request for organ donation. A number of factors have been offered to explain this reluctance, including health care professionals' discomfort with death, concern about overburdening a bereaved family, or a lack of awareness about the urgent need for organs. Whether due to psychological factors, legal concerns, or simply disorganized wallets, many opportunities for organ donation are lost.

In response to the organ shortage, Congress enacted "routine inquiry" legislation in 1986, mandating that hospitals receiving Medicare or Medicaid reimbursement establish protocols to ask families of potential organ donors whether they would consider organ donation on behalf of their loved ones. Despite this law and similar laws enacted by more than 30 states, organ donation has remained static during the past several years. In some localities, it has actually declined.

DONOR NUMBERS HAVE DECLINED

The stabilization or decline in the number of organs available for transplant has been attributed to several factors. The availability of organs depends on the prevalence of certain kinds of injury or disease. Organs cannot be donated by people who die of infectious diseases or illnesses, such as cancer, that compromise their organs. Thus, broad demographic and illness trends can lead to a smaller pool of potential donors. According to a 1992 study by Roger Evans and his colleagues in the *Journal of the American Medical Association (JAMA)*, AIDS alone has diminished the pool of potential organ donors by 10 percent.

The most likely candidates for organ donation are people who die in motor vehicle accidents, since they typically die from a traumatic head injury, leaving other organs intact. Other possible candidates include people who die of aneurysms, cerebral hemorrhages, or injuries such as gunshot wounds. Medical ethicist Arthur Caplan, among others, has pointed to changes in public safety laws as well as social attitudes as another contributing cause of the shortage of organ donations. By curbing behaviors such as high-speed driving, driving while intoxicated, not fastening seat belts, and underage drinking, these changes have saved many lives—simultaneously decreasing the number of potential candidates for organ donation. The Evans study concluded that, even employing liberal criteria for donor selection, there will be no more than 29,000 potential donors annually, with more likely figures ranging from 6,900 to 10,700. About 4,300 people join waiting lists for organs each year.

EQUITABLE ALLOCATION

In addition to the serious shortage of available organs, our society faces another challenge: how to decide who gets one. The 1993 GAO report was highly critical of the United Network for Organ Sharing (UNOS), the organization that coordinates transplantation services nationwide, and the Department of Health and Human Services (DHHS), which oversees UNOS, for failing to ensure that organs are allocated strictly on the basis of medical criteria. A private agency, UNOS operates under contract with the federal government. Individual transplant centers and regional organ-provider organizations must belong to UNOS in order to receive Medicare or Medicaid funding.

The GAO report indicated that organs are often allocated to recipients who happen to be on the right transplant center's list, rather than those who are medically most eligible. This works to the advantage of people who are able to get on more than one waiting list by seeking treatment from doctors at more than one center. Rep. Henry Waxman (D-Calif.) has noted that wealthy foreigners are somehow able to receive organs that are not available to U.S. citizens and permanent resident aliens.

Recent studies have also documented significant disparities between the proportions of white and black Americans receiving organs for transplant and the amount of time they spend waiting for transplants. According to a recent *JAMA* article by Robert Gaston et al., in 1990, African-Americans represented 31 percent of Americans suffering from end-stage renal disease, even though they comprise only 12 percent of the population as a whole. Yet they received only 22 percent of the cadaveric kidney transplants. African-Americans waited an average of 14 months for such transplants, whereas the average waiting period for white Americans was 8 months.

A Dramatic Increase in Available Organs

Despite widespread efforts to promote organ donation, the number of people who give their prior consent, usually through a donor card or driver's license, remains disappointingly low. Needed is a new law reversing the presumption of the current organ donation law, to presume consent.

The adoption of such a law in three European countries has resulted in a dramatic increase in the availability of donor organs. In Belgium, which enacted its presumed consent law in 1986, the total number of organs available for transplant increased 183% between 1984 and 1988, and has continued to rise. In Austria, organ availability *quadrupled* after the present presumed consent law was implemented.

Alan H. Berger, *Animal People*, September 1995.

Some physicians have argued that this imbalance simply reflects the application of strict medical criteria in finding a match between donor and recipient. Physicians use a six-point antigen-matching scale to identify the most suitable recipient for an organ; a perfect six-point match is more likely to result in a successful transplant than a three- or four-point match. Since antigens are genetically determined, persons of different racial groups are unlikely to have complete antigen matching. But reliance on antigen matching as a major factor in organ allocation has been challenged on scientific and ethical grounds. In many cases, no six-point match is available. How, then, should physicians decide between giving the organ to a white person who achieves a four-point match or an African-American with a three-point match? The allocation of organs raises uncomfortable questions about balancing medical and social criteria. . . .

An Alternative Ethic

For many years, proponents of the current organ-donation system have argued that all that is needed to create an adequate supply of transplantable organs is to educate the public and, to a lesser extent, health care professionals, about the need for organ donation. So far, however, this approach has not worked. And even if potential donors could be more efficiently recruited, the Evans study noted, the desperate demand for kidneys would continue to exceed the supply.

It is time to consider another approach to organ procurement and allocation. Instead of treating organ donation as an act of individual altruism, we must view it as an act of community service and support it as such. We should institute a system in which all mentally competent individuals over the age of 18 would be presumed to consent to the retrieval of their organs at the time of death but that provides numerous opportunities for individuals to opt out. At the same time, we should provide compensation for this act of community service, just as we provide stipends, subsidized education, and health benefits to those who serve in the military or the Peace Corps.

Merely to mention the words "presumed consent" and "compensated donation" is to raise ethical eyebrows. However, a system of presumed consent to compensated organ donation is a rational response to the present organ shortage. Without compromising the voluntary nature of organ donation, it would increase rates of donation and possibly expand the pool of potential donors.

OPTING OUT

A model statute I drafted provides for six possible occasions on which individuals could object to organ donation: when obtaining or renewing a driver's license; filing an income tax return; applying for public benefits, such as food stamps; making a routine visit to a hospital or doctor's office; executing a living will or health care proxy document; and responding to a specific request by a health care professional. Multiple ways for opting out are essential to ensuring that all people, regardless of their educational and income levels and cultural backgrounds, have equal opportunity to decide whether to participate. The names of individuals who object to donating their organs will be recorded in a national computerized registry, which will be updated on a daily basis and protected by appropriate backup systems to ensure confidentiality and guarantee that all objections are preserved.

No doubt, if such a statute were enacted, some religious, civic, and civil liberties groups would urge their members to opt out of the presumed-consent system. Such dissent is welcome, for it will provide an opportunity to promote free and open debate about organ donation and educate people about the issues involved.

THE POOL OF POTENTIAL DONORS WOULD INCREASE

The presumed-consent system would eliminate many existing barriers to organ donation. Health care providers would no longer have to confront a grieving family with the need to make a quick decision about organ donation, because that decision would be out of the family's hands. Instead, they could tap into the national registry to confirm the presumption of consent. Medical personnel could begin the process of preparing a deceased individual's body for organ transplantation—by injecting cooling solutions into the major arteries, for example—without waiting to find a donor card or the next of kin, which would enhance the viability of organs for transplant. Such measures would not be unethical if the underlying presumption was one of consent rather than refusal.

In addition to improving rates of organ retrieval, the presumption of consent would increase the pool of potential donors. For instance, physicians would be allowed to retrieve organs from terminally ill people who had decided to be disconnected from life support systems—a measure that engendered controversy at the Pittsburgh University Medical Center. In their 1992 study of potential organ donors, Evans and his colleagues considered only those potential donors who died in a hospital, after efforts to sustain their lives through artificial life support failed. If one were to expand the pool to include patients who ask to be taken off respirators as well as so-called non-heart-beating donors (those who die outside the hospital whose circulation and respiration is not artificially maintained), the number of available organs could increase substantially.

The concept of presumed consent is not new. It has been proposed by numerous commentators over the last 25 years. In fact, presumed consent to the donation of specific organs, most often the cornea and the pituitary gland, has been adopted by more than 20 states, resulting in the restoration of sight to more than a half-million people. Several European countries as well as Israel, New Zealand, Singapore, and Tunisia have already instituted a system of presumed consent for kidneys and other organs, resulting in significant overall increases in the supply of organs.

"The essential ethical advantage of required response is its undiluted loyalty to the value of individual autonomy."

CONSENT FOR ORGAN DONATION SHOULD BE REQUIRED

Presumed Consent Subcommittee of the UNOS Ethics Committee

The Presumed Consent Subcommittee of the United Network for Organ Sharing (UNOS) was formed to study the ethics of presumed consent, a policy that assumes a potential organ donor would have consented to donate his or her organs if he or she had been asked. The following viewpoint, excerpted from the subcommittee's report, maintains that presumed consent has serious ethical problems. It recommends a policy of required response—in which all adult Americans would be required to indicate their willingness to be an organ donor—be adopted. The subcommittee argues that required response would respect an individual's choice concerning organ donation and would increase the number of organ donors as people become more accepting of the procedure. UNOS is the national organization of organ procurement and transplant centers through which all organs for transplant must be cleared.

As you read, consider the following questions:

1. What are the main objections to presumed consent, according to the subcommittee?
2. Why is routine salvaging unethical, in the subcommittee's opinion?
3. According to the author, how will the policy of required response eventually lead to one of presumed consent?

Reprinted, with permission, from "An Evaluation of the Ethics of Presumed Consent and a Proposal Based on Required Response," by the Presumed Consent Subcommittee of the Ethics Committee, United Network for Organ Sharing, June 30, 1993.

The Presumed Consent Subcommittee of the UNOS [United Network for Organ Sharing] Ethics Committee was charged with evaluating the ethics of presumed consent as a legal-policy regimen for the regulation of the donation of cadaveric organs and tissues for transplantation. . . . In this paper we as a Subcommittee evaluate presumed consent from an ethical perspective and propose an alternative organ donation reform called "required response."

PRESUMED CONSENT

We begin with the following definition:

Public policy based on presumed consent would offer every adult the opportunity to express and have recorded by publicly accountable authorities his or her refusal to be a donor of solid organs and tissues. A clinically and legally indicated candidate for cadaveric organ and tissue recovery is presumed to have consented to organ and tissue recovery if he or she had not registered a refusal.

In the above definition of presumed consent, there is no allowance for the donor's family to interfere with the donation process. This is the strong version of presumed consent. . . . A weak version of presumed consent requires the permission of the donor's family, if the family can be located, before organs and tissues are removed. Proponents of presumed consent (sometimes referred to as "implied" consent) argue that the policy, if accompanied by public education and an efficient mechanism for recording and transmitting donation refusals, would increase the supply of organs while simultaneously respecting the individual's right to "opt out" of organ donation. . . .

PREVIOUS UNOS RESEARCH

Presumed consent, as one of several contending reform policies, has been considered previously by other UNOS committees and members. The UNOS Ad Hoc Donations Committee evaluated the public's receptivity to presumed consent legislation in its January 1991 telephone poll of 801 individuals. When asked "Whether physicians should be able to act on implied consent," 38% said "yes," 55% said "no," and 7% were undecided. The Ad Hoc Committee suggested that many (33%) of the respondents may not have fully understood the concept of presumed consent by objecting to presumed consent on the grounds that "a person should make the choice to give consent." In the view of the Ad Hoc Committee, "the individual has made a choice by not objecting to donation" and therefore respondents should not object to presumed consent on the basis that it precludes personal choice.

The 1992 National Kidney Foundation/UNOS survey would appear to support the assumption that spirited public education in the qualities of presumed consent would need to be conducted as a necessary, if not sufficient, condition for its acceptance. J. Childress, Edwin B. Kyle Professor of Religious Ethics, University of Virginia, and an At Large UNOS Ethics Committee member, underscored this practical point in emphasizing the potential for donors to act on their fears and distrust by "opting out" or "dissent" in such numbers that presumed consent would "actually reduce the number of donated organs."

THE ETHICS OF PRESUMED CONSENT

Generally, advocates of presumed consent advance the following in support of their position:

• Efficiency is good. Increasing the supply of organs—that is, supply-side efficiency—is a worthwhile goal. It is sufficiently important to collect more organs that other goals and values, within limits, may be compromised.

• Asking for consent can be cruel. Presumed consent would obviate the need to ask the donor's family for consent at a time of family's painful grieving.

• Individual conscience can be respected. Presumed consent respects the principle of individual choice by giving objectors to organ donation an opportunity to empower their anti-donation preference.

• Individuals owe society the effort to register their objection. Individuals who object to organ donation should be burdened with the task of registering their preference to the public authorities because organ donation is, presumptively, socially desirable. The burden of communicating objection should be placed on objectors to organ donation.

Presumed consent, advocates argue, combines the principles of supply-side efficiency, respect for individual conscience, and the individual's positive, yet qualified, duty to promote the good of society.

PRACTICAL OBJECTIONS

Opponents of presumed consent base their position on the following presuppositions:

• There will be false positives, that is, persons who were "presumed" to consent but who, in fact, objected to donation. Under a policy of "presumed consent," some individuals who do object to organ donation in principle will not register their preference with public authorities because of one of many factors. For instance, individuals on the margins of society might not learn of their option to register their refusal. Furthermore, individuals have differential access to the mechanism for registering refusal, as in the case of itinerant persons who may not receive a postcard informing them of the opting-out alternative.

• Problems in registering and transmitting objection status. The mechanism for registering and transmitting objection status is likely to be inadequate. Only a nationwide database of objectors is ethically justified because individuals may suffer irreversible cessation of brain function outside their state of residence. There is uncertainty whether mailed-in objection notices will be entered on the database and whether the information will be distributed to organ procurement organizations in a timely fashion.

FAMILY OBJECTIONS MUST BE ACCEPTED

William F. May recalled a tale from the Brothers Grimm in which a young man who is incapable of horror and does not shrink back from the dead attempts even to play with a corpse and is sent away "to learn how to shudder." If families are often reluctant to authorize organ donation after the death of a loved one, that reluctance ought to be honored—lest we collectively forget how to shudder. Indeed, I do not think it wise even to act upon the deceased person's previously stated willingness to be a donor in the face of family reluctance or objection. Our society's desperate attempt to find ways to live longer should not be allowed to override a deep-seated and difficult to articulate sense of the importance of the body, even the dead body.

Gilbert Meilaender, First Things, April 1996.

• Individual autonomy speaks to a core value. Asking individuals to publicly express their objection to donation does not respect the individual's right not to choose. Individuals do not have a social duty to express an objection.

• To decide whether to consent is not a dichotomous choice. Individuals should have the right to delegate the decision to family members. Presumed consent would authorize collection of organs of a non-objector who had trusted his family to make the decision.

Opponents, then, have practical objections to presumed consent based on the predictably positive, if undetermined, probability that individual donation preferences will not be respected in the event of donation candidacy.

Advocates and opponents of presumed consent are not distinguished by their divergent assessments of the risk that some persons who object to donation will become donors under the presumed consent regime. Rather, the origin of divergence lies in the ethical assessment of tolerable risk. Advocates of presumed consent find permissible cases of false positives. Such cases are excusable because (i) individual objectors ultimately have the responsibility to register their objections and (ii) false positives which arise due to mechanical breakdowns must be weighed against the greater good of increasing the supply of organs. Opponents, in contrast, perceive a statist, non-individualistic intent behind presumed consent. That is, opponents perceive that advocates of presumed consent can predict—before the policy is implemented—that presumed consent will remove organs from persons who objected to donation. Respect for individual conscience, for policy opponents, is a core value that should supersede the social utilitarianism underlying presumed consent.

THE SUBCOMMITTEE'S POSITION ON PRESUMED CONSENT

Three main considerations guided us.

First, the practicality of the policy must be questioned given that public opinion surveys suggest its unpopularity. The NKF/ UNOS survey found support at approximately 37%. A 1985 Gallup survey placed public support at 7%. More profoundly, the policy stands to contradict a profound respect a majority of Americans reserve for the value of individualism, as evidenced in the the following pronouncement by David Ogden:

> Presumed consent is not quite the American way. It is relatively coercive, compared to the more classical freedom of choice that characterizes our way of life. Consent should be positive, not implied.

In the Subcommittee's view, the anti-statist, individualistic perspective is sufficiently distributed in the general population to make problematic the acceptance of presumed consent.

Second, the Subcommittee was unimpressed with mechanisms in place in countries which employ presumed consent to protect the rights of objectors to donation. These mechanisms often appear to offer only superficial respect for individual autonomy. The mechanistic difficulties convince us that the quality of "consent" likely to be "presumed" would fail the practical challenge of matching individual preferences for donation with candidacy for donation. We as a Subcommittee challenge the integrity of the notion of "presumed consent." Our challenge is based on the fact that data make clear that consent cannot be presumed. Focus groups organized in the NKF/UNOS Organ Donation Study confirmed the findings of national public opinion surveys that a significant portion of the public is opposed to donation on grounds of distrust of the medical community in general and the organ donation and allocation process in particular.

The third consideration was the Subcommittee's positive assessment of the alternative of "required response." In our view, the alternative can significantly lead to an increase in the supply of organs without risking the violation of the principle of individual autonomy by removing organs from persons who objected to donation but did not have the preference recorded by the proper authority.

The ethical challenges facing "presumed consent" are considerable. They are not, however, insurmountable. The Subcommittee takes an active interest in states' experimentation with presumed consent policy. Part of the ethical test for the states is this: To not use the concept of "presumed consent" to rationalize the acquisition of organs from persons who may have had an objection to donation. States should invest heavily in educating the public in the consequences of not registering an objection, in facilitating the registering of an objection, and in assuring that procurement organizations are made aware of the identities of objectors on a timely basis.

ROUTINE SALVAGING

Routine salvaging is a policy originally proposed by Jesse Dukeminier and David Sanders. The effect of routine salvaging on the practice of organ procurement would be similar to procurement relying on presumed consent. In either case, organs could be taken without the explicit consent of the donor's family or donor (as indicated, for example, by a signed donor card).

The ethical underpinnings, however, are quite different. The policy of routine salvaging is inconsistent with liberal individualism. Liberal societies assume that the individual, not the state, should control his or her physical disposition. A liberal society respects this principle by asking for the consent of the donor before organs are recovered. Exceptions to liberal individualism must meet a severe test, as in wartime when the coercive military draft is premised on the need to serve vital national interests. Exceptions to liberal individualism must meet the further test of being the only measures which can plausibly attain the community's objectives.

Presumed consent relies on the claim that there is a basis for a presumption that the deceased would have agreed to donating organs had he or she been asked. Routine salvaging, in contrast, does not assume consent is needed. It presupposes the subordination of the individual to the state-led national community, as exemplified by the procurement law in France which codifies the ethic of the "Good Samaritan." Many proposals for routine salvaging soften their approach by permitting individuals who object to having organs procured to "opt out" by registering an objection to organ procurement.

For the United States, reforming the organ donation system on the basis of routine salvaging gives more authority to the state-led national community than public opinion—and American political culture—would allow at the present time. The reform would require abandoning the current commitment to the importance of the individual, at least for matters of determining how the body is to be treated after death.

Since empirical evidence makes clear that (i) we cannot presently presume the consent of Americans to have their organs procured after death and (ii) most Americans appear unwilling to support routine salvaging, a third option seems to this Subcommittee to be preferable, a policy we shall call "required response."

REQUIRED RESPONSE

This section will describe the Subcommittee's proposed alternative to presumed consent and routine salvaging and then discuss its ethical advantages over the two previous alternatives. In the comparative analysis, presumed consent and required response will be emphasized owing to their greater salience in the current policy context.

The policy status quo is a state-centered approach relying on the use of the back of driver's licenses, applications for driver's licenses, or the distribution of donor cards to be carried with or attached to the driver's license. The approach is uncoordinated across the states: Not only is there no centralized collection of donation preferences but not even the same data points are collected (i.e., the variations include consent for removal of specific organs, all organs, and all tissues). A policy of required response would replace wasteful uncoordinated state-level programs with a uniform method of collecting and disseminating donation preferences to procurement organizations. A national approach is needed to assure the routine and uniform collection of donation preference data and its dissemination to organ procurement specialists.

Required response intends to accelerate the historical increase in the number of Americans who have indicated a willingness to be organ donors. In 1992 approximately 33% of Americans had signed a donor card, compared to 16% in 1985. The need for required response is seen in a result of the NKF/UNOS Organ Donation Survey: Respondents who had not designated a willingness to donate were most likely to cite the fact that they had "never been asked to" (52%). Required response would address this most obvious of reasons why individuals have not designated themselves as willing to donate. . . .

CHARACTERISTICS OF REQUIRED RESPONSE

Under a legal regime of required response, all adults would be required by public authorities to express their preferences regarding organ donation. Individuals will have the opportunity to indicate a willingness or objection to donation. Moreover, the individual would have the option to delegate the donation decision to his or her next of kin or designated surrogate. Donation-regarding preferences would be recorded in a National Donor Registry (NDR), a centralized database accessible by organ procurement organizations. These preferences will carry legal weight. Following death declaration, the OPO would access the NDR to ascertain the donor's preference on donation of organs and tissues. The OPO will have the legal authority to excise organs from a deceased person who had expressed a pro-donation preference. This recorded preference would be shown to the donor's family in order to acquire the cooperation of this key set of actors in the donation process.

While respecting the individual's prerogative to "opt in or out" of the donation process, required response would increase the supply of donated organs by decreasing the frequency of refusals by donor families and by granting additional legal protection to OPOs. We expect families of donors to less frequently present an obstacle to donation because of the presentation of evidence that the decedent had a pro-donation preference. The Subcommittee's assumption, based on previous survey research, is that the primary reason more people do not sign their donor cards is because no authority had asked them. Hence the following conclusion: Required response would increase the percentage of donation events in which the OPO had substantial evidence that the donor had a pro-donation preference. In terms of legal immunity, required response would also protect the OPO in the event that the donor's family cannot be reached and the donor had expressed a preference for donation.

In short, the efficacy of required response would come about as the result of reducing uncertainty of the donor's wishes by (i) recording the donor's preferences routinely and (ii) making those preferences accessible to OPOs which have a need to know this information on a timely basis.

The Subcommittee proposes the policy of required response as the first part of a larger reform strategy. Over time, ideally, the legal regime regulating organ donation will approach the policy of "presumed consent" wherein organs and tissue are recovered without active consent-seeking on the part of OPOs. The envisioned policy evolution is as follows: As adults increasingly "opt-in" to the donation system by expressing "yes" via required response, the practical necessity of checking the database recording preferences will diminish. The evolution is for a societal consensus on transplant donation to emerge, as recorded through required response, so that consent may be safely "presumed" because of universal approval of organ donation. . . .

THE ETHICAL ADVANTAGE

The essential ethical advantage of required response is its undiluted loyalty to the value of individual autonomy. By giving every adult an opportunity to opt-out of the donation system, required response respects the individual's "right" to stand apart from society. On this dimension, required response is distinct from presumed consent because the latter offers less protection against the risk of collecting organs from persons who held reservations toward organ donation. This distinctiveness of required response is also the source of its major limitation because it is uncertain what percentage of the adult population would elect to opt-out of the system. If not accompanied by an effective public education campaign, required response could backfire by empowering a substantial bloc of anti-donation attitudes.

The loyalty of required response to the value of individual autonomy, however, should not be overstated, lest we neglect to underscore the term "required" in the policy's title. Society, as represented in the state, would take it upon itself to require individuals to express their preferences for or against organ donation. In a real sense, the provision constitutes a coerced burden, not to mention the burden accruing from public spending on the program of required response. The justification for this added burden is that it will empower individual preferences in the context of organ donation while respecting the right of individuals to remain "whole" in death.

The Subcommittee concludes that reform of the organ donation process should not be based on the presumed consent model. Ethically, presumed consent offers inadequate safeguards for protecting the individual autonomy of prospective donors.

Presumed consent too closely approximates "routine salvaging" in practice, although in rhetoric it pays homage to the value of individualism inherent in the consent model.

The Subcommittee recommends the policy of required response as an alternative reform. Under required response, individual adults must express a preference regarding donation to the public authorities. The recording and dissemination of this preference in the event of death would help persuade the decedent's next of kin of the desirability of organ donation. Family refusals to donate constitute a major source of lost donors. Ethically, required response emphasizes the autonomy of the individual, making unnecessary any presumption of the individual's willingness to donate.

| "We should not allow sentimentalism
| for particular kinds of animals to
| block procedures which could save or
| enhance many human lives."

ANIMAL-TO-HUMAN ORGAN TRANSPLANTS COULD SAVE LIVES

Jennifer Cunningham

Animal-to-human organ transplants are ethical because a human life is more important than the life of an animal, asserts Jennifer Cunningham in the following viewpoint. Human interests should come before those of animals, she contends; if an animal's organ is needed to save a life, then it should be used. Moreover, regulations that restrict animal-to-human transplants unless the procedure will produce a clear benefit for humans are ill advised, Cunningham argues, because many of the operation's benefits are not immediately apparent. Cunningham is a regular contributor to Living Marxism, a monthly British magazine.

As you read, consider the following questions:

1. What percentage of genes are shared between chimpanzees and humans, according to the author?
2. According to the Nuffield Council on Bioethics, why are animal-to-human organ transplants unethical?
3. In Cunningham's opinion, why is the Nuffield Council's argument against primate-to-human transplants illogical?

Reprinted, with permission, from "Planet of the Apes?" by Jennifer Cunningham, Living Marxism, June 1996.

Human-to-human organ transplantation has become almost routine. The problem of rejection of donor organs that inhibited transplantation efforts in the 1960s has been largely overcome—due to a remarkable progress in tissue typing (matching donor and recipient to get immunological compatibility) and the development of effective immunosuppressive drugs.

Now a different problem has arisen: there are insufficient human organs for everyone who needs one. Around 5000 patients are on the waiting list for transplants in Britain, but because of the shortage of donated organs less than 3000 human organ transplants were performed in 1995. This has led to increased interest in the use of animal organs for transplantation into humans, or xenotransplantation (transplanting tissues from one species to another)—a procedure now made far more possible by scientific advances.

ANIMAL-TO-HUMAN ORGAN TRANSPLANTS

Transplant pioneers attempting animal-to-human organ transplants in the 1960s experienced dramatic failures. Many recipients died on the operating table, principally due to the rapid rejection of animal tissues by the human immune system. But progress has been made. In particular, the use of primate (monkey and ape) organs, developed exclusively in the United States, is now quite feasible.

The genetic relatedness of primates and humans makes their tissues more immunocompatible with ours than those of other animals; for example, we share more than 98 per cent of our genes with chimpanzees. A patient who received a chimpanzee kidney in 1964 survived nine months. In 1984, baby Fae survived 20 days after she was given a baboon heart, and in 1992 a patient with a baboon's liver lived 10 months.

In a highly publicised case in December 1995, American researchers in San Francisco transplanted baboon bone marrow into Jeff Getty, an AIDS patient. This effort to boost Getty's immune system relied on the fact that baboon immune cells are naturally resistant to the HIV virus. Although the graft failed to take, it did the patient no harm and in fact he appeared to be healthier by several measures than he was before the procedure. Hopefully, further trials will follow.

All this is good news, and offers hope for many people. All the more shocking, then, that there is a good chance that such procedures will soon be banned in the United Kingdom, and that related research will be severely curtailed.

Such a ban was recommended in 1996 by the Nuffield

Council on Bioethics, Britain's leading voice on bioethics, a body funded by the Medical Research Council and the Wellcome Trust among others. In their report *Animal-to-Human Transplants: The Ethics of Xenotransplantation*, Nuffield's experts raised a warning about disease transmission. But even if this problem was resolved, they said, such transplants would remain unethical because they would violate the rights of baboons and other primates. Nuffield's stance is a major victory for animal rights and animal welfare organisations—and a major setback for humanity. It is also an insult. The Nuffield Council has, in effect if not by intention, put the lives of transplant patients on a par with those of primates.

THE JEWISH VIEW

[The question is asked:] "is the use of nonhuman primates ethical?" The question raises issues about the killing of animals, the raising of animals in captivity, and the treatment of animals in general. The corpus of Jewish law has much to say about the appropriate treatment of animals. Provided that the baboons receive appropriate treatment, and given careful assurance against extinction of a species, Judaism would hold the use of animal parts to be not only justifiable but preferable to the use of human body parts.

Stacy K. Offner, *Making the Rounds in Health, Faith, & Ethics*, October 9, 1995.

Nuffield recommends that pig organs be used instead of primates'. Advances in genetic engineering have made it possible for pig organs to be modified in order to limit the immune reaction of the human host. This is to be welcomed. There are some instances in which pig organs might even be preferable to primate ones. But there is no hiding the fact that in many cases an organ from a pig will be the second best option. Nuffield knows this. The simple fact is that it has caved in to the animal rights lobby, who sent in by far the largest group of submissions to the working party preparing the report.

It is not unusual for mainstream ethics committees to attempt to take on board the views of hardline critics of certain scientific procedures. Usually, the intention is to water down the criticism and allow the procedure to continue, even if it does so under a cloud of suspicion. What is different and so disturbing this time is that the group drawn together by Nuffield has crossed the line and endorsed a substantial argument of the animal rights critics. Reading between the lines, it is clear that this decision was not reached without some argument. But that is all by-the-by now, for the animal rights campaigners have their endorsement.

HUMAN WELFARE SHOULD COME FIRST

The pity is that the issue should be an easy one to explain: humans are special, are not to be equated with primates, and our interests should come first. Unfortunately, the Nuffield Council seems to lack the confidence to make this elementary point.

The divide that matters is between humanity and the animal kingdom as a whole, not between humanity and the primates on one side and pigs and the rest of the animal kingdom on the other. Contrary to the claims made by leading proponent of animal rights Peter Singer in his *Declaration on Great Apes*, which are echoed in the report from Nuffield, primates are no different from the rest of the animal kingdom as regards their limited capacities. The gulf between human and primate is unbridgeable in terms of our capacity for conscious thought, voluntary control of our behaviour and our ability to learn and advance. All of these differences set us apart from primates and other animals.

Let us get the issue into some perspective: as the Nuffield report itself points out, baboons, the likely source from which hearts would be taken if the procedure were allowed, are regarded as pests in many parts of the world. Are we to let concern for the 'rights' of pests cost human lives? Yes we are, it would seem, if Nuffield has its way.

THE ANIMAL RIGHTS LOBBY'S NEXT STEP

Having achieved this concession, the animal rights lobby will now seek to push home its advantage. The next step, as outlined by Singer in his *The Great Ape Project*, will be to question the use of primates in all experimental procedures. After that, a broader case will be made for extending rights and protections to all animals.

At the moment, it is legal to use primates in experimental procedures which benefit humanity, even if this leads to the death of the primate concerned. Nuffield has endorsed this position. One obvious such procedure is xenotransplantation trials. To test out the possibility of pig-to-human transplants, we need to try experiments in which hearts are taken from pigs and placed in primates, as these provide the best guide to the difficulties that will arise when we try to place pig hearts in humans.

While Nuffield defends these experiments, as it must if it is to recommend the use of pig hearts in humans, it has made the job of doing so far harder by endorsing the animal rights case for primates. For if logic matters on these questions, the logic of

Nuffield's argument would be to ban such experiments as well. Indeed, the logic of Nuffield's argument should surely be that the experiments are more of a problem than the simple killing of primates for their hearts. The experiments can cause distress to primates prior to an early death; killing primates for their organs, on the other hand, causes none, assuming anaesthetic is used. All that is lost is life and liberty—and Nuffield itself, by endorsing the use of primates in experiments, is clearly accepting that primates do not have a sufficiently developed sense of self to value these things.

A BROADER THREAT TO RESEARCH

Nuffield's concession to the animal rights campaigners carries with it a broader threat to research in the whole field of xenotransplantation, and beyond. The Nuffield report argues that animal rights and animal welfare should also be a consideration when pigs and other animals are involved. They say that the needs of humans definitely override this only when it is a life for a life. However, if the benefits to humanity are not so immediately obvious, the report goes on to say, then consideration for animals must be given more weight: 'the likely adverse effects on animals must be weighed against the benefits likely to accrue from their use.'

This might seem like a subtle way of placating the opposition while allowing the experiments to continue. Indeed, that might well have been the intention. But there is a problem. In some cases the benefits will not be obvious. What is more, it is often the case that benefits arise in unforeseen ways from experimental procedures. Nuffield's approach threatens to restrict experiments in which the benefits are unclear, and in doing so it might lead to humanity missing out on unforeseen gains.

SOME POSSIBILITIES WORTH EXPLORING

We can already glimpse some possibilities which are worth exploring experimentally. For example, the therapeutic avenues of both genetic engineering and the testing of new drug therapies to minimise xenotransplantation rejection may have applications far beyond transplant programmes. They could provide answers to a number of diseases involving thrombosis and inflammatory reactions which cause major tissue damage and impaired function, including autoimmune diseases (in which the body produces antibodies against its own tissues).

Fritz Bach, a Harvard Medical School professor involved in developing genetically engineered therapies in xenotransplantation, has pointed out that 'research into xenotransplantation presents exciting prospects for treating organ failure':

> It also offers insights into issues common to medicine as a whole. From tackling the problem of thrombosis and inflammation in rejection grafts, for example, we are likely to be able to introduce genes into a patient's endothelial cells via the blood to treat a segment of diseased vessel or other tissues. The results of xenotransplantation research should provide broad benefits in treating human disease.

Of course, nobody can be certain that the results of the experimental work will bring the benefits Bach outlines, but we shall never know unless we try to find out. Unfortunately, Nuffield's equivocation on experimental procedures casts a shadow over such work.

SENTIMENTALISM

Causing unnecessary distress to animals is inhumane, and scientists working in the field take all the steps they can to minimise it. But we should not allow sentimentalism for particular kinds of animals to block procedures which could save or enhance many human lives. Rather, a positive case should be made for animal experiments which emphasises the benefits and potential benefits they offer for people.

The Nuffield Council has given in to sentimentalism in its report. Thankfully, it is not yet law, and others may yet see sense in time. The government is to be given advice on the subject of xenotransplantation by a committee headed by Professor Ian Kennedy. The Nuffield report will be its starting point, but let us hope that this committee has not been so swayed by the animal rights lobby that the interests of humans are placed secondary to those of primates.

In America, where primates are used in transplants, the case of Jeff Getty, the AIDS patient given baboon bone marrow, has forced some of Hollywood's leading lights to decide which cause they care most about: animal rights or AIDS. Such cases should make people in Britain think too: are we really going to let people suffer and die unnecessarily in order to protect the 'interests' of baboons?

"[Animal-to-human organ transplants] have proved to be extremely costly failures that may pose serious health risks to the public."

ANIMAL-TO-HUMAN ORGAN TRANSPLANTS ARE DANGEROUS AND UNETHICAL

People for the Ethical Treatment of Animals

Xenografts are organ transplants in which an animal organ is transplanted into a human patient. In the following viewpoint, the anti-animal experimentation organization People for the Ethical Treatment of Animals (PETA) argues that animal organs should not be transplanted into humans. No animal-to-human transplants have succeeded, PETA asserts. Moreover, the organization contends, transplanting animal organs into humans may transfer deadly viruses to the human species. PETA maintains that more effort should be directed at convincing people to become organ donors than pursuing xenografts.

As you read, consider the following questions:

1. How many animals have been used as organ donors for humans since 1905, according to PETA?
2. Why did many medical ethicists condemn Baby Fae's transplant surgeon, in PETA's opinion?
3. According to PETA, how do xenografts affect other health programs?

Reprinted, with permission, from "Xenografts: Frankenstein Science," Animal Experiments Fact Sheet No. 14, of People for the Ethical Treatment of Animals, April 1996.

Xenografts are surgical transplants in which donor and recipient are members of different species. The success rate for xenografts is zero. Transplantation of vital organs and other body parts, such as bone marrow, taken from other-than-human animals has been attempted as part of experimental treatments for degenerative organ diseases and viral infections like hepatitis and AIDS. After several decades of research, xenografts have proved to be extremely costly failures that may pose serious health risks to the public.

A BLOODY TRAIL

Since 1905, at least 34 pigs, chimpanzees, monkeys, and baboons have been made the unwilling "donors" of kidneys, hearts, livers, and bone marrow for transplantation into humans. The misery inflicted on such experimental animals begins at birth, with delivery by surgical hysterectomy, after which they are placed in an "isolette" in an attempt to keep them free of infectious agents. Animals are subjected to the sensory deprivation of a sterile laboratory environment and denied all social interaction with members of their own species. When the time comes for them to "donate" their organs, they are killed.

Every one of these experiments has failed, with most recipients dying within a few hours, days, or weeks.

BAD SCIENCE

The human immune system is designed to identify and reject foreign objects. Human-to-human transplants have relied on immunosuppressive drugs to control rejection of the transplanted organ. Genetic differences make transplants from other species particularly noticeable to the human immune system. Even chimpanzees, our closest relatives, are six times as different from us as we are from each other, and the risk of rejecting a baboon organ is 25 times greater than for an unmatched human organ. Xenograft researchers have developed increasingly powerful immunosuppressive therapies to try to overcome this natural reaction. The drawback is that these treatments create an immune deficiency that leaves the recipient vulnerable to often fatal infections.

HIDDEN DANGERS

In several recent xenograft experiments, researchers have cited the differences among species to try to justify the use of animal organs. In 1992, a team led by Dr. Thomas Starzl of the University of Pittsburgh transplanted a baboon liver into a 35-year-old man who was suffering from hepatitis B. The experimenters reasoned that since the hepatitis virus does not cause liver damage in baboons, a baboon liver would increase his chances of survival. Two months later, the patient died of a massive brain hemorrhage.

In 1995, AIDS patient Jeff Getty received a transplant of bone marrow taken from a baboon. Baboons infected with the Human Immunodeficiency Virus (HIV), the virus presumed to cause AIDS, do not develop the life-threatening immune deficiency that characterizes human AIDS. Bone marrow is an important component of the immune system, and Getty's doctors hypothesized that by transferring this component to their patient they could create a "parallel" immune system that would fight the virus. But just weeks after the transplant, the doctors were forced to admit that the experiment had failed and no trace of the baboon cells could be found in the patient.

ANIMAL-TO-HUMAN ORGAN TRANSPLANTS ARE A FAILURE

Donor	Organ	Length of Survival	No. Cases	Year
Chimpanzee	Kidney	<9 months	12	1964
Monkey	Kidney	10 days	1	1964
Baboon	Kidney	4.5 days	1	1964
Baboon	Kidney	<2 months	6	1964
Chimpanzee	Heart	<1 day	1	1964
Chimpanzee	Liver	<14 days	3	1969–74
Baboon	Heart	<1 day	1	1977
Chimpanzee	Heart	4 days	1	1977
Baboon	Heart	4 weeks	1	1985
Baboon	Liver	70 days, 26 days	2	1993

AV Magazine, Fall 1996.

Prior to approving the Getty experiment, the Food and Drug Administration held a conference with experts in immunology to discuss dangers and potential benefits. There was general agreement that the procedure was more likely to kill the patient than to help him. In fact, many in the scientific community are calling for a moratorium on all xenografts because of the danger of unleashing new diseases into the human population. Many microbes that are completely harmless in one species cause disease in others. Baboons, for example, routinely carry infectious agents that are harmful or deadly to humans. Among them are

Yersinia pestis, which causes bubonic plague, the Marburg virus, and the lethal Ebola virus and hantavirus. In addition to known pathogens, animals may also harbor as-yet-unidentified viruses, bacteria, and parasites which could prove deadly to people. Many human epidemics, AIDS included, can probably be traced to microbes "jumping" from one species to another.

Informed Consent?

As with any hazardous medical procedure, xenograft recipients are required to sign an informed consent form before undergoing the procedure, stating that the patient understands the risks involved and the alternatives available. It is doubtful that desperately ill patients are given all the facts when considering xenograft procedures. Many believe their doctors are attempting to save their lives, rather than performing futile experiments on them. In 1984, doctors at Loma Linda University in California transplanted a baboon heart into an infant born with serious heart defects. "Baby Fae" died 20 days later. Afterwards, an independent review panel determined that there were at least three other options—all more promising than a xenograft—available to treat her condition. The baby's mother, who was alone and virtually destitute, was never informed of these options. Many medical ethicists condemned Dr. Leonard Bailey, who performed the experiment, for leading Baby Fae's mother to believe that the doomed experiment offered hope for her baby's survival.

Costly Failures

In addition to the toll in human and animal lives, xenografts divert precious resources away from truly life-saving efforts to treat disease. Each xenograft procedure costs between $250,000 and $300,000 to perform. The University of Pittsburgh's experimental transplant program alone receives more than $8 million each year in funding, largely through federal grants from the National Institutes of Health. Meanwhile, many promising new treatments for AIDS and other life-threatening diseases go unexplored because of lack of funding. National organ donor procurement programs receive less than half a million dollars annually.

Even basic programs which have proved to save lives, like those that provide housing, primary care, and treatment to people with AIDS, have suffered cutbacks due to resource constraints. Most of the diseases for which xenografts have been proposed, including AIDS, hepatitis B, and other degenerative organ diseases, are preventable, yet prevention programs receive little to no public funding.

Advocates of cross-species transplants point to the scarcity of human organ donors to justify continued efforts in this field. Every year, thousands of Americans are buried with organs that are suitable for donation, far exceeding the 3,400 who die while on organ donor waiting lists. European organ donor policies assume that every person is an organ donor unless otherwise specified. The burden rests with individuals (or their families) if they do not wish to donate their organs. Even within the current system, patients have a better chance of long-term survival by waiting for a last-minute human organ than by choosing a xenograft.

| "What's obviously bad . . . is imprisoning or killing people because of their beliefs, not using any resulting corpses to save lives."

USING ORGANS FROM EXECUTED PRISONERS IS ETHICAL

Robert Wright

Robert Wright argues in the following viewpoint that removing the organs from executed criminals for transplantation is a practical and moral way to ease the shortage of organ donors. He maintains that using the death of a guilty person is an ethical way to save the life of an innocent person. What is immoral about the situation, Wright contends, is executing prisoners for their beliefs, not for the use of their organs afterwards. Wright is a contributing editor for the *New Republic*, a weekly liberal magazine.

As you read, consider the following questions:

1. Who is Harry Wu and why is he important in the debate about buying and selling human organs, according to Wright?
2. In Wright's opinion, why are Americans in no position to complain about the inegalitarian effects of organ allocation in China?
3. What are some questions that bother the author about using the organs of executed criminals for transplantation?

Reprinted by permission of the *New Republic* from "The Trouble with Harry," by Robert Wright, *New Republic*, July 31, 1995; ©1995, The New Republic, Inc.

Editor's note: Harry Wu was a political prisoner in China for nineteen years before becoming a naturalized U.S. citizen in 1985. He secretly returned to China three times in the early 1990s to expose human rights abuses. On his fourth attempt, he was arrested and charged with espionage. He was convicted of spying in July 1995 and expelled from China.

Remember those two Americans who wandered haplessly across the Iraqi border in March 1995 and now sit in an Iraqi prison? [They were released in July 1995.] What were their names again? You needn't worry about the name "Harry Wu" fading from the nation's consciousness quite so fast. There are several reasons for this, and some are valid. Before his fateful attempt to re-enter China, Wu had worked fearlessly to expose the gruesome interior of Chinese prisons. Most famously, he had gathered evidence that Chinese officials sell the organs of executed prisoners, sometimes even rescheduling executions to meet peak demand. Such feats give Wu a legitimate claim to our lasting attention.

More dubious is the way news about Wu and his findings has been further amplified, and sometimes warped, by aging cold warriors like Jesse Helms, whose worldview lost its simple clarity back when the Berlin Wall fell in 1989. For them Wu is not merely someone who has shed valuable light on important problems; he is a gift from God—someone who has brought Satan back into their lives. It was Helms who convened the May 1995 hearings in which Wu rehashed earlier revelations about organ-selling (and Helms who used the occasion to trot out anecdotage of unclear relevance about Chinese fetus eaters). And it is Helms, among others, who will now want to make the immediate release of Wu paramount, even if that risks sending China back into a cold-war shell. China is, after all, a nation that sells the organs of its prisoners.

Clearly, the Chinese penal system is abhorrent. But that's true of many nations we've stayed on speaking terms with. (I don't recall Helms investigating the Shah's prisons.) If Helms is going to use things like organ-selling to label China uniquely evil, can we at least get clear on his logic? What exactly is it about this organ-selling business that's bad?

A DEBATABLE QUESTION

Presumably it's not the mere idea of using a guilty person's death to save an innocent person's life. If after Ted Bundy's execution you could have given his liver to some child who would otherwise die, would you have done so? Maybe you consider the question debatable, but surely you don't consider people who take the utilitarian side of the argument totalitarian monsters. Of course, China doesn't execute only Ted Bundys. China has political prisoners and has been known to kill them. Obviously, that's bad. But what's *obviously* bad about it is imprisoning or killing people because of their beliefs, not using any resulting corpses to save lives. So too with the issue, emphasized in the Helms hearings, of large-scale livestock theft being a capital crime in China: the problem is that theft entails death, not that death entails surgery.

AN OPPORTUNITY TO MAKE AMENDS

We wantonly squander priceless opportunities to study ourselves and our living brains, as well as new ways to make us wiser, healthier, and happier. Worse yet, in our "most enlightened" way of serving justice, we don't even think about making the attempt. So we sanctimoniously keep snuffing out the lives of criminals, many of whom acknowledge their transgression and sincerely desire to somehow make amends. They are eager to give society *real* retribution by donating their organs and by helping science unlock some of nature's deepest secrets by submitting to otherwise impossible experimentation.

But society will not allow it, and doctors refuse to accept it. In callously overriding the personal autonomy of the condemned by denying them the privilege of choice, we inflict on them the worst kind of suffering—far more agonizing than any physical pain—the crushing pain of a tortured mind and a turbulent soul denied any hope of requital.

This is forcefully driven home in a recent letter to me written by a fifty-year-old inmate awaiting electrocution on Georgia's death row: "It's cruel . . . to deny me the chance to donate my organs and make that degree of restitution. I am forced to meet my maker having taken a life and being denied the chance to give life to people so desperately in need. *I am forced to exit this world with a troubled heart and anxious mind*" (italics added).

Jack Kevorkian, *Truth Seeker*, Vol. 121, No. 5, 1994.

Is it the *selling* of organs—"to wealthy Asians"—that's so creepy? Surely Americans are in no position to complain about using the profit motive to save lives (even if prison wardens aren't the ones who in our system make the profit). And surely we can't complain about the inegalitarian effect of market-allocated medical resources; here, as in China, the rich and powerful get the best health care, including lifesaving breaks. Mickey

Mantle is a long-time alcohol abuser—a fact that, according to the guidelines which supposedly govern organ donations in America, should have complicated his recent quest for a liver. But Mantle got a new liver faster than you can say "going, going, *gone!*" Meanwhile, somewhere in America, some penniless uninsured sap walked into an emergency room with alcohol on his breath, complaining of pain around his liver. What do you suppose became of him?

As for execution dates being moved up to accommodate the needs of organ recipients: If accelerating Ted Bundy's death by a week would save the life of your son or daughter or sibling, would the idea acquire some moral plausibility? Again: you may answer no, but can you really call people who answer yes Stalinist goons, or even un-American? In any event, the Jesse Helmses of the world are all for accelerating executions—not to save anyone's life, just on principle.

PRISONER CONSENT

Human rights advocates make a big issue of "prisoner consent" to donate organs. They seem to think that removing someone's kidneys without permission is a violation of bodily dignity in a way that already having killed them without permission wasn't. Well, maybe. But surely this is a culture-bound belief, not some obvious universal truth. If we're going to claim to have found a bright moral line between (*a*) killing people and (*b*) also taking their kidneys, we should pay more attention to nations without capital punishment that claim to see a bright line between (*a*) killing people and (*b*) not killing them. Their line looks brighter than ours. (For the record: China claims to forbid organ transplants without the consent of prisoners or their relatives.)

There are some nagging questions that bother even a bloodless utilitarian like me. The main one is whether the profit motive (further) corrupts the judicial system, inflating the number of death sentences handed down. Wu has no evidence to this effect, and the best guess is that organ-selling results from freelancing prison officials, not a nationally coordinated plan. Still, this is a crucial question, and if Helms had used his hearings to ask it, he would have done a public service. But his sole aim is mind-numbing propaganda, and it seems to work. Just this week, NPR's [National Public Radio] "Morning Edition" reported that Wu has gathered "evidence that Chinese prisoners were being executed to provide donor organs for wealthy Asians." This is, indeed, the way Helms tells the story. But surely a journalist should add that, so far as Wu knows, all prisoners "executed to provide donor organs" were going to be executed anyway.

A COMPLICATED ISSUE

I doubt this column will wholly alter anyone's opinion about selling Chinese prisoners' organs. But you may now agree that we don't have enough data to deem the practice immoral in some universal, self-evident sense. Or, at least, you may now consider the issue more complicated than before. If so, that's progress. Jesse Helms would like to keep things simple: China is evil, beyond the pale. Well, what China is is pretty awful—better, on balance, than five years ago, but much worse than we'd like it to be. The overriding question should be: How can we benignly influence the arduous process of getting it from here to there?

As Helms and Harry Wu's other powerful friends try to blur this issue by emotionalizing his case, let's keep one thing clear: Wu didn't, like the two guys in Iraq, stumble innocently into the clutches of evil. When he returned to China, it was clear—to him and to colleagues who warned him—that he ran the risk of arrest. Of course we should still work steadfastly to get him out of prison. But we shouldn't, as the cold warriors want, subordinate a good part of our foreign policy to that goal. You don't have to be a utilitarian to think that the future of the world outweighs the future of Harry Wu. Indeed, judging by the way Wu has chosen to live his life, it's far from clear that he'd disagree.

"[A] former police official ... said that ... he never knew of any prisoner giving consent before his organs were harvested."

USING ORGANS FROM EXECUTED PRISONERS IS UNETHICAL

Harry Wu

Harry Wu is a Chinese dissident and human rights activist who became a naturalized U.S. citizen in 1985. In the following viewpoint, Wu maintains that Chinese prison officials are illegally selling the organs of executed prisoners for transplantation into wealthy Asians and U.S. citizens. Such a policy is unethical, he contends, because the prisoners have not given their consent for their organs to be donated.

As you read, consider the following questions:

1. According to Wu, what percentage of kidneys used in Chinese transplant operations in 1994 came from executed prisoners?
2. What are the three cases that permit the removal of organs from the body of an executed Chinese prisoner, as cited by Wu?
3. Why are the three rules governing organ removal from executed Chinese prisoners meaningless, according to the author?

Reprinted by permission of the author from "A Grim Organ Harvest in China's Prisons," by Harry Wu Hongda, *Open Magazine*, January 1995.

Editor's note: China is executing more prisoners each year, reports Amnesty International—1,079 in 1992 and 1,419 in 1993. Human-rights advocates charge that the Chinese government is committing legalized murder to harvest body organs from healthy prisoners. Chinese dissident and human-rights activist Harry Wu Hongda and Sue Lloyd-Roberts of the British Broadcasting Corporation (BBC) went to China to investigate. In the following article, Wu describes his findings. The Chinese government has denied his charges.

In China, human organs have become merchandise available to the privileged. There is a great demand for human organs such as kidneys among high Communist Party officials, who receive faster and better-quality health care than do ordinary citizens. As the level of medical technology has improved, so has the number of organ transplants from executed prisoners. According to published surveys, at least 1,400 to 1,500 kidney transplants were performed in China in 1993. No longer a well-kept secret, the supply of such marketable human organs has been extended to Hong Kong and to other countries.

No reliable information is available about the exact number of organ transplants done in the 1980s, but the official Chinese news agency, Xinhua, has reported that, by October, 1994, nearly 10,000 kidney transplants had been performed in some 90 hospitals throughout the country. Where did these kidneys come from? We estimate that 90 percent of them came from executed prisoners.

PRISONERS AS AN ORGAN SOURCE

Under the guise of seeking help for a relative in need of a kidney transplant, I met with officials and staff at several hospitals. At Number 7 People's Hospital in Zhengzhou, Henan Province, a staff member named Li told me that he had handled executed prisoners' organs for years. Li cautioned that information about organ transplantation "should be kept secret from foreigners. . . . [The organs] all come from prisoners, death-row prisoners. . . . We buy the corpses. . . . Everything is approved." Li said that one Japanese patient had paid $30,000 for a kidney.

He described the procedure: "We make arrangements with the executioners to shoot in the head so that the prisoner dies very quickly, instantly, and the survival rate of organs is considerably higher [than from shooting through the heart]. . . . We drive the surgical van directly to the execution site. . . . As soon as the prisoner is executed . . . [and] upon completion of necessary procedures by the police and the court, the body is ours. . . . We buy the whole body. . . . From a legal point of view, once a prisoner has been shot, he no longer exists as a human being."

At the West China University of Medical Sciences in Chengdu, the capital of Sichuan Province, Professor Yang, the director of urology, said that kidney transplants are performed several times a month. "We don't sell kidneys. . . . The kidneys come from brain-dead people," he assured us. Wu Jingping, head of the hospital's external affairs section, gave us a tour of the hospital and fielded questions. Asked to define the term "brain-dead," she replied, "I cannot say exactly. Each country has its own standard, and, therefore, the definition is different. . . . In the U.S., even the minute of death and such trivial matters all seem to be tied to the issue of so-called human rights. It's very difficult. We act according to our laws and reality. . . . The source of our kidneys may be donors who died in traffic accidents or brain-dead people. If the donors are brain-dead, we contact the appropriate government units to find out when we can obtain the organs. State policy does not allow us to contact our donors. . . . But we do guarantee that our kidney donors are healthy and that the organs are of excellent quality."

AN ENORMOUS POTENTIAL FOR ABUSE

Advocates for a death row donor program in the United States argue that China's abuses could never be repeated under the American criminal justice system. Heads in the sand, they ignore the fact that habeas corpus is being stripped to a meaningless shell; that blacks are four times more likely to receive the death penalty than whites; and that actual innocence is no longer an appealable issue. In a land where prosecutors routinely withhold exculpatory evidence, and 15-year-olds are given life sentences for drugs, the potential for abuse of a death row donor program is enormous. The people cry for vengeance and tax-cuts in equal measure. A death row donor program could bring them both.

Lane Nelson, *Angolite*, January/February 1995.

Wu then made the following offer: "In two to three weeks, we can get a living kidney. . . . A team of surgeons will be dispatched for removal and delivery of the organ at a fee of $9,500–$11,860. . . . We get customers from Hong Kong, Taiwan, the U.S., and from all over the world."

The Organ Transplantation Research Center of Tongji University of Medical Sciences in Wuhan City, Hubei Province, is the largest facility of its kind in China. One of its patients told me:

"All five of us in this hospital had our kidney transplants done on the same day. . . . All came from young prisoners, all under 25 and very healthy. . . . They were executed at 11 a.m., and we had our operations at 2 p.m."

THE GOVERNMENT'S ROLE

Selling organs is strictly prohibited by Chinese law. The Chinese Communist Party holds that it is poverty and capitalism that drive the trade in human organs and that to permit their sale would result in criminal gangs murdering people just for their organs. There has never been a known case of such gangs. In any event, China's medical system is controlled by the state. The trade in human organs would be virtually impossible unless the government allowed it.

The 1984 legalization of the prison harvesting, first made public in 1990, permits the removal of organs from executed prisoners in three cases: if the prisoner's body is not claimed, if the prisoner has consented to the organ removal, or if the prisoner's family has given its consent. In reality, however, these rules are meaningless. According to Chinese law, no prisoner may be treated as a death-row inmate until the Supreme People's Court makes a final ruling on his case. Therefore, technically, before that point no one is permitted to ask a prisoner to sign any document consenting to donate his organs or to conduct the medical tests necessary to prepare for organ transplantation.

Moreover, in China executions are carried out promptly— that is, immediately after the judge has delivered the verdict. The prisoner is then taken to the execution site and shot. There is no time for the authorities to get a consent form signed. Former police official Gao Peiqi of Shenzhen City said that, in the 10 years he worked at the police bureau, he never knew of any prisoner giving consent before his organs were harvested.

In Beijing, said Police Deputy Commander Yang Guang, "executed prisoners' families are not allowed to pick up the bodies. . . . Almost every corpse is cut open, organs are removed, and the bodies are cremated."

While alive, prisoners in the labor camps are forced to work in the name of reform and "to create wealth for the nation." They reclaim wastelands, build roads, dig reservoirs, and manufacture products for export. When dead, even their bodies are used to make additional profits for the Chinese government.

PERIODICAL BIBLIOGRAPHY

The following articles have been selected to supplement the diverse views presented in this chapter. Addresses are provided for periodicals not indexed in the *Readers' Guide to Periodical Literature*, the *Alternative Press Index*, the *Social Sciences Index*, or the *Index to Legal Periodicals and Books*.

Council on Ethical and Judicial Affairs, American Medical Association	"The Use of Anencephalic Neonates as Organ Donors," *JAMA*, May 24–31, 1995. Available from Subscriber Services Center, 515 N. State St., Chicago, IL 60610.
Economist	"Buddy Can You Spare a Lung?" January 25, 1997.
Steven Alan Edwards	"Pork Liver, Anyone?" *Technology Review*, July 1996.
Paul C. Fox	"Babies and Body Parts," *First Things*, December 1994. Available from 156 Fifth Ave., Suite 400, New York, NY 10010.
Ron Hamel	"Organ Allocation Should Be an Equal-Opportunity Procedure," *U.S. Catholic*, January 1997.
Issues and Controversies On File	"Organ Allocation," May 16, 1997.
Kennedy Institute of Ethics Journal	Special issue on the ethical, psychosocial, and public policy implications of procuring organs from non–heart-beating cadavers, June 1993. Available from 2715 N. Charles St., Baltimore, MD 21218-4319.
Merrill Matthews Jr.	"Have a Heart, but Pay for It," *Insight*, January 9, 1995. Available from 3600 New York Ave. NE, Washington, DC 20002.
Gilbert Meilaender	"Second Thoughts About Body Parts," *First Things*, April 1996.
Takeshi Umehara	"Descartes, Brain Death, and Organ Transplants: A Japanese View," *New Perspectives Quarterly*, Winter 1994.
Richard L. Worsnop	"Organ Transplants," *CQ Researcher*, August 11, 1995. Available from 1414 22nd St. NW, Washington, DC 20037.

CHAPTER 3

ARE REPRODUCTIVE TECHNOLOGIES ETHICAL?

Chapter Preface

The birth of Kenneth, Alexis, Natalie, Kelsey, Brandon, Nathanial, and Joel McCaughey in Iowa in November 1997—the world's first surviving set of septuplets—was called a miracle by their parents (Kenny and Bobbi McCaughey), their doctors, and much of the world. The McCaughey septuplets are part of a national trend: The number of multiple births involving three or more babies has tripled since 1980 and quadrupled since 1971.

Like many babies of multiple births, the McCaughey septuplets were conceived when their mother, Bobbi McCaughey, 29, took the powerful fertility drug Pergonal. While fertility treatments such as McCaughey's offer hope for millions of men and women who want to become parents, the drugs also raise ethical and health care concerns. Health care professionals are concerned that fertility specialists may not advise infertile couples of the risks they and their future babies face during treatment, pregnancy, and afterward. Babies born in multiple births are usually premature and have a higher risk of developing numerous health problems. Doctors often advise women to selectively abort some fetuses to give the remaining fetuses a better chance of survival, but many disregard this advice. Bernard Lieberman, a fertility doctor in Great Neck, New York, explains, "Once they get pregnant, they don't want to do anything to change things. You tell them there are risks, but they feel they can handle anything. If they can get the golden ring, they want to take it."

Fertility experts counter that women like Bobbi McCaughey, who refused to selectively abort any of her fetuses because they were a gift from God, are rare. Approximately 90 percent of women impregnated with four or more fetuses do choose selective abortion to limit the number of babies they will carry. As a result, in the United States there are only forty-seven sets of quintuplets, three sets of sextuplets, and now one set of septuplets.

For many infertile couples, the mere possibility of becoming a parent is worth the risk, the uncertainty, and the expense of fertility treatments. In the following chapter, the authors examine several ethical issues related to reproduction.

> "The best legal approach to reproductive technologies and contracts that violate women's bodily integrity . . . is abolition, not regulation."

REPRODUCTIVE TECHNOLOGIES SHOULD BE BANNED

Janice G. Raymond

In the following viewpoint, Janice G. Raymond contends that reproductive technologies such as in vitro fertilization and surrogacy are a form of violence against women because they technologically ravage women's bodies. She maintains that regulating these procedures will not protect women's integrity or prevent people from "renting" women's reproductive organs. The only way to protect women from medical abuse and exploitation, Raymond argues, is to ban the technology. Raymond is the author of *Women as Wombs: Reproductive Technologies and the Battle over Women's Freedom*, from which the following viewpoint is taken.

As you read, consider the following questions:

1. How does a proprietary right to one's body differ from a substantive right, according to Raymond?
2. In the author's view, how do reproductive technologies demean women's integrity?
3. According to the author, how do laws regulating reproductive technologies actually end up promoting them?

The articulation of reproductive rights has been mired in proprietary language. The right to control one's body too often frames the body as a possession and as capital to dispose of as the individual wishes. This view of rights analogizes the body to private property. To say I own my body is substantively different from saying I am my body. In the latter articulation, the body becomes more than a private space that the person is free to do with as she pleases. It becomes the ground of the self that has integrity, dignity, and worth—more than a use value.

Theories about owning the body help objectify and commodify women's bodies, both for others and the woman herself, creating a distance between a woman's self and a woman's body. A *proprietary right* to my body allows me to submit it to the control of others or to do with it what I please, no matter how those actions undermine not only my dignity, my integrity, and my ability to act but also the dignity, integrity, and abilities of others as well. A *substantive right* to my body means the body is more than a mere possession and raises the fundamental issue of the relationship between my body and my self, and my self to the class of women worldwide.

Prostitution and surrogacy are based on the notion that a man can buy or rent a woman's body, as in a market exchange or real estate transaction, and that a woman has the right to sell or rent her own body for money. The body, however, is not property, and therefore it is not transferable in a market sense. Yet reproductive liberalism, in North America, is locked into an oppressive legal language and reality of rights that derives from a male-dominant tradition of property rights, which institutionalizes a female body as a possession. . . .

"Natural" Rights

Within the long history of rights discourse, rights have also been essentialized as "natural" rights. Natural rights have historically been used in both conservative and radical defenses of what is perceived as given in the human condition. The right to procreate has been conceived as a natural right, and, by extension, technological reproduction has been recently promoted as the means to fulfill one's natural right to procreate. Thus the male-dominant tradition of property rights converges with a version of natural rights proclaiming a natural right to procreate, a natural right to a child, a natural right to use any means necessary to procreate, and thereby a natural right to use any person necessary to procreate.

When procreation is defined as a natural right, it is viewed as deriving from a natural instinct, comparable to eating and sleeping. Attempts to institutionalize procreation as a natural right divest the person procreating of moral responsibility, so that anything a man or woman does to reproduce is treated as an instinctive response beyond the control of human will and human relations. One way that the right to procreate becomes a law of nature is that, as a right, it becomes grounded in a natural need, that is, a compelling paternal urge or maternal instinct that demands an outlet. The right to procreate, portrayed as a natural right, renaturalizes motherhood and reproduction and grounds men's rights to "their" children in the natural order.

The challenge is to recognize the material contribution that women make to reproduction and pregnancy while at the same time not essentializing that contribution as natural female destiny. The challenge is also to argue that this contribution alone does not constitute the primary action or agency of female reproduction but grounds, in unique ways, the relationship of woman to fetus. The challenge is not to expand men's already prevalent rights over women's bodies by reinstitutionalizing male "genetic fulfillment" as a justification for reproductive technologies and contracts.

It has long been the task of feminism to challenge the natural and show it to be political. Reproductive behavior, like any other behavior, can and must be subject to an analysis embedded in human social and political relations. . . .

THE INTEGRITY OF WOMEN

As reproductive technologies and contracts proliferate, women are increasingly viewed as means to another's fulfillment, health, well-being, or population goals. In fetal tissue research, abortions become the handmaidens to the salvaging of fetal tissue for medical use; in surrogacy women are hired wombs contracted for procreative use; in IVF [in vitro fertilization], wives are used to bear children, often for husbands who have infertility problems and thus cannot procreate naturally and normally or because of the societal prescription that women must reproduce at any cost to themselves.

The new reproductive technologies reinforce the perception that, apart from their ability to procreate, women have no independent or intrinsic value. An ethics of integrity asserts that women are ends in themselves with dignity and integrity of person, that is, women are independent, integral beings, not breeders. This seems to be a quaint notion in an age where it increasingly becomes difficult for women to define the limits of what must be endured and sacrificed in many situations: for a pregnancy; for not becoming pregnant; for fetal benefit; for medical research and the conquest of disease; and for unrelated men who must have "their own" biological children. The new reproductive technologies reinforce the conditional value of women in medical treatment, law, and public policy. Woman's independent integrity is set aside.

THE LACK OF INTEGRITY

Integrity is not intangible; it has a material reality. It is socioeconomic as well as existential, physical as well as spiritual. It includes a woman's work and health as well as her needs and beliefs, all of which should not be subordinated to reproduction. In the whole debate over reproductive technologies, few talk about women's own need for bodily and spiritual integrity. Technological reproduction and surrogacy promote the view that medical research, male genetic fulfillment, women's supposed desperate need to have children, as well as the creeping perception and validation of the fetus as independent person or patient have more integrity than a woman has in her own person. Women, in contrast, have no value, independent of and unconditioned by sexuality and reproduction. Western women have come to be seen as owing children to themselves, to their male partners, and to those with whom they have signed a contract. And women in developing countries have come to be seen as either owing children they cannot care for to the Western world, who can, or as targets/acceptors of population control and contraceptive drug testing. In the reproductive realm, others' interests have become paramount, and what a woman owes to herself, independent of her ability to procreate, is ignored.

This lack of integrity has graphic consequences for women's health and well-being. When multiple tests, technological interventions, and drug cocktails are an intrinsic part of new reproductive treatment, these treatments undermine, in a most physical way, women's self-determination. A woman's life, work, and health are demoted when they do not mesh with her reproductive worth. Next to procreation, reinforced in Western technological reproduction as women's greatest need, these other needs are perceived as trivial.

DIVIDED WOMEN

The new reproductive technologies reflect a view of women as decentered subjects and social beings. The material outcome of such a view is a concrete carving up of women into body parts, specifically, into wombs, eggs, and follicles. But the worst thing about this decentering of woman as subject is that a woman is divided from her own perceptions of herself, of her own body and of her issue. As one so-called surrogate phrased it, "I'm only baby-sitting for their child." In addition, surrogacy decenters motherhood into categories of genetic, gestational, and social. What better way of dividing women from themselves and each other?

Recentering women as subjects—individual subjects with bodily integrity, and subjects with other women in resistance to male dominance and in relation to each other—is the radical feminist challenge to the postmodernist decentering of the female body and spirit, and to the disintegration of women's dignity and integrity inherent in new reproductive procedures. Integrity and dignity are at once transcendent and concrete values. Unless integrity is recognized in terms of women's particular needs, actions, and relationships, it is little more than an empty notion—"nonsense upon stilts," as the eighteenth-century philosopher Jeremy Bentham phrased it.

In an age of technological reproduction and commodified reproductive contracts, women need a principle that goes beyond reproductive freedom. Any concept of rights, as a cluster of claims made by women for social justice, must derive its principal moral warrant from the concept of integrity. The right to bodily integrity is particularly grounded in women's history since it is women in all countries who have been abused sexually and reproductively through the body. For women, the principle of bodily integrity is not intangible or symbolic but very historical, material, and cross-cultural. The ultimate tragedy of technological reproduction is that women are made to negate their own bodies, treating their bodies as instruments for their own or someone else's reproductive goals and splitting their bodies from their selves.

REGULATION

As a legal approach to technological and contractual reproduction, many have advocated regulation, that is, encumbering new reproductive technologies and arrangements with certain legal restrictions and bringing them more within the purview of state and/or federal guidelines. Many reproductive rights groups have cited the dangers of these technologies for women but nonetheless advocate regulation as a solution. Basically, the regulatory approach leaves the technologies intact while making them less haphazard. It restricts the more egregious abuses of these technologies by legislating the conditions and the contexts in which they can be used and by watchdogging the ways in which these technologies are abused, for example, when a woman is given [the long-term contraceptive] Norplant without her consent. Regulation functions as quality control rather than as critical challenge.

Regulation is a perceived rational response advocating restriction rather than abolition, and within the dominant medical and commercial ecology of reproductive technologies and contracts, scientists, lawyers, and entrepreneurs have made a plea for this kind of legislation. Regulation is exactly what the supporters and developers of technological reproduction want. It gives the surrogate brokers, for example, a stable marketing environment and makes the process of surrogacy more convenient for the client and broker. It also gives the IVF clinics a way of quality-controlling their success rates so that only the most successful centers survive and the competition is edged out. Regulation thus amounts to self-regulation as, for example, in the American Fertility Association's report on new reproductive procedures.

The regulatory approach is also based on a sense of the inevitability of the new reproductive technologies. The message is that it is useless to prevent such procedures since they have already gained prevailing ground; that many women want and need them; and that prohibition will drive them underground. Even if outlawing surrogacy, for example, did drive it underground, the number of surrogate arrangements would be minuscule compared to the explosive growth of surrogacy that would result from permissive regulation. Yet this sense of inevitability has given way to a perception of legal necessity leading to continued use and legitimation of new reproductive procedures. Is becomes ought. Caution rather than resistance becomes the norm. Regulation encourages adaptation rather than a search for alternatives or an outright rejection of a technology.

MOMENTUM

In the United States, there has always been more of an institutional momentum for regulation than abolition. Part of this momentum can be attributed to the value that Americans place on choice and laissez-faire individualism, but it is also bound up with the perception that to prohibit any of these new reproductive procedures is technological McCarthyism—a repressive, retrogressive censorship of progress and a gross intrusion into the reproductive lives of individuals who may need the techniques.

In the case of surrogacy, many state legislatures have crafted or are in the process of considering regulatory legislation that will get rid of the grosser inequities of the surrogate contract. Some of these regulatory bills allow the so-called surrogate to change her mind after the child is born, but only if she is willing to contest her claim in court and most likely to endure a custody battle. Thus she must hire a lawyer and have the financial wherewithal to challenge the greater legal and financial advantages of the sperm source. Other bills restrict any money from changing hands as a payment for reproductive services but allow money to be exchanged for "necessary expenses" or as a gift. Thus these very limits, enacted supposedly to protect the surrogate, do not provide her with the concrete *means* of protection from abuse that are available only to the powerful, that is, to the sperm source or the contracting couple or the brokerage agency.

Some Procedures Should Be Banned

Will brain-dead or dying females become egg donors the way they are now kidney and liver donors? Will we harvest eggs to conceive our own grandchildren?

We need some ethical stop signs. One stop sign goes up at the idea of using fetal eggs at all. Another stop sign should go up at the sight of the dollar sign. In no way should eggs or sperm be bought and sold in the marketplace.

Ellen Goodman, *Liberal Opinion Week*, January 17, 1994.

Regulatory surrogacy legislation has tightened up not only the contract, but also the supervision and regulation of the woman's behavior while pregnant. As in legalized prostitution where the state becomes the brothel, so too in legalized surrogacy the state becomes the broker. According to a report from the United Nations Educational, Scientific, and Cultural Organization, "The regulations governing prostitution (medical checkups, cards and brothels) were historically one of the main causes of the prostitution of women, and still are, because they do not allow them to abandon this activity and return to their social group. Because of the regulations, they come to form a separate category of women living on the fringes of society, who are vulnerable and 'marked for life.'" Likewise, regulatory surrogacy legislation brands a certain class of women as surrogate breeders. Laws that claim to regulate surrogacy end up promoting it.

Finally, regulation saves women from perhaps some of the more abusive aspects of the new reproductive technologies, but as a private privilege, not as a political human right. It provides no public protection for women, as women, against medical invasions of bodily integrity; it fails to prevent a new version of reproductive servitude from taking root as reproductive choice; and it encourages the exporting of surrogacy to countries where women's bodies are cheaper and there are no regulations.

REGULATIONS DO NOT PROTECT WOMEN

If we take seriously the right of women to bodily integrity, we must also urge the passage of legislation against the new reproductive procedures that is premised on a more substantive right to personal and political integrity. Such legislation must address not merely the effects of technological reproduction but the causes as well and must acknowledge the violation of a woman's bodily integrity. As Katha Pollitt wrote, "Feminists who think regulation would protect the mother miss the whole point of the maternity contract, which is precisely to deprive her of the protections she would have if she had signed nothing."

In examining environmental legislation in the United States, H. Patricia Hynes asks the question whether more environmental laws guarantee more environmental protection. The Federal Insecticide, Fungicide, and Rodenticide Act (FIFRA) gave the Environmental Protection Agency (EPA) the right to review all new pesticides before they could be sold and used and to review all new uses for old pesticides. In looking at the way in which FIFRA was enforced, however, Hynes found the law gave only the appearance and language of protection but not necessarily the reality of it. Because the intentionality of the law was to register chemicals and their uses, to close the more glaring loopholes that environmental activists of the 1960s had identified, and to keep chemicals on the market without letting them run rampant in agriculture, she maintains that "it placed a mantle of protection around the use of chemical pesticides."

Citing FIFRA's lack of ecological intentionality, Hynes contends that the law could have been written to promote a sustainable agriculture without chemicals that maximized, instead, the use of organic farming, biological controls, and integrated pest management (IPM). It could have contained no loophole allowing the manufacture or sale of chemicals banned in the United States in other, particularly Third World, countries. Hynes asserts that a law that had ecological intentionality "would intend to protect people and global ecology, not the chemical market. It would be a law intent on 'risk elimination, reduction, and minimization,' not risk management. This is what I mean by intentionality."

Regulations that place only certain limits on contractual and technological reproduction lack a similar intentionality. This kind of regulatory legislation intends only to manage the risks to women, not to eliminate those risks. And, as . . . with other reproductive drugs such as Depo-Provera, when a treatment or technology is banned for use in the United States, it is often exported to women in developing countries.

ABOLITION

Ultimately, I contend that the best legal approach to reproductive technologies and contracts that violate women's bodily integrity—such as IVF and its offshoots, egg donation, sex predetermination, fetal reduction, fetal tissue use for research and transplants, surrogacy, sterilization abuse, and invasive injectable and implantable contraception of Third World women—is abolition, not regulation. The starting point for the protection of women's bodily integrity is the abolition of technological reproduction by penalizing its vendors and purveyors and by preventing women from being technologically ravaged.

Before legislation, however, we must strengthen feminist action and activism at all levels. Action has to be the foundation and base for any legislation that is gender specific and international. Technological reproduction is a transnational, as well as a national, traffic in women that is promoted by organized medicine, marketing, and media. Any interventions at the national level must also be enforced internationally, and any laws enacted must not limit women's rights in other areas of female existence.

As one concrete example, women need an International Convention against medical exploitation developed by governmental and nongovernmental organizations (NGOs) that would declare women's right to bodily integrity, support women's established right to human dignity and physical well-being, and work to prohibit the expansionism of contractual and technological reproduction. Perhaps set in a larger context of medical violations of women's human rights, such a convention would specifically recognize contractual and technological reproduction as a violation of women's human rights, addressing its role in promoting an international reproductive traffic in women, and making clear that it constitutes a severe form of sexual and reproductive exploitation.

No radical feminist believes that legislation itself will bring an end to women's sexual and reproductive subordination. Legislation can often be subverted for male-dominant purposes, but regulatory legislation makes that subversion all the more likely.

Regulatory legislation encourages reams of rules and restrictions having the potential to generate legal conflicts that end up in layer upon layer of litigation. It is easy to imagine an accretion of reforms in relation to surrogacy, for instance, that, instead of effecting transformation of the conditions that draw women into surrogacy, further normalizes, rationalizes, and institutionalizes reproductive servitude. Regulatory legislation manages rather than stops the traffic in women and children, like a blinking traffic light that slows traffic, but only at certain points, and then allows it to start up again at its normal pace. A radical feminist politics takes seriously the need to provide women with a full stop to this battle over women's bodies. A radical feminist politics demands technological justice.

"[The woman entering a fertility program] assumes that the state should have a role in this arena, but for her, the much more limited role of regulator is sufficient."

REPRODUCTIVE TECHNOLOGIES SHOULD NOT BE BANNED

Rickie Solinger

Fertility treatments give hundreds of thousands of infertile women the opportunity to become mothers, maintains Rickie Solinger in the following viewpoint. The fact that these women want to be mothers so badly that they will put up with the uncertainty, the pain, and the risks inherent in the procedures should be enough to keep the technology legal, she asserts. Solinger is the author of *Wake Up Little Susie: Single Pregnancy and Race Before Roe v. Wade*, *The Abortionist: A Woman Against the Law*, and *Abortion Wars: A Half Century of Struggle, 1950–2000*.

As you read, consider the following questions:

1. What are some of the ways that Solinger admits women can be exploited by reproductive technologies?
2. How are women in fertility programs similar to women who have abortions, in the author's view?
3. What fertility issues cut to the heart of gender and class politics, according to Solinger?

Reprinted, by permission, from "Baby Love," by Rickie Solinger, *In These Times*, September 19, 1994.

R eports of technological breakthroughs in reproductive technologies have tended to focus on the sensational and the singular: on the putative grotesqueries of post-menopausal pregnancies; and on surrogacy cases, which are invariably transformed
into melodrama, described as if gender, class and sometimes race
exploitation were not at their heart. The media trendsetter, of
course, was the "Baby M" case, reported as if it were about one
lowdown, unstable and insufficiently maternal female welching
on the good-faith deal she made with a proper middle-class
couple—lacking only a baby in their quest for perfection.

The media dishes out these tales of perversity with relish; but
the big impact of the new technologies is on the lives of ordinary women, hundreds of thousands of them, who have partici-
pated in fertility-enhancing programs in recent years. These
women, who for one reason or another are apparently unable to
conceive in the usual way, undergo treatments ranging from IUI
(intra-uterine insemination) to egg harvesting, embryo implantation, embryo and egg freezing, the micro-injection of sperm
and the micro-manipulation of ova.

THE BROADER IMPLICATIONS

There has been a great deal of controversy among feminists,
most often expressed in heated political terms, about the broader
implications of such treatments. Such discussion generally proceeds as if it is possible to embrace or reject any given modality
of procreation for straightforwardly political reasons.

But, in this arena as in so many others, the personal is always
threatening to trump the political—in ways that might be famil-
iar, say, to progressives who feel compelled to go to extraordinary expense and other inconveniences in order to raise their
children in a safe neighborhood with good schools, despite
their commitment to improving the lot of all children in society.
In a capitalist society, it is the rare individual who forgoes on
principle the chance to buy what one values—in this instance
motherhood—if one has the resources, even when it takes a
special effort to fit an essentially personal choice into a deeply
held politics of justice.

And so, to begin with, I'd better identify my own reproductive history: I have two biological children conceived through
intercourse. It may also be relevant that I have a close relative
deeply enmeshed in the full array of new reproductive technology treatments. I say this because I have the feeling that readers
of this kind of article are, like me, always sleuthing the subtext.
Is the writer herself a mother? And if so, what kind? A biological

mother? An adoptive mother? A technologically assisted mother? Or is she a voluntarily child-free person?

STARK DIFFERENCES

The differences between those supporting and those opposing the new technologies is stark. Those who oppose them insist that the new technologies constitute a new form of violence against women, alienating them from their reproductive processes, reducing them to what critic Janice Raymond, author of *Women as Wombs*, calls "experimental raw material" or "womb environments." Supporters, such as Carol Sternhell, director of women's studies at New York University, argue that the technologies can be potentially liberating for women. "All the new alternative forms of family building are . . . challenges to our culture's dominant ideas about family," Sternhell suggests.

Raymond and the other critics can draw upon a great deal of history to back up their opposition to the new technologies. One need only recall the horrifying examples of thalidomide and the Dalkon Shield to prove that real danger can lurk in the heart of technology's promise to women desperate to manage their fertility. And it is clear that technologically assisted conception has been overhyped. The statistics are terrible, yet desperate women keep coming, a fact suggesting that the customers are actually being duped and even coerced into undergoing treatments that are not only physically risky but often futile.

Equally troublingly, the new technologies use up vast social and financial resources that could potentially be better spent solving existing problems such as high infant mortality rates in some parts of the United States and around the globe. (In the United States alone, fertility clinics do $2 billion of business a year.) And the technologies pose tougher issues for the ethicists. They mandate a "normalcy" standard for fetuses: all participants in the programs have the right to demand perfect babies, so fetuses that fail the test will be selectively eliminated.

In addition, the mere existence of the new technologies creates new worldwide inequities. The procedures are terribly expensive: in vitro fertilization, for example, costs $10,000 or more. And so there are multiple new opportunities for exploitation, both of women desperate to be pregnant and of poor women who, out of an extreme lack of resources, can be pressed into service as egg donors or so-called surrogate mothers.

The new technologies, Raymond suggests, are dangerous to women and to feminism because they take power and control over fertility away from desperate women and hand it over to doctors and technicians who manage and profit from the infertility empire. "Women as a class have a stake in reclaiming the female body," Raymond argues, "by refusing to yield control of it to men, to the fetus, to the state, and most recently to those liberals who advocate that women control our bodies by giving up control."

Given this house of horrors (and the sci-fi scenarios anyone can conjure up, based on what seems to be possible and acceptable in the realm of reproduction today), the theorists believe that the only effective check on the evils inherent in the new technologies is a curiously "liberal" one—that the state must outlaw the whole business on the grounds that these technologies are necessarily used in ways that are unethical, dangerous for women, costly and out of sync with the common good.

While the feminists who categorically oppose the new technologies are a relatively homogeneous group, those who support them share no common analysis or creed. No single ideology fits the diverse perspectives of researchers, doctors, business types and participants in fertility programs. And, of course, the doctors and technicians who develop and deliver the new technologies and the average women who buy them may or may not identify with feminism in any form.

THE RIGHTS OF INDIVIDUAL WOMEN

While Raymond and her colleagues concentrate on the big picture, the supporters of the new technologies focus on the rights of individual women. They may sometimes have the less powerful argument, medically and politically. But I am struck by their references to the sheer number of women moving through infertility programs—women ready to make sacrifices and take risks simply to be able to give birth. In some ways, their desire for control over their own reproductive capacities is not all that different than that of the countless women who sought abortions even when a large measure of social opprobrium was attached to women trying to determine their fate that way.

The woman entering a fertility program simply wants to be a mother, probably in pretty much the same way that most other women, feminist or not, want to be mothers. She wants to be a mother so badly (maybe partly because of the cultural mandate that presses women into motherhood, partly because motherhood seems so genuinely, emotionally grand) that even though she knows something about the lousy stats, the painful procedures, the possible risks, she enrolls in a fertility program anyway, glad to have the choice to do so, and glad to have the resources to pay for it. The odds tell her there is a good chance that at the end of the process she will be frustrated, disgusted, depressed and much poorer—though not necessarily sorry she tried everything she could.

VOLUNTARY CHOICE

Advocates of assisted reproductive technology concede . . . that IVF [in vitro fertilization] and its high-tech cousins can be painful, both physically and mentally. However, they are quick to add, infertile women elect to participate in these technologies knowing the risks. The pain is the price infertile women choose to pay for expanded reproductive choices.

"These technologies offer expanded reproductive opportunities for women," explains Bernard Rosen, a philosophy professor at Ohio State University. "There is some harm to women involved, but this is harm that is self-inflicted, voluntarily chosen. It would be paternalistic to close these technologies down and bar access to them under the auspices of protecting women from themselves. We act paternalistically with children because they don't know what's good for them. That's not the case here. Women understand what's involved and choose to proceed anyway."

Kelly Kershner, *USA Today*, May 1996.

This woman may also see herself as a feminist, someone who cares about ethics and justice and issues of equity. She simply wants her life to meet her expectations, and having a baby is a key expectation. And so she justifies her participation in the program on roughly the same principles as her like-minded friends when they explain why they choose to live in safe neighborhoods or send their children to private schools or colleges or why they use so much of their disposable income to pay for summer vacations instead of, let's say, sending all their excess dollars to organizations devoted to ending world hunger.

What's more—and this is the most painful part—she doesn't believe it is her personal responsibility to engage in orphan-saving just because she or her partner is infertile, or lesbian, any more than it is the responsibility of the lawyer couple next door with one conventionally conceived 6-year-old and tons of money. She is concerned about the high infant mortality rate in the United States and abroad, but she doesn't see how her forbearance from participating in a fertility-enhancing program will reduce the rate of infant deaths. She doesn't believe that her infertility or her sexual orientation requires her to redress this particular human problem. She herself would find paying another woman to be a "surrogate mother" repugnant and unacceptable. Like the theorists, she assumes that the state should have a role in this arena, but for her, the much more limited role of regulator is sufficient.

GENDER AND CLASS POLITICS

Given the competition between the logic of the opponents of reproductive technology and the strength of the desire of unwillingly childless women to become pregnant, how does one formulate a position regarding the new technologies? Surely we have to find a position that allows us to reject the medicocultural mandates that rigidly define infertility as a disease requiring a medical "cure" and that leaves it to the infertility establishment alone to define what is and is not a legitimate mode of procreation. And certainly we must insist that the possibility of male infertility be equally scrutinized in each case where appropriate, and treated accordingly.

Just as important, we need to evaluate the controversy between the supporters and the opponents of the new technologies in light of what we know about the politics of parental worthiness in the United States at the end of the 20th century and the enduring race and class biases that continue to shape these politics. Specifically, it would not do to consider the politics of fertility without attention to the fact that the new technologies can contribute, on the one hand, to the enduring anxiety about poor and non-white women who have "too many" children and must have their fertility controlled, while, on the other hand, it drums up sympathetic concern for "deserving" white middle-class women beset by infertility problems who must be given the chance to enhance their child-bearing possibilities.

These issues cut to the heart of gender and class politics in this era. Together with the politics of abortion and welfare of which they are a part, they define the huge, problematic terrain in which many women now live, a terrain substantially unreconstructed after 20 years in which feminist politics has had an impact on many facets of our national life.

SIZING UP THE OPTIONS

And yet, to construct a meaningful position with regard to the new technologies, one must listen carefully to the voices of women who use them. We must ask why women keep on seeking out and undergoing fertility treatments, despite the poor statistics and the political implications.

And it would be best if we could imagine that these legions of women filing into burgeoning infertility programs around the country are just like those of us who conceived in the old-fashioned way. They've sized up the options, and they've sized up their hearts, realizing that the costs (emotional, financial, medical and political) of the new technologies—like the costs of living through one's child's adolescence or paying for a child's college education—are very high. But no one can tell them—or me—that it's not worth it. Nor, in the end, does it seem fair to me to impose a demographic politics of justice on the backs of women who simply want the same thing that I got without even trying.

"There is nothing different, in kind, from a surrogate renting out her womb and other women who routinely rent out other aspects of their bodies in employment contracts."

SURROGATE MOTHERHOOD IS ETHICAL

Wendy McElroy

One objection to surrogate motherhood—in which one woman bears a child for another—revolves around the issue of informed consent for the surrogate contract. In the following viewpoint, Wendy McElroy argues that claims that a surrogate mother is unable to give informed consent to her pregnancy are invalid. She contends that what opponents of surrogate motherhood are really objecting to is a woman's financial gain from the procedure. McElroy is the author of XXX: A Woman's Right to Pornography and Sexual Correctness: The Gender-Feminist Attack on Women.

As you read, consider the following questions:
1. What are the two basic points on which feminist objections to surrogacy are based, according to McElroy?
2. What are the three examples of a surrogate's lack of informed consent, according to the court as cited by the author?
3. What are the true issues surrounding reproductive technologies, in McElroy's opinion?

Reprinted, with permission, from "Breeder Reactionaries," by Wendy McElroy, *Reason*, December 1994.

"59-Year-Old Woman Gives Birth to Twins on Christmas Day!"

Although it reads like one, that's not a headline from the *National Enquirer*. In 1994, reputable newspapers around the globe rushed to report that a 59-year-old British businesswoman had produced two healthy children from donated eggs which had been implanted in her uterus. She was soon overshadowed by a pregnant 62-year-old Italian woman, who wanted a baby to replace her only child, a son who had died in an accident.

Then a black woman gave birth to a white baby and the world confronted a host of new questions: Should parents be allowed to choose the race of their children? Or the sex? Should "designer" babies be encouraged? Or should the new reproductive technologies that allow such possibilities be banned, as several European nations are now attempting to do?

MORE CHOICES

The controversial procedures causing such a flap encompass a number of fully achieved technologies as well as some still in the development stages. They include: sperm donation, by which a woman is impregnated with sperm from someone other than her partner; egg donation, by which one women conceives with an egg donated by another; sperm and egg freezing; embryo adoption, by which a donated egg and sperm are cultured into an embryo; embryo freezing; and embryo screening. The world has certainly come a long way since Louise Brown became the first test-tube baby in 1978.

The main appeal of reproductive technologies is that they give people more choices and more flexibility in a domain previously ruled by biological chance and limits. And, sensational headlines notwithstanding, the typical beneficiaries of reproductive technologies are individuals in their child-bearing years. Still, the proliferation of new options means that the social implications of the new reproductive technologies are staggering. By the year 2000, for instance, more than 2 million children will have been born as a result of artificial insemination, estimates Roxanne Felshuch of IDANT Laboratories. Essentially, women can reset their biological clocks at will. Instead of having children during their peak career years, women can wait until retirement to raise a family. A single infant can now have more than two parents, all of whom might die of old age before he or she begins to teethe. If recent experiments on mice are an indication of things to come, a woman could abort a female fetus and, using its ovaries and eggs, later give birth to her own grandchild.

The prospect of such a reproduction revolution raises important and vexing ethical questions. For example, with two possible sets of "parents," how should the courts adjudicate custody claims? What will prevent governments from commandeering this science to produce "better" citizens? Will women be pressured to abort "defective" fetuses? Who will define a defect?

And, because they often utilize donors and surrogates, the new reproductive technologies also raise many serious questions about individual rights and contract law. Does a donor or a surrogate have any rights beyond sharply delimited contractual obligations? Is it possible to contract out motherhood—or fatherhood—itself? Congress and the courts have begun to address these questions and, if 1987's "Baby M" case is any indication, the final answers are certain to be long and hard in coming.

These are the sort of questions that will alter the reproduction debate in the twenty-first century. Indeed, they promise to alter reproduction itself. Women can now choose to have children when, where, and with whomever they want.

The Feminist Detractors

Such fundamental change inevitably inspires champions and detractors and, in the cacophony surrounding the new reproductive technologies, you would think feminists would be among the staunchest advocates for freeing a woman's body from the restrictions of nature. This, after all, has been one of the main goals of the feminist movement since its inception. As Shulamith Firestone wrote in the 1970 feminist classic, The Dialectic of Sex: The Case for Feminist Revolution, "The first demand for any alternative system must be . . . the freeing of women from the tyranny of their reproductive biology by every means available."

The new reproductive technologies, like effective contraception and access to legal abortion, seem to provide women with the "choice" central to virtually all brands of feminism. So aren't they part and parcel of the "reproductive freedom" that was so hotly contested at the United Nations' International Conference on Population and Development held in 1994 in Cairo? You would think only the pope and other reproductive traditionalists could be critical of such technologies. And you would think feminists would shout with joy now that their long-time rallying cry—"A woman's body, a woman's right"—is on the verge of fulfillment.

But you would be wrong. When high-profile feminists have commented on the topic at all, they have been outspoken in their attacks on new reproductive technologies ranging from innovations in birth-control methods to refinements of in vitro techniques. Consider the words of Janice Raymond, professor of women's studies at the University of Massachusetts and author of *Women as Wombs*. Raymond disparages the technologies as "reproductive abuse," a product of the "spermatic economy of sex and breeding" or "spermocracy," and "medicalized pornography."

SURROGACY SHOULD NOT BE BANNED

If liberal feminists tend to overemphasize women's ability to make free choices, radical feminists tend to overemphasize the status of women as victims. In their desire to protect women from abuse, radical feminists repeatedly ask whose interests does surrogate motherhood serve. They claim that no matter which of women's traditional sexual or reproductive services we consider, a case can be made that, in providing the service, more women have probably been harmed than benefitted. Nevertheless, banning commercial surrogate motherhood (the form of surrogacy that most troubles radical feminists) would not necessarily benefit women. On the contrary, a ban on commercial surrogate motherhood would tend to drive the practice underground where women's best interests would be even more poorly served than they are above ground, so to speak. Rather than resorting to a remedy that, by the way, gives legal and medical authorities *more* rather than *less* control over women, one would think that radical feminists would prefer to use consciousness-raising techniques to eliminate the practice of commercial surrogate motherhood. If women neither hire surrogate mothers nor agree to work as surrogate mothers, the surrogate motherhood industry will collapse.

Rosemarie Tong, *Kennedy Institute of Ethics Journal*, March 1996.

This rejection has nothing to do with the ethical questions posed above. Critics such as Raymond are radical feminists who consider men and women separate political classes, with interests that dramatically—and necessarily—conflict. Within the radical feminist ideological belief system, anything developed within the "patriarchy"—the "seamless web of male oppression" that radical feminists say characterizes our world—must be condemned, regardless of the apparent benefits for women. . . .

SURROGATE MOTHERHOOD

The most dramatic expression of radical feminists' contempt for individual choice is their passionate rejection of surrogate motherhood, by which one woman agrees to bear a child for another. In essence, they call for the prohibition of surrogacy contracts, because such an arrangement is said to convert women into breeding stock against their will.

In testifying before the House Judiciary Committee of Michigan in October 1987, Janice Raymond railed against surrogacy contracts: "[They] should be made unenforceable as a matter of public policy . . . they reinforce the subordination of women by making women into reproductive objects and reproductive commodities." Notice that Raymond characterizes women as passive objects and contracts as active agents. Although the woman in fact makes the contract, Raymond speaks as if the situation were the reverse.

The radical feminist case against surrogacy contracts has been spelled out in detail by Phyllis Chesler in her 1990 essay "Mothers on Trial: Custody and the 'Baby M' Case," published in the collection *The Sexual Liberals and the Attack on Feminism*. This was the custody battle which took place in 1987 before the New Jersey Superior Court. The surrogate mother sought custody of the child conceived with sperm provided by a couple who had contracted her services.

"Some feminists," wrote Chesler, "said, 'We must have a right to make contracts. It's very important. If a woman can change her mind about this contract—if it isn't enforced—we'll lose that right!'. . . They didn't consider that a contract that is both immoral and illegal isn't and shouldn't be enforceable. They didn't consider that businessmen make and break contracts every second. . . . Only a woman who, like all women, is seen as nothing but a surrogate uterus, is supposed to live up to—or be held down for—the most punitive, most de-humanizing of contracts. No one else. Certainly no man."

Two Feminist Objections

The radical feminist objections against surrogacy contracts rest on two basic points, which are commonly raised against all forms of reproductive technology. First, the woman is selling herself into a form of slavery; and second, the woman cannot possibly give informed consent because she does not know how she will feel later toward the child she is bearing.

As to the first objection, it can be easily argued that there is nothing different, in kind, from a surrogate renting out her womb and other women who routinely rent out other aspects of their bodies in employment contracts: doctors, computer programmers, secretaries. The real question at issue is, What constitutes slavery?

The essence of slavery is what has been called "alienation of the will"—that is, you transfer over to another person not merely the limited use of your body, but all moral and legal jurisdiction over it. In effect, you transfer title to yourself as a human being. But if you signed such a contract, you would instantly lose all responsibility for living up to its terms, because you would no longer be a legal entity capable of being bound by contracts. In this way, a "slavery contract" is a contradiction in terms. All that can be contracted out are services.

The second objection to surrogacy contracts—that a woman cannot give informed consent—similarly raises general questions of contract law. And on this point, the legal system at times seems to agree with the feminists. Although in the Baby M case, Judge Harvey Sorkow found in favor of the biological father and against the surrogate mother, his ruling implicitly criticized surrogacy contracts: "[The surrogate mother] never makes a totally voluntary, informed decision, for quite clearly any decision prior to the baby's birth is, in the most important sense, uninformed, and any decision after that, compelled by a pre-existing contractual commitment, the threat of a lawsuit, and the inducement of a $10,000 payment is less than totally voluntary. Her interests are of little concern to those who controlled this transaction."

THE RULING INVALIDATES ALL CONTRACTS

But this ruling does not so much invalidate surrogacy contracts as it invalidates the possibility of any contract whatsoever between human beings. The court wrongly identifies contractual obligations, voluntarily entered into, as somehow coercive. Consider what the court views as a lack of informed consent.

First, the surrogate doesn't know how she will feel about the baby she is carrying until it is born. A similar statement could be made about almost any contract. If I sell my family home, for example, I do not know how much I will miss the memories and associations it contains until the house is gone. If I am commissioned to paint a landscape, I don't know how emotionally attached I might become to the painting until it has been executed. To claim that a woman can change her mind about a contract, with impunity, simply because she has second thoughts, is to say no contract exists at all.

Second, the surrogate is said to be "compelled by a pre-existing agreement" and "the threat of a lawsuit." These two factors are almost the definition of what constitutes a contract: namely, an agreement that binds parties to certain actions and leaves them vulnerable to damages if they fail to follow through. If these factors are inherently coercive, then contracts themselves are coercion.

Third, the interests of the surrogate "are of little concern to those who controlled the transaction." Again, this is true of all contracts, which are binding agreements between people who are pursuing their own perceived best interests. If the surrogate is of age and in her right mind, it is assumed that she's looking out for herself. If the surrogate later discovers that keeping the baby is in her actual self-interest, she can breach the contract and pay the damages involved.

The feminist rejection of surrogacy, then, is just another assault on women's right to make "wrong" choices and on the free market, which is the arena of her choices.

This becomes clear whenever radical feminists waffle on what they call "limited individual situations"—such as one sister carrying a baby for an infertile sibling. This, some maintain, should be tolerated for compassionate reasons, on the same level as a bone marrow transplant between relatives.

For instance, in the book *New Approaches to Human Reproduction*, editor Linda M. Whiteford makes a distinction between commercial surrogacy and the altruistic kind. "Commercial surrogacy exploits socio-economic class differences," argues Whiteford, "using financial need and emotional need as currency. The exchange of money transforms surrogacy from an altruistic gift between sisters or friends into baby selling or womb renting."

But "humanitarian" surrogacy is still the medicalization of childbirth. Here the object of radical feminist condemnation becomes clear: It is not reproductive technology per se, but the free market that is the true evil. Women may compassionately lend their wombs, but they should never be allowed to materially profit by the process.

Why? Because such profiteering would exploit the wombs of underprivileged women. In other words, if a surrogate truly needs money, her contracts are invalid on the grounds of socio-economic coercion. But it is precisely those who need money who most need the right to contract for it. To deny a poor woman the right to sell her services—whether as a waitress or a surrogate—deals a death blow to her economic chances. Her services and labor may be the only things she has to leverage herself out of poverty. If anything, she needs the right to contract far more than rich and powerful women do.

A WOMAN'S RIGHT

The true issue surrounding the new reproductive technologies remains "a woman's body, a woman's right." In essence, radical feminists wish to alter feminism's most famous slogan to read: "A woman's body . . . sometimes a woman's right."

But however fuzzy radical feminists may be in arguing against the new reproductive technologies, they are crystal clear about their end goal. Remember: Radical feminism is a call for revolution, not for reform. As Gloria Bowles and Renate Duelli Klein put it in their introduction to the anthology *Theories of Women's Studies*, "The present structure of education (and the nature of societal institutions at large) can [n]ever accommodate feminist claims because its very existence depends on the perpetuation of patriarchal assumptions and values. . . . What we are at is nothing less than an intellectual revolution: we challenge the dominant culture at its source."

Similarly, radical feminists do not seek to regulate reproductive contracts and procedures. Instead, they demand their abolition. They seek to outlaw increasingly widespread practices such as surrogacy, in vitro fertilization, and the implantation of contraceptives. They call for legal sanctions against anyone who sells or provides such services—e.g., doctors and hospitals—and a cessation of research in this area.

While such demands for "technological justice" may indeed be radical, it is difficult to see them as particularly "feminist."

> "The main objection to commercial
> surrogacy is that it is the equivalent
> of baby selling, a practice that is
> inherently morally objectionable."

SURROGATE MOTHERHOOD IS UNETHICAL

Scott B. Rae

The practice of surrogate mothering, in which one woman is impregnated with another couple's embryo and bears them a child, is nothing more than legalized baby selling and is therefore morally objectionable, according to Scott B. Rae in the following viewpoint. Rae contends that the fee paid to the surrogate mother is not for her gestational services, as advocates claim, but is a payment for her waiver of parental rights. Therefore, he argues, surrogate motherhood should be abolished. Rae is the author of several books on ethics, including *The Ethics of Commercial Surrogate Motherhood: Brave New Families?* from which this viewpoint is excerpted.

As you read, consider the following questions:

1. According to the author, why does a reduced fee for a miscarriage or stillborn birth by a surrogate mother indicate that the contract is for baby selling?
2. Why are the three differences between surrogacy and black market adoptions irrelevant to the discussion of surrogacy, in Rae's opinion?
3. In the author's view, why is a comparison between surrogacy and artificial insemination by donor invalid?

In the *Baby* M case, the New Jersey Supreme Court equated surrogacy with baby selling, in violation of the state's adoption laws. The lower court had maintained that surrogacy cannot be baby selling since one of the parties involved is the natural father. The lower court ruled that the adoption laws did not contemplate surrogacy arrangements, and thus that extending them to surrogacy was invalid. The state Supreme Court sharply disagreed, defining surrogacy as inherently the sale of children, rejecting any attempts to evade what the court considered obvious.

THE ETHICS OF COMMERCIAL SURROGACY

The differences between the two decisions have helped set the parameters for the debate over the ethics of commercial surrogacy. The argument in favor of allowing payment of a fee to surrogates beyond their reasonable expenses has taken one of two forms. First, it is argued that commercial surrogacy is essentially not equivalent to baby selling. Instead, the fee is payment for gestational services rendered. Second, it is granted that surrogacy does constitute baby selling, but the argument is made on the grounds that surrogacy is qualitatively different from the types of situations that the baby selling laws were designed to prevent. This viewpoint will argue that commercial surrogacy is indeed the sale of children, and that the differences between surrogacy and black market adoptions do not justify allowing for payment of a fee to surrogates. Thus, commercial surrogacy should be prohibited, and consideration paid to surrogates should only be for necessary medical expenses and other expenses associated with the pregnancy.

Twenty-five states currently have laws that prohibit the exchange of consideration for adoption of a child. These laws were enacted to prevent economically and emotionally vulnerable birth mothers from being coerced into giving up children for adoption that under non-coercive circumstances they would not otherwise give up. The abuses and excesses of black market adoptions were, and still are, the target of these laws. As applied to surrogacy, however, these laws have been interpreted by the courts in different ways. For example, in Michigan and New Jersey, the laws have been applied to prohibit any commercialization of surrogacy. But in Kentucky, the courts have ruled that surrogacy does not fall under the heading of baby selling because the natural father cannot buy back what is already his. Kentucky's interpretation of adoption statutes seems to be the exception rather than the rule, since the surrogacy laws in the states that have enacted them are generally consistent with existing adoption laws.

AN ARGUMENT IN FAVOR OF COMMERCIAL SURROGACY

The Fee Is for Services Rendered, Not for the Sale of a Child. Though this argument takes various forms, proponents insist that surrogacy is not inherently baby selling, since the fee that is paid to the surrogate is for her gestational services, and thus constitutes simply another expense for the contracting couple, parallel to the medical and legal expenses involved. This argument assumes sensitivity to existing adoption laws, being careful to delineate exactly the things for which the fee pays, and insuring that the transfer of parental rights is not included under that heading. Most surrogacy contracts are structured to relate the fee to the specific gestational services rendered by the surrogate, and those who frame the contracts are careful not to make any mention of surrendering parental rights as part of the services for which the fee is paid.

Among the various forms that this argument can take, William Laufer suggests that the contracting couple does not buy the child, but rather buys the woman's egg and rents her womb, emphatically denying that the couple pays for an adoption. Avi Katz suggests that the fee pays for the entire process, not just the final step in it, and thus calls surrogacy contracts to bear a child, not contracts to sell a child. Karen Marie Sly terms surrogacy not baby selling, but prenatal baby-sitting, and the surrogate has the right to rent her womb for a fee. This definition of surrogacy is the foundation for her argument that prohibiting commercial surrogacy violates a woman's constitutional right to contract. Lori Andrews draws a parallel between the fee paid to surrogates and the other payments to those involved in helping relieve infertility. She states, "Prohibiting payment to the surrogate is as much an interference with the couple's reproductive rights as passing a law which bans payment to doctors who perform in vitro fertilization or a law which bans payment to pharmacists for contraceptives."

She parallels that analogy with an analogy drawn between childrearing and childbearing. It is legitimate to pay for all kinds of services involved in childrearing, from wet nurses to day care. Since childrearing, not childbearing, is the more influential element in the child's well being in the long run, if it is justifiable to pay people for childrearing, then surely it is valid to pay them for childbearing. Finally, Christine Sistare insists that all the attention being paid to baby selling is a "red herring" that distracts from the real issue of a woman's autonomy and a male fear that women's reproductive capacities will no longer be available cheaply or on demand.

EVALUATION OF THE ARGUMENT

The argument that the surrogacy fee is for services and not for the sale of a child fails to take into account both the nature of the surrogacy contract and the intended end of a surrogacy arrangement. Most surrogacy contracts are structured around the product, not the process or the service of surrogacy. For example, the Stern-Whitehead contract specified that only in the event that Mary Beth Whitehead delivered a healthy baby to the Sterns would she be paid the entire $10,000 fee. If she miscarried prior to the fifth month of pregnancy, she would receive no fee, though all medical expenses would be paid. If she miscarried after the fifth month, or if the child was stillborn, she would only receive $1,000 of the fee. The contract was oriented to delivery of the end product, not the service rendered in the process. Normally, the majority of the fee (usually half), if not all of it (as was the case with the Stern-Whitehead case), is withheld until parental rights are actually waived and the custody of the child is turned over to the contracting couple. Thus, it is difficult to see how the fee can be for gestational services only when the service itself is not the final intent of the contract. Payment is made upon the surrogate fulfilling all the necessary responsibilities to insure the transfer of parental rights. Alexander M. Capron and Margaret J. Radin of the University of Southern California Law Center suggest that the claim that the fee is for gestational services alone is merely a disguise that serves to hide the true intent of the contract. They state, "The claim that the payment to the surrogate is merely for 'gestational services' is just a pretense, since payment is made 'upon surrender of custody' of the child and for 'carrying out obligations' under the agreement. These include taking all steps necessary to establish the biological father's paternity and to transfer all parental rights to the biological father and his mate.". . .

BABY SELLING

Commercial surrogacy is indeed baby selling and should be prohibited. Given the long tradition in the United States against the sale of human beings, as with slavery and with children through adoption laws, the burden is on the advocates of commercial surrogacy to show either that it does not involve the sale of children or that it is an acceptable form of it. Most of the arguments in favor of commercial surrogacy are sensitive to the charge of baby selling, and supporters go to considerable lengths to show that it is not, or that if it is, it is benign in its effects. . . .

There is not much controversy in American society concerning the morality of selling children. Most agree that children should not be objects of barter, both for utilitarian and deontological reasons. The real debate in surrogacy is whether the practice does indeed constitute the sale of children, and if it does, whether this makes a morally significant difference. The conclusion of this viewpoint is that surrogacy is the equivalent of selling children, and does not constitute an acceptable form of baby selling.

"HOW MUCH IS THAT BABY IN THE WINDOW?"

The first argument made by proponents of commercial surrogacy is that the fee paid to the surrogate is payment for gestational services, not for the sale of a child. Yet upon closer examination, a substantial portion of the fee pays for the willingness of the surrogate to waive parental rights to the child she is carrying. Many surrogacy contracts include provisions that the balance of the fee, if not all of it, will be held in escrow until the arrangement is completed, that is, until the child is turned over to the contracting couple and adopted by the natural father's wife. These contracts also often include provisions that the surrogate will receive less of the fee should she miscarry or give birth to a stillborn child. The contract and payment schedule are oriented to the product of the arrangement, not to the process. If it were process oriented, the surrogate would receive the same fee whether she turned over the child or not, a situation inconceivable to surrogacy brokers. Thus, the way the fee is paid indicates that it is indeed for the waiver of parental rights, precisely the thing that adoption laws were written to preclude, since such a waiver for a fee constitutes baby selling.

Black Market Adoptions

A second argument attempts to distance surrogacy from the practice that the adoption laws were written to discourage, black market adoptions. Proponents suggest that there are major differences between the two practices. . . . The differences were either overstated or not relevant to the discussion of surrogacy. For example, one major difference is that the adopting father is the child's natural father, as opposed to a stranger. However, genetics alone does not necessarily make for a better parent, and simply because the natural father is involved in the transaction does not make it any less of a transaction. He is not the sole owner of the child, but a joint tenant with the surrogate. He is, in effect, buying out the surrogate's rights to the child with the fee. A further difference is that surrogacy is concerned with the child's best interests as opposed to black market adoptions which are solely financially driven. Yet this overstates the difference, since the only psychological screening done in surrogacy is on the surrogate, and normally the only screening done on the contracting couple is financial. A third difference is that in surrogacy, coercion of the surrogate cannot take place since the agreement is entered into prior to the onset of pregnancy. Thus there is no unwanted pregnancy that might coerce a young unwed mother, for example, to give her child up when she would not do so under less coercive circumstances. But to suggest that surrogacy is free from coercion overstates the case, since once the pregnancy begins and the surrogate decides she wants to keep the child, she may have a wanted pregnancy and an unwanted contract that will force her to give up the child she is carrying.

A third argument attempts to draw a parallel between AID [artificial insemination by donor] and surrogacy. Proponents of commercial surrogacy insist that since AID is legitimate, and men can be paid a nominal amount for sperm donation, women should also be able to engage in surrogacy for a fee. But the more appropriate parallel to AID is not surrogacy, but egg donation. Equal protection only requires that women be able to donate their eggs for a small fee in the same way that men donate their sperm. . . .

THE COMMODIFICATION OF CHILDREN

Further arguments include the fact that children are not treated as commodities in surrogacy and that money changes hands in some adoption proceedings. It is true that the majority of children born to surrogates are well treated by their new families. But the fact remains that they are still being bought and sold. Even though there were certainly slaves who were treated well, that hardly justifies the sale of human beings. In response to the concept of money changing hands in some adoption proceedings, the permitted exchange of money in adoption occurs between two already existing parents, not between two people who have been strangers prior to the surrogacy arrangement being organized. Further, the exchange of cash, as in surrogacy, has been banned even between already existing family members. The consideration being exchanged in the cases being used to support this argument was forgiveness of a debt or a child support obligation, not a cash deal as is the case in surrogacy.

The most obvious argument against commercial surrogacy is that it constitutes the sale of children, violating adoption laws in many states as well as the Thirteenth Amendment. Commercial surrogacy is prohibited because it involves the commodification of children, that is, it is one of the blocked exchanges, blocked because of society's desire to protect certain areas of social life from the realm of the market. Baby selling is blocked because babies are market inalienable, that is, because human beings cannot be bought and sold without doing violence to an essential aspect of personhood.

SURROGATE EXPLOITATION

Further arguments against commercial surrogacy include the notions that women's reproductive capacities should not be subject to the dictates of the market. However, it is not clear that surrogacy involves a morally objectionable market transaction: only the sale of the child that results from the agreement is inherently morally objectionable. What makes the commodification of women's reproductive services argument more compelling is the potential for exploitation of the surrogate. Although such exploitation has not materialized so far, there is evidence of surrogacy brokers marketing surrogacy among poor women, particularly those in the Third World, and thus the potential for exploiting women is real.

The main objection to commercial surrogacy is that it is the equivalent of baby selling, a practice that is inherently morally objectionable, because human beings are not objects of barter or commerce. Any attempt to show that surrogacy does not constitute child selling fails to account for the realities of the surrogacy contract. Thus, public policy should be formulated to prohibit a fee to surrogates beyond reasonable medical expenses and perhaps lost wages due to the pregnancy. Any fee to surrogacy brokers to set up a commercial surrogacy arrangement should likewise be prohibited.

| "Late-life childbearing is an entirely different matter for old geezers compared with geezerettes."

POSTMENOPAUSAL PREGNANCIES SHOULD BE BANNED

Part I: Barbara Ehrenreich; Part II: *Philadelphia Daily News*

An increasing number of postmenopausal women are becoming pregnant through in vitro fertilization. In Part I of the following two-part viewpoint, syndicated columnist Barbara Ehrenreich argues that elderly women may not be capable of the physical demands of childrearing. In Part II, the editors of the *Philadelphia Daily News* assert that in a time when millions of Americans do not have adequate health care, it is selfish to devote so many resources to a procedure that will benefit few people.

As you read, consider the following questions:

1. According to Ehrenreich, what would be the result if men became pregnant?
2. In Ehrenreich's opinion, why is pregnancy becoming more difficult?
3. According to the editors of the *Philadelphia Daily News*, what is the goal of science?

Part I: Reprinted, with permission, from "So's Your Old Lady," by Barbara Ehrenreich, *Nation*, January 31, 1994. Part II: Reprinted, with permission, from the January 4, 1994, *Philadelphia Daily News* editorial "Impregnating the Elderly: Is It Wise?"

I

So far the debate over elderly mothers has centered on the issue of whether a 75-year-old, possibly senile and walker-
bound, is a fit guardian for a child who has reached the gun-
toting, coke-snorting stage. This is an interesting question to
ponder, but the real issue has to do with the mental competency
of any woman who would volunteer for pregnancy, especially
when she has the reasonable excuse of old age. Are such women
feminist heroines, as some of the sisters are arguing? Or are they
so deeply disturbed that any resulting offspring should be re-
manded to foster care at the moment of birth?

PREGNANCY IS DIFFERENT

Some will say I am indifferent to the sufferings of the elderly infertile population, which craves nothing so much as a few tod-
dlers to brighten up life in the nursing home. But the advocates
of late-life parturition know nothing of, or else have mercifully
forgotten, the experience of pregnancy itself: the nightmarish
symptoms, the ghastly sequelae that can leave a woman disfig-
ured for life. If men had to endure even a fraction of this in the
cause of reproduction—the nausea, stretch marks, lethargy,
hemorrhoids, varicose veins—you may be sure that the Right-
to-Life movement would fold overnight.

Furthermore, and contrary to the impression created by Demi
Moore and others in the pregnant-pinup line of work, pregnancy has been getting harder, not easier, over time. Two decades
ago, when I was making my own contribution to the continu-
ance of the species, pregnancy was considered so simple that
even a 15-year-old could pull it off. True, there were a few prohibitions—as against bungee-jumping and kick-boxing in the
final months—but generally one was encouraged to treat the
whole thing as if it were nothing more than a bout of inexplica-
ble obesity. Doctors warned against the consumption of food,
which could add permanent poundage and lead one's husband
to wander, but they had nothing against alcohol, which was
known to have a soothing effect on the uterine lining.

Today, however, a medically correct pregnancy resembles a
stay in a drug detox ward operated by one of [former Cambo-
dian dictator] Pol Pot's successors. It is impossible to enter any
venue where alcohol might possibly be imbibed without en-
countering signs warning how one little nip could make your
baby turn out cross-eyed and pinheaded. Self-respecting women
are reduced to carrying a flask disguised as liquid iron supple-

ment in order to survive the endless well-meaning lectures on the teratogenic [monstrous] effects of aspirin and coffee and undercooked meat. As for smoking: You might as well snatch an infant from its carriage and publicly strangle it as reach into your maternity smock and pull out a fag.

GEEZERS VERSUS GEEZERETTES

The argument is that if doddering old men can have babies, why shouldn't we? But late-life childbearing is an entirely different matter for old geezers compared with geezerettes. Not only does a man get to skip pregnancy but the eventual child is genetically related to him. Not so with a 59-year-old mom, who is forced to carry a child conceived—through some sort of high-tech hanky-panky—by her husband and *another woman*. Imagine being approached by your husband: "Uh, my girlfriend and I would like to have a child together, but she's awfully vain about her figure, so we were wondering if uh . . ."

Then there is the inevitable outcome, so brilliantly portrayed in the movie *Honey, I Blew Up the Kid*. Not long ago, childraising was sufficiently undemanding that it could be left to servants or to women who were otherwise employed full time at spinning, sheepherding and the like. Today, however, the whole business has gotten so complicated and psychologically perilous that able-bodied young couples are routinely reduced to cowering wrecks by some seven-foot toddler.

But who knows? Perhaps it makes sense to relegate childbearing to the wearers of adult diapers and elasticized polyester slacks. The young and the sound-minded have other options in life, and there's no reason those nursing homes couldn't double as nursery schools, with the same calm, professional staff tending both baby and mom.

II

Science keeps marching forward. Unfortunately, it most frequently marches where the market is.

There is a market for human beings, especially children. This is despite the feeling that the world may have fully enough people.

So science gallumphs on, on a crusade to allow everyone on Earth to reproduce, no matter their age or physical state.

Most recently, researchers in the United Kingdom report success in fertilizing eggs taken from aborted female fetuses. This surpasses the glory days of grave-robbing, involving the theft of body parts from those who are not only dead, but also have never been born.

This report follows the successful birth of twins in 1993 to a 59-year-old English woman who had been artificially fertilized via petri dish. Pregnancy among the post-menopausal, previously merely a bad dream, is now a reality, if a medically chancy one.

Perhaps it's a good thing to try and even the odds. Many infertile people would make good parents. Many suffer because of their infertility.

5-20

"A 63-year-old giving birth raises an interesting question . . . should people who are out of their minds have children?"

And maybe some day there will be a cosmic human equity, in which all people are immortal, highly intelligent, athletic, invulnerable to illness or injury and wise enough to make Yoda look like Butthead.

The implications of genetic engineering are enough to bewilder the best among us. So are the implications of science providing such services, as it has in Britain, where it was possible for a black woman with a husband of mixed race to bear a white child.

THE INTEGRITY OF HUMAN BEINGS

The integrity of human beings should be worth something. The drive to reproduce among all creatures is a basic quest for immortality, of one's genes at least. It doesn't have a lot to do with modern notions of equity.

Why indeed? Why not totally re-engineer mammalian biology while we're at it? The difference in the ability to procreate at advanced age is programmed in. It wasn't a plot by the male power structure. Redressing it shouldn't damage anything, although it might make more sense to spend our time and treasure to perfect the biology we've got.

Leaving aside the philosophical arguments (except to denounce harvesting eggs from the dead as ghoulish), there are important issues to consider as universal health care approaches.

Is it sensible for a nation with millions of people lacking even the most basic medical care to allow enormous quantities of its resources to provide so small a benefit? Perhaps there are lots of 60-year-old women who would love to have babies, but what do we do about the babies who are already here and in need of medical care?

"Banning [postmenopausal] pregnancies provides, at best, the illusion that we have done something to foster the goal of responsible parenthood."

POSTMENOPAUSAL PREGNANCIES SHOULD NOT BE BANNED

Lawrence M. Hinman

The age of prospective parents is not the important issue in the debate over postmenopausal pregnancies, argues Lawrence M. Hinman in the following viewpoint. What is important, he contends, is whether the parents can meet the child's needs. Banning reproductive technologies for women past menopause would only harm those who are ready and able to meet the responsibilities of parenthood. Hinman, a professor of philosophy and ethics at the University of San Diego, is the author of *Ethics: A Pluralistic Approach to Moral Theory* and *Contemporary Moral Issues*.

As you read, consider the following questions:

1. What must prospective parents ask themselves, in Hinman's view?
2. The author believes that prohibiting fertility clinics from helping postmenopausal women become pregnant would not work. How does he prove this by citing the Keh case?
3. In Hinman's opinion, why should society not accept a reproductive laissez-faire policy?

Reprinted, by permission, from "What Really Counts in Parenthood?" by Lawrence M. Hinman, *San Diego Union-Tribune*, April 30, 1997.

"**O**ur age doesn't matter," Arceli Keh told *The Express*, a British tabloid, in April 1997. "We feel young at heart, and we love our child. Isn't that what counts?"

It's a good question. Keh, a Filipino woman from Highland, a suburb of San Bernardino, California, gave birth in 1996 to Cynthia, a healthy baby girl—at the age of 63—and rekindled the debate about childbearing after menopause. The last such case was Rosanna Della Corte, an Italian woman who had given birth at the age of 62 in 1994.

MORAL QUESTIONS

How are we to make sense of this, especially from a moral point of view? Do we simply say, as some have, that if it's technologically possible, then it's morally permissible? Or that, since men have been fathering children at ever more advanced ages, women should be permitted to do the same thing? (We might christen this "The Tony Randall Argument," in honor of the 77-year-old actor who is a new father in 1997.) Or do we say that such births are simply selfish acts that put the desires of the parents ahead of any consideration about the well-being of the children? Or do we see this as yet one more reflection of our society's unrelenting quest for eternal youth?

We need to step back from the question to gain enough perspective to answer it. When we bring a child into the world, we are creating a network of responsibilities, with the child at its center. They are responsibilities to nourish, to protect, to educate and to love. There is no easy answer to the question of whether Keh and her 60-year-old husband, Isagani, were right to bring this baby girl into the world. But if there is an answer, it is to be found by focusing on the question of whether they—the two parents and the extended family of which they are a part—can meet those responsibilities of nourishment, protection, education and love.

Once we begin to see the issue in terms of meeting this nexus of responsibilities, we see that we have much to learn from the Kehs. We do not need at this point to worry about whether they will be able to meet those responsibilities. There is good evidence to suggest that they, and their extended family, take this obligation very seriously and that their daughter will grow up within a loving family committed to her welfare.

WHAT COUNTS?

The Kehs' decision forces all of us to ask, "What counts?"

What counts, for example, when one partner in a marriage

knows that he or she is at risk for the recurrence of cancer? Certainly this raises questions about longevity and quality of life akin to those posed by the birth of Cynthia Keh. A prospective parent, either female or male, must ask whether the responsibilities to nurture, protect, educate and love their potential child will be met.

Similarly, men who wish to become fathers later in life must ask themselves the same question. They are creating a little bundle of responsibilities, and it is incumbent upon them to make every effort to ensure that those responsibilities are met.

Older Is Better

There is no evidence in the psychological literature to indicate that older parents are unfit parents. In fact, some evidence suggests that because they tend to bring economic tranquility and emotional stability to baby-rearing, they are better parents.

Such advantages, not to mention the blissful enthusiasm for parenthood that is the hallmark of most graying mothers and fathers, may outweigh drawbacks associated with anxiety about health and stamina.

Linda Wolfe, *San Diego Union-Tribune*, January 4, 1994.

For those who are disturbed by the Kehs' decision to have a child so late in life, the response should not be to outlaw such pregnancies by forbidding fertility clinics to assist women over a certain age. (This, in fact, would not have prevented the Kehs from having a baby, since Arceli Keh had falsified medical records indicating that she was only 50 years old.) Such legislative and regulatory responses single out a narrow range of cases (postmenopausal assisted pregnancies) and ban them, presumably on the grounds that the parents will not be able to care adequately for the child.

But this misses the point: we need to foster throughout our society a strong conviction that bringing a child into the world creates profound and deeply binding responsibilities for the nurturance, protection, education and love of that child. That is the point we need to remind ourselves about constantly. Banning such pregnancies provides, at best, the illusion that we have done something to foster the goal of responsible parenthood. At worst, it harms persons who deeply desire to become parents and who want to assume and meet the responsibilities of parenthood.

The Central Issue

For those who are not disturbed by the Kehs' decision, the response should not be to condone some kind of reproductive laissez-faire policy, saying that "anything goes" in this realm. After all, such a policy will simply result in a world in which, if people have the money and if the technology is available, they can do whatever they want. This response, too, misses the central issue: how can parents meet the responsibilities they create by bringing a new life into the world?

The laissez-faire option opens the door to human cloning and other possibilities we can hardly imagine, but offers us no guidance about why some ways of living are morally better than others.

Finally, we should note that the question the Kehs face is the question all parents face: Will they be able to provide for their children the nurturance, the protection, the education and—most of all—the love that will enable those children to navigate the perilous journey to adulthood?

In the face of that question, we all recognize our fallibility and the fragility of human life. We can but wish them and their daughter well in the years to come.

What counts most of all is asking the question, repeatedly and honestly, about one's own responsibilities to one's own children and to the next generation as a whole. The real tragedy begins when we stop asking the question, "What counts?"

"Why should it be more dignified to decompose at once, rather than to be used for bringing a child into existence?"

POSTMORTEM PREGNANCIES ARE ETHICAL

Christoph Anstötz

Christoph Anstötz is a professor at the University of Dortmund, Germany, who specializes in the ethical problems in the education of severely mentally retarded students. In the following viewpoint, Anstötz discusses a case in which a pregnant German woman who was brain-dead was sustained on a life-support system until her baby was born. Anstötz asserts that maintaining a brain-dead woman on life-support to prolong a pregnancy does not rob the woman of her dignity.

As you read, consider the following questions:

1. How did the doctors caring for Marion Ploch's fetus put a value on the life of her fetus, according to Anstötz?
2. What was the reaction of the German public to the news that doctors were trying to sustain Marion Ploch's pregnancy, according to the author?
3. What is needed, in Anstötz's opinion, to help German doctors deal with similar ethical dilemmas?

Reprinted from "Should a Brain-Dead Pregnant Woman Carry Her Child to Full Term? The Case of the 'Erlanger Baby,'" by Christoph Anstötz, *Bioethics*, vol. 7, no. 4, July 1993, by permission of Blackwell Publishers Ltd., Oxford.

In October 1992, a young woman died in a car accident. She was pregnant and her fetus appeared to be unhurt, so a decision had to be made: should the mother's body be artificially supported in order to give the fetus a chance to live? The situation became a public question that split Germany in two. One side demanded that the young woman—and her child—be left to die in dignity. The other side referred to the unborn child's right to live and therefore wanted the body of the woman maintained until the fetus could be born. . . .

THE CASE

At noon on 5th October, 1992, Marion Ploch, a dental assistant, was on her way home from work. She was 13 weeks pregnant. On a road between Feucht and Altdorf, two towns in the south of the Federal Republic of Germany, she crashed her car against a tree. About a quarter of an hour later the ambulance arrived. Because she was suffering from a fractured skull, the young woman was taken by helicopter to the university hospital in Erlangen. There she was treated at the intensive care unit. On the same day her parents, Gabriele and Hans Ploch, were informed that Marion had no chance of survival. They told the magazine Stern that during the first days after the accident they came into contact with nearly twenty different doctors of the hospital. At first the doctors wanted to get their approval for organ donation. The doctors who made this request knew about the pregnancy, but they saw no chance of survival for the fetus. The parents refused to make Marion's organs available for donation. Later other doctors came with other views. They also regarded Marion's situation as hopeless. On the evidence of comparable cases in the literature they thought, however, that the fetus would have a real chance of survival. At this time the doctors sought the parents' agreement to keeping Marion coupled to the apparatus that was maintaining her bodily functions. The father of the child was unknown and did not appear in the days that followed.

On the 8th of October the doctors confirmed that brain death had occurred, but did not turn off the respirator. On October 9, Marion's parents sent a cry for help to the Bild-Zeitung, a mass-circulation newspaper. German newspapers picked up this theme and the case was taken up and became known as the "Erlanger Baby" case. Amid emotional public discussion, the doctors did everything possible to keep the fetus alive. The birth was planned for March 1993, by Caesarean section. On November 17, however, the daily paper TAZ reported:

On 16.11.1992 at 00.10 a spontaneous abortion happened to Marion P. The fetus . . . who was alive until just before the miscarriage, was born dead. The reason for the spontaneous abortion needs further clarification, but the parents have refused an autopsy of the mother and of the fetus.

At this time Marion Ploch's parents were both reported to be ill with the stress of the past few weeks.

Justification

On October 11, after the Bild-Zeitung had been informed of the case by the parents of Marion Ploch, a reporter from that newspaper called one of the doctors of the Erlangen hospital. He asked for a statement from the clinic by the next afternoon. Under considerable time pressure, a committee met the next morning. After the parents finally had agreed to the plan of the doctors, the committee decided to continue the respiration of Marion Ploch until the fetus could be born. The assistant medical director and professor of surgery at the university hospital, Johannes Scheele, later said that "on the grounds of proportionality . . . it is probably reasonable to impose on the mother, through the use of her body, for the benefit of the child." And in another newspaper he argued: "There really isn't any question whether it should be tried or not . . . more than that, we don't see any ethical reason simply to let the embryo die." The clinic's director, Franz Paul Gall, agreed with his colleague: "The child's right to live demands also the use of modern and technological aids."

In a detailed interview with the same newspaper, Professor Hans-Bernhard Wuermeling defended the decision, which he had supported in his function as the clinic's legal advisor. A long-standing member of the "Juristenvereinigung Lebensschutz" (Association of Jurists to Protect Life), he asserts that: "Respect for the dead body is no absolute ethical demand, as the right to life is." In a strict sense, Wuermeling couldn't have seen the right to live as an absolute one, because later on he referred to important restrictions based on the proportionality of the means used and the results gained. In his opinion this relationship between effort and success would be jeopardized if, for example, a handicap were detected: "In my view it is justifiable to abandon the whole treatment, if impairments appear." And he explained: "This would be no killing, but the ending of a measure, which would not have been started, if it had been known what would happen."

The treating doctors, on the other hand, expressed doubts about the idea of stopping respiration if the fetus was found to be impaired: "It is not up to us to decide if a life is valuable," Dr Johannes Scheele said. But this position, too, is not as unequivocal as it sounds because doctors who defend it make their decision depend on the effort that continuation of pregnancy in the dead woman requires: "If Marion Ploch's kidneys fail, a dialysis machine would not be rolled to the deathbed, nor a heart-lung machine in case of further complications." In saying that they would not step up medical efforts to sustain Marion Ploch's body, what else are the doctors doing but weighing up costs and putting a value on the life of the fetus?

THE LAW IS SILENT

The decision whether to switch off the machines was a purely ethical issue, because German law seems silent in a case of this kind. Torsten Lund of the Institute for Philosophy of Law at the University of Munich pointed out: "There is nothing about this in the penal codes. It is an extreme case, which has never occurred in Germany before." Before the most recent reform of Section 218, concerning abortion, the penal code spoke about "killing of the body-fruit." This expression might have been seen as giving legal direction. In its present form, however, the law speaks of "termination of pregnancy." This presupposes a living mother, whose interests are to be weighted against the interests of the developing child. Insofar as there are no criminal sanctions to protect the life of the fetus, the section confers no legal right on the fetus to be kept alive.

The law also offers little support on another aspect of the case. Nowhere does the law lay down who shall represent the presumed interests of a brain-dead pregnant woman. Judge Gerold Wahl, of the court with jurisdiction in the case, assigned a relative to look after the dead Marion Ploch. He grounded his decision on the "Betreuungsgesetz" (Guardianship Law), which regulates the representations of interests of (living!) intellectually disabled people. The parents of the dead pregnant woman, Gabriele and Hans Ploch, were appointed to protect the interests of the growing child. This is the usual procedure with pregnant patients in a coma. Those appointed by the courts in this manner would have to be consulted before any decision were made.

THE PUBLIC REACTION

In his "Report from Germany: Bioethics and Academic Freedom," published in 1990, Peter Singer showed the astonishing reluctance of many people in Germany—even those with university education—to discuss subtle moral problems in a rational, factual and serious manner. Similarly in the case of the "Er-langer Baby," the discussion often became emotional, at times even fanatical.

Dr Johannes Scheele, for example, had some extremely un-pleasant experiences: "On the desk of Professor Scheele the opinions of the people are piled up, thirty letters every day: "SS-Nazi Pig," "Concentration Camp Dr Mengele," "Dr Franken-stein." In this way many citizens expressed their views that the respiration of the brain-dead pregnant woman should not be continued. When it became known that Marion Ploch's body was given physical exercises, as is usually done with coma pa-tients to prevent stiffening of the limbs, a large graffiti appeared on the wall of the university hospital: "Zur Leichengymnastik" ("To the gymnastics for corpses"). And a few steps further: "Now human—instead of animal—experiments." The Viennese psychologist Springer-Kremser condemned the doctors' attempt as a "shameless human experiment . . . a perversion of the oath of Hippocrates . . . And we have already seen in this century what perversion German brains are capable of."

Shortly after the case first became public, the Bild-Zeitung con-ducted a phone-in opinion poll on the question "Is it right for a dead woman to have a child?" The result: 33,436 readers thought that the dead Marion should not give birth to her child, while 7,302 callers considered that Marion should bring her child into existence. The Berliner Morgenpost reported a nation-wide protest of the "Greens" and other organizations, who de-manded an immediate halt to the "human experiment." In a short time they gathered 7,000 signatures and passed them to the Minister of Women's Affairs, Angela Merkel, and the Minis-ter of Justice, Sabine Leutheusser-Schnarrenberger. Another dec-laration came from the Institute for Medical Psychology of the University of Munich, signed by 21 academics: "It is not clear whether interests of power and misguided scientific ambitions were the relevant motives. But there can be no doubt that the goals are being sought under degrading circumstances."

WOMEN'S VIEWS

Hanna Wolf, spokeswoman for Women's Affairs of the Lower House of the Federal Parliament, comments in the Bild-Zeitung: "What is happening in this clinic is a scandal and inhuman. The mother is degraded to a nutrient fluid, disposable after use." She told the Berliner Morgenpost that she was asking the government "if maintaining the physical functions on the grounds of pregnancy violates the human dignity guaranteed by article one of the constitution." Other female politicians of different political parties said that the "border of what is tolerable for a civilized society has been exceeded," and that "the dignity of the dead woman . . . is violated in an unacceptable way." They demanded that "the 'Erlanger case' must lead to a new ethical discussion on a political level, too." Professor Andrea Abele-Brehm, Director of the Institute for Psychology at the University of Erlangen and a representative of female employees there, criticized the male composition of the committee and said, "It cannot be right that the horror-vision of a female corpse as an 'incubator' becomes reality without any female comment." Alice Schwarzer, a dedicated leader of the women's movement in Germany, preferred attacks with publicity effects to rational analyses: "The Pope will like it—women as incubators. I think it's perverse."

SAVING THE FETUS IS NOT IMMORAL

Surely, it is not unreasonable to think in the absence of any evidence to the contrary that a mother would want an effort to be made to save her fetus. And if a husband, parents or other family members decide that the attempt to save the fetus is the right thing to do, it is hard to see why others would say that maintaining the body on machines to allow the fetus to develop is disrespectful to the mother.

Using a cadaver to save the life of a developing fetus is risky, unusual and maybe even macabre. But it is not immoral.

Arthur Caplan, St. Paul Pioneer Press, August 23, 1993.

The churches were equally active. In Nürnberg, in the "Lorenz-kirche," a special divine-service was organized to provide an opportunity for commentary on the case. Many theologians expressed their points of view in talk-shows and also in the print-media. Everybody sought their answer to the question whether it is permissible to switch off the life-support for Marion Ploch. On this the prevailing theological assessment of brain death played an important role. Wilhelm Polster, the chaplain for the intensive care unit of the university hospital in Erlangen, rejected the definition of death in terms of the death of the brain: "I don't accept the medical statements," he said. "For me a dead woman is someone who lies there white and stiff. In the end nobody knows when the soul leaves the body." The Catholic hospital chaplain Rainer Denkler, whose task it would have been to give the last rites to Marion Ploch, saw this differently: "The soul is the personality. As long as somebody is lying in a coma, there still is a capacity for a relationship. In her (Marion Ploch's) case the soul has departed." Because the last rites are given before death, the priest only spoke a prayer. He added: "The possibilities of modern intensive care have in this case passed beyond a border given by nature and, for the faithful, given by god." The *Bild-Zeitung* headlined one of its stories: "Whoever interferes with Creation will one day be punished."

UNCERTAINTIES ABOUT MEDICAL TECHNOLOGY

In Germany the discussion of subtle problems seems to slip easily to a level of personal defamation, thoughtless parallels with the Nazi-era, graffiti and so on. But less drastic means of carrying on a discussion also disturb the development of reasonable solutions. Talking about a woman as a "birth machine" or "nutrient fluid" prevents a rational analysis of a problematical situation. In part such phenomena may be explained by general uncertainties towards new possibilities in modern medical technology. Brain death has for many years been widely accepted in Germany as a medical and legal criterion of death. But the case of Marion Ploch shows that there are obviously psychological difficulties in drawing the relevant ethical consequences from it. At first even factual questions arose. So Dr Julius Hackethal, well known from the euthanasia discussion in Germany, brought a charge against Dr Johannes Scheele for causing "bodily harm, poisoning and maltreatment of a patient in his care," adding that: "The expression 'brain death' is a verbal construction avoiding the heart of the matter. In fact only the cortex of the patient does not function, but the rest of the brain works very well. She is alive." And in other articles he said: "The patient lives—under intensive torture and the worst nightmare." This view, however, was not widely shared. Referring to the comment of Hans-Bernhard Wuermeling, an expert in medical law, the *Nürnberger Nachrichten* wrote: "In the case of the 18-year-old Marion P. all parts of the brain are dead . . . including the lower and older parts. Therefore the basis of the charge is not applicable." In addition the public prosecutor refused to accept the charge, which Julius Hackethal subsequently unsuccessfully tried to bring again.

NO CLUE TO HER WISHES

The general view was that since the accident, Marion Ploch's body had been and always would be without any awareness. This meant that the minimal prerequisites for considering Marion Ploch's actual interests were lacking. By assigning an aunt to stand for Marion Ploch's interests when considering whether

treatment should be discontinued, the court denied this ir-
refutable fact. The law that the court applied was made for living
intellectually disabled people and not for the dead. Of course
there are interests beyond death which are to be respected—in
case of a will, for example. But in regard to the actual situation,
there were no clues about Marion Ploch's wishes. There was
nothing anyone could directly refer to, in order to defend her
interests. Despite this, it was emphasized again and again that
her dignity required that the apparatus be switched off and she
be allowed to die. But why should it be more dignified to decompose at once, rather than to be used for bringing a child
into existence? And how can somebody who is already dead be
allowed to die? According to Hans-Bernhard Wuermeling the
answer is easy: "People get upset because they don't accept brain
death as death." The previously cited view of Wilhelm Polster
confirms this simple explanation with rare clarity: "I don't accept the medical statements. . . . For me a dead woman is someone who lies there white and stiff. " Since Marion Ploch was not
white and stiff, she couldn't really be dead. Therefore she had a
moral status which was more like that of a living than a dead
human being. In this context the concept of human dignity
played an important role. Usually, however, "human dignity"
was invoked in order to give personal attitudes some moral relevance. In rejecting the charge brought by Dr Julius Hackethal,
the public prosecutor spoke about the "right not to be kept artificially alive, deducted from the principle of human dignity."

Is the idea really absurd, that Marion Ploch would have agreed
to give her child a chance to live? Would she thereby have in-
jured her own dignity? In this discussion "human dignity" was
used like a joker. Those who had no arguments could still play
human dignity as the last card in their hand. For example the Süd-
deutsche Zeitung wrote: "Maybe it is possible to keep the child alive.
But everything is already lost: the woman's dignity, the child's
dignity and the dignity of death—in favour of science.". . .

ETHICAL PROBLEMS

The case of the "Erlanger Baby" gave rise to many questions. Because of the amount of publicity it received, many people in our
country are . . . confronted with the new possibilities of modern
medicine and their ethical problems. . . . The zeal shown in favour
of the right to life of the "Erlanger baby," however, did not corre-
spond in any way to what might have been expected, given this
background. Often the same groups who opposed . . . euthanasia
now resisted the continuation of the "death-pregnancy"—and

again they used the tactic of reminding us of the Nazi era, but this time against the course of action that was intended to preserve human life. Even those fighting for the right to life of the unborn child who—like Hans Bernhard Wuermeling—spoke about an absolute right to life, put restrictions on this right, referring to the possibility that the fetus might be handicapped, and also to possible complications with the mother and the resulting increased costs. On the testing ground of real cases like the "Erlanger baby" we can see what is left of the absolute sanctity of life position.

But this case had another outcome. After the death of the Erlanger baby on November 16, there was an outcry against "medical experimental ambitions." The parents now objected that their consent to maintaining the body functions of their daughter was not given freely. The doctors had told the parents that if they refused consent, they risked losing custody. "It seemed like a blackmail" the parents told *Stern*.

Dr Scheele and Dr Würmeling denied this claim. The initial predications of the chance that the fetus would survive were also disputed. Dr Scheele talked about a "first prize in the lottery." But the parents understood this differently, they claimed, when they agreed to the innovatory treatment. Questions about the borderlines of medical experimentation and the consequences of the case were answered by the clinical director Franz Paul Gall: "In medicine there can be no borders given by the society . . . medicine knows its borderlines itself, and they will continue to expand." This quotation was repeated in different news media. Statements like this show that German doctors need more help—if necessary, from the law—to understand the distinction between medical competence and ethical competence. A good starting point might be the setting up of some institutional controls over ethical decisions in medicine.

| "There is something distinctly creepy about keeping a corpse from decaying so that a fetus can continue to grow inside it."

POSTMORTEM PREGNANCIES ARE UNETHICAL

Hilde Lindemann Nelson

Technological advances have allowed doctors to keep a pregnant, brain-dead woman alive long enough to safely carry her baby to term. These pregnancies are called postmortem pregnancies. Arguments advocating such practices are invalid, contends Hilde Lindemann Nelson in the following viewpoint. She asserts that sustaining the pregnancy does not always benefit the fetus and oftentimes imposes a substantial burden on the mother. Furthermore, Nelson argues, neither the law nor morality compel physicians to sustain a postmortem pregnancy. Nelson is a research associate and former associate editor of the *Hastings Center Report*, a bimonthly journal on ethical issues in medicine, the life sciences, and the professions.

As you read, consider the following questions:

1. What are the three reasons cited by the author that might oblige a physician to attempt to sustain a postmortem pregnancy?
2. Why should a physician not assume that a brain-dead woman would want her pregnancy sustained, in Nelson's opinion?
3. According to Nelson, what is the state's interest in sustaining a postmortem pregnancy?

Reprinted from "The Architect and the Bee: Some Reflections on Postmortem Pregnancy," by Hilde Lindemann Nelson, *Bioethics*, vol. 8, no. 3, July 1994, by permission of Blackwell Publishers Ltd., Oxford.

S everal years ago a graduate student at Michigan State University presented a paper on transgenic animals. At one point in the discussion that followed somebody intoned, "The problem is such a novel one that we haven't the appropriate moral language to describe it."

"Yes we do," retorted the philosopher Martin Benjamin. "The word is *creepy*. We call it creepy!"

Benjamin's term of art can just as readily be applied to postmortem pregnancy. There is something distinctly creepy about keeping a corpse from decaying so that a fetus can continue to grow inside it, about bringing forth a child from the flesh of the living dead. On the other hand, we might think of this practice as salvaging what we can from the wreckage of an untimely disaster. After all, what is creepy here is a process aimed at a quite ordinary outcome, not the outcome itself. We might think of this practice, like other disgusting medical or surgical procedures that are performed every day, as putting to rights something that has gone badly wrong. If we can't save the mother, don't we at least owe the fetus a chance to be born? Isn't that what the mother too would have wanted?

In this viewpoint I examine the case of women who die during the first or second trimester of pregnancy, since the third trimester requires a separate moral and legal analysis. I offer [three] possible grounds for a duty on the part of physicians to sustain early pregnancies in the newly dead, but find all of them inadequate. . . .

PRONOUNCED DEAD AND PREGNANT

The first successful attempt to bring a postmortem pregnancy to term is generally taken to be the American one reported by William P. Dillon and colleagues at Buffalo, New York, in February of 1981—a case in which a 26-week-old infant was delivered 5 days after its mother was pronounced brain dead. In San Francisco in March 1983 a baby boy was delivered 61 days after maternal brain death, and in July of that same year in Roanoke, Virginia, a baby was born 84 days after its mother was pronounced dead. A baby was born to a brain-dead women late in pregnancy in Finland in 1984. In Santa Clara, California, in July 1986 a healthy baby girl was born 53 days after her mother, Marie Henderson, died of a brain tumor. Conley Hilliker, of Champlain, New York, grew inside his mother's brain-dead body for 107 days before cesarean delivery on 29 March 1988. In 1989 a San Bernardino, California, baby was delivered alive at 27 weeks' gestation to a brain-dead teenager who had been on life-support for about 60 days. And in the most recent case of this kind a baby was delivered by cesarean section in Oakland, California, on 3 August 1993, 105 days after his mother, Trisha Marshall, was declared brain dead. She had been shot in the head during an attempted burglary when in the seventeenth week of pregnancy.

Two unsuccessful attempts at postmortem pregnancy were also widely reported. In August 1986 a boy weighing 17 ounces was delivered dead three months prematurely from the body of Donna Piazzi in Augusta, Georgia. Postmortem gestation in this case, which was complicated by a dispute between the fetus's father (who wanted life support continued) and Ms. Piazzi's husband (who did not), lasted 49 days. In October 1992 in Erlangen, Germany, Marion Ploch was pronounced brain dead when 15 weeks pregnant; her body was kept on life support for 42 days until it miscarried.

Of the ten cases just catalogued, seven involved pregnant women who we can say with confidence were not married to their fetus's father; the written reports of the other three cases make no mention of a husband one way or another. In at least one instance the identity of the father was unknown. Requests to continue the pregnancy were initiated by the fathers in some cases and the woman's parents in others—sometimes as a result of pressure brought to bear by the physicians.

THE BABY IN THE BODY

What exactly must a health care team do to sustain a postmortem pregnancy? Consider the San Francisco, 1983, case mentioned above, which was written up in 1988 by the woman's physicians in the *Journal of the American Medical Association*. When the 27-year-old patient presented at the hospital with headaches and disorientation and four hours later suffered a generalized seizure and cardiac arrest, she was given cardiopulmonary resuscitation and placed on a ventilator in the intensive care unit, where, after two days, she was pronounced brain dead. Injections of vasopressin were required to control the massive case of diabetes that developed soon after, and two antibiotics were given to treat a urinary tract infection. A feeding tube, surgically implanted in the woman's abdomen, required careful monitoring because it is a vector for further bacterial infection. A transfusion of packed red blood cells was given.

After two weeks the cadaver was transferred to Moffitt Hospital at the University of California at San Francisco, where ventilator support was continued. Caregivers at Moffitt Hospital expended every effort to regulate bodily functions which are ordinarily governed by the brain. To improve the extremely low blood pressure they used plasma expanders and a combination of vasopressors. Fluctuations of bodily temperature were stabilized by heating and cooling blankets. The persistent symptoms of diabetes responded to a vasopressin infusion, and hypothyroidism and cortisol deficiency were dealt with by administering thyroxine and cortisol. To avoid the risk of abdominal infection, nasogastric feeding was attempted; when it failed, a feeding tube had to be implanted again. Hyperglycemia developed and was treated with a continuous infusion of insulin.

An Unwholesome Proposal

Our technical capacity to manipulate physiology seems less and less grounded in either reality or good sense. Should we stop for a minute to think about the implication of keeping the body of a brain-dead pregnant woman functioning so that an embryo or fetus can grow or develop, no matter what the former prospective mother might have wanted? A fetus near term, assuming it has not been severely damaged by whatever injury killed the mother, can probably survive with immediate delivery. Beyond this already uncommon circumstance, no material or symbolic meaning I try to assign to a dead woman's enduring interests, the putative interests of a preterm fetus, or the interests of the father or other family members, and no consideration of resources allows me to feel wholesome about sustaining dead bodies to "grow" fetuses.

Joel E. Frader, Journal of Clinical Ethics, Winter 1993.

Fetal heart tones were monitored at every shift and obstetric sonograms were performed at two-week intervals. The body was injected with betamethasone sodium phosphate on a weekly basis and nonstress tests were performed twice a week. Enterococcal bacteremia developed and required two different regimens of antibiotics before the infection cleared up.

In the last few days of the pregnancy, a staphylococcus aureus infection developed and was treated, but because a sonogram indicated the fetus had not grown in the last two weeks and because of the recurrent infections, the physicians decided to deliver the fetus by cesarean section at 31 weeks' gestation. At this point the woman had been dead for 61 days.

The respirator was shut off as soon as the delivery was completed and the woman's heart stopped beating shortly thereafter. An autopsy revealed that her brain was decayed to such an extent that no tissue analysis was possible. The child was admitted to the neonatal intensive care unit, where he did well despite a mild case of respiratory distress syndrome. At three weeks of age he was transferred to a hospital nearer his father's home.

The cost of maintaining a postmortem pregnancy in a county hospital in California in 1993 was $3,200 per day. Further costs will depend on the condition of the infant after delivery. She or he may require weeks of intensive care before being discharged from the hospital, depending on the degree of maturity at birth and whether there was permanent damage due to oxygen deprivation or some other cause.

IS SHE DEAD?

A preliminary question to consider before exploring possible grounds for a duty to continue pregnancies of this kind is whether the woman is actually dead. Does it make sense to say this of someone whose heart is beating, whose kidneys and liver are functioning, and in whose uterus there is a placenta that is actively nourishing a growing fetus? If an organism fitting this description is dead, what can we possibly mean by 'living'? Medical technology has blurred the distinctions between the living, the dying, and the dead, and this has caused a great deal of conceptual confusion. It is not necessary, however, to enter the debate over brain death, or to distinguish between the death of the person and the death of the body, to agree that the woman cannot be restored to consciousness and has become permanently incapable of purposeful activity—to agree, moreover, that as soon as artificial support is withdrawn, organic activity will cease and decay set in. It is perhaps useful to remember that even under the older heart-lung criteria the body harbors living cells and other signs of life when pronounced dead, that neither heart-lung nor brain criteria is compatible with the integration of organic systems, and that the original purpose of brain-death criteria was to establish the point at which treatment could be stopped. Asking whether one ought to call brain death a very serious terminal illness, part of the dying process, or death, then, is to ask what one ought to do with a body in this state.

I shall continue to call her dead, although I do not think the answer to the question of what to do with the body will differ materially from what it would be if I were to say she is insentient and irreversibly dying. My own suspicion is that it makes sense to talk of "early death"—the phase after brain death in which organs are still salvageable and fetal life can be sustained—and "middle death," which is compatible with cellular life, but I shall not attempt here to argue for this view. I do want to underscore the point that the pregnancies under discussion are those in which the fetus is not able to live outside the woman's body, not those in which the fetus could do so but would be better off if the pregnancy could be continued for a few more weeks.

THREE DUTIES

One assumption undergirding efforts to sustain postmortem pregnancies seems to be that the fetus, no matter how immature, is a person with interests and rights—or, minimally, that as the pregnancy has been allowed to continue, the actions of the present ought to be guided by consideration for the welfare of the unborn child. On this assumption one would treat the fetus as if it were like any other person in need of emergency care, and that in fact is what seems to be happening. The physicians who managed the first successful postmortem pregnancy appeared to be acting out of a belief that a duty to rescue the fetus required it. The second time such a case was written up in the medical literature, the physician-authors stated this belief explicitly. So did the chairman of the hospital ethics committee in the most recent U.S. case, and a district attorney in Nuremberg, Germany, Gerd Neubeck, was quoted in *Stern* to the effect that withdrawing life support from Marion Ploch was a punishable offense and would certainly be prosecuted, very likely to the fullest extent of the law.

Are physicians in fact obliged to bring such fetuses to term? On what grounds might such an obligation rest? I can think of [three] possibilities. The duty might be a matter of respecting the woman's wishes, there might be a duty to the state, [or] a duty might be based in beneficence toward the fetus. . . . Each possibility must be examined in turn.

A DUTY TO RESPECT THE WOMAN'S WISHES

Wouldn't any mother want physicians to try to save her baby? Put this way, the answer to the question ought surely to be yes. It is possible, of course, that the pregnancy was unintended and unwanted, forced on her by rape or lesser forms of intimidation. It certainly won't do to assume that because the woman did not have an abortion she has chosen to continue the pregnancy: her personal code, poverty, or lack of access to the procedure might have blocked this option. Nor should one paint too romantic a picture of women's unalloyed desire to sacrifice themselves for their children. But it would be depressing if, in the absence of clear evidence, the default assumption had to be that a pregnant woman did not wish to be pregnant or bear her child, and that she did not love her baby enough to save its life when it was possible to do so.

This is, however, not to say that most women in the early stages of pregnancy would want the pregnancy continued if they knew they were going to die tomorrow. Postmortem pregnancy, as we have seen, involves serious and sustained invasion into the woman's body. The pregnant woman, if she could be consulted, might not at all want these prolonged bodily invasions. Even if in life and health she joyfully and willingly assented to the pregnancy, we cannot assume that now, under very different circumstances, she would desire intensive support of her cadaver to achieve that end. While she might have wanted, for example, to bring a third child into a close and loving two-parent family, she might not at all have wanted to burden with a third child a grieving single parent who is already overwhelmed by the care of the two who exist. Nor would she necessarily have wanted to produce a motherless child—particularly if, as our catalog of cases suggests, the father's ability and willingness to rear the child can't be counted on. Furthermore, because a beating-heart cadaver looks as if it lives, and because it cannot be buried while the pregnancy is being sustained, those grieving her loss will be left with an additional kind of suffering that she may well have wanted to spare them—the distress of not knowing how to mourn.

For these reasons and others, a physician cannot simply assume the woman would want her pregnancy continued after brain death. Clear evidence would be required to justify such an assumption. It would follow that a duty to continue the pregnancy cannot be grounded in what the woman is presumed, without warrant, to have wished.

A DUTY TO THE STATE

Does the state have an interest in bringing a fetus to term, and may it press a woman's cadaver into service as an incubator to achieve that end? . . .

The U.S. Supreme Court has repeatedly affirmed that the state has no interest in fetal life until "viability," the point at which the fetus is "potentially able to live outside the mother's womb, albeit with artificial aid." Viability is left to physicians' best medical judgment; nor need the physician report the factors she relied on in determining that a fetus was not viable.

The Court's stance is not merely a device for resolving the

conflict of interest between a living woman and the fetus she does not wish to carry. It is also an affirmation of bodily privacy, an assurance that there is a limit to how far a person's body can be invaded at the state's behest. The state has some interest here: It may insist on an autopsy under certain restricted circumstances, for example, but greater levels of invasion have not ordinarily been justified. As the *Quinlan* court remarked in 1976 when contemplating precisely the kind of intensive nursing care, antibiotics, respirator, catheter, and feeding tube required for a postmortem pregnancy, "the state's interest *contra* weakens and the individual's right to privacy grows as the degree of bodily invasion increases and the prognosis dims." The prognosis for a woman who is dead is very dim indeed. . . .

A Duty Based in Beneficence

If physicians have no legal duty, might we nevertheless say of the woman herself that she has a moral duty to incubate the fetus within her dead body—a duty that is based in beneficence and that physicians are morally bound to honor? Even after death it is possible to exercise moral agency: a last will and testament permits a person to become someone else's benefactor, as does an organ donation card. Might, then, the pregnant woman have a duty to be her fetus's benefactor? A duty of beneficence is generally taken to consist of two parts: the action must offer (1) a clear gain to others and (2) only moderate risk to the benefactor. . . .

At a casual glance, the benefit [the fetus of a brain-dead mother] receives looks substantial: its life is saved, whereas without continued support inside its mother's body it will surely die. A closer look, however, reveals a difficulty. The odds against bringing the fetus to full term are extraordinarily bad; I have seen no report that it has ever been done. As one of the earliest commentators somewhat incoherently put it, "Attempts to prolong maternal life in the face of brain death are expensive, frustrating, and ultimately futile. Therefore, a fetus of 28 weeks or beyond should be delivered as soon as practicable after confirmation of brain death."

This is to say that children born from postmortem pregnancies will be premature—sometimes quite severely premature—and so are at risk for serious ailments, ranging from brain damage to lung disorders. Their growth may be stunted, their lungs too brittle to breathe without a respirator, severe visual damage is not uncommon. They may be subject to repeated respiratory infections and many have problems digesting food. The Office of Technology Assessment reports that for every 100 very low birthweight infants (those weighing between 1500 and 750 grams at birth), 27 will die before hospital discharge, 16 will be seriously or moderately disabled, and 57 will be normal children, though some will experience mild difficulty in learning. Infants born at less than 29 weeks gestation (often weighing less than 750 grams) are especially at risk for brain bleeds; a Johns Hopkins study found that 90 percent of the babies weighing under 1000 grams had cerebral hemorrhages—36 percent of them severe. An Australian study of babies born between 23 and 28 weeks gestation reported that 8 of 12 infants with severe hemorrhage (67 percent) developed major disabilities. . . .

THE RISK TO THE BENEFACTOR

The other half of the condition—that the action pose only moderate risk to the benefactor—also turns out to be less straightforward than a casual glance would indicate. While it is tempting to say that a cadaver has no interests and for this reason cannot be harmed, this is arguing too loosely. The once-living woman who is now a cadaver has a number of interests that outlast her lifetime: she has an interest in having certain directives carried out, such as those relating to the disposition of her property or her organs. She has an interest in respectful treatment of her body. She has an interest in preserving her good reputation, and in public acknowledgment of her lasting achievements. She has an interest in discharging certain obligations, such as paying her debts or providing for the care of her children and promoting their well-being.

While some of these interests and obligations have no bearing on an involuntary postmortem pregnancy, others do. And because the woman can no longer correct others' mistaken views of what those interests are, a certain precision of understanding becomes particularly important. Robert Veatch once suggested that if a woman had signed an organ donation card and died while pregnant, it would be ethically permissible to sustain the pregnancy even over the objections of her family. But this is an unacceptably broad interpretation of what the woman has consented to. It is one thing to have organs taken out of one's body before burial, and quite another to have that body subjected to unremitting intensive treatment for weeks and even months. Proxy decisionmakers are at times forced to reconstruct someone's wishes by analogizing from what they know of the person, but too loose an analogy argues that they are not taking the person's interests seriously. . . .

A Creepy Pregnancy

In short, I find no general basis in preference, in law, [or] in beneficence to continue a pregnancy after the woman is dead. While the arguments I used to arrive at this conclusion are probably not strong enough to prohibit these pregnancies, no physician or family member need presume that either law or morality compels their continuation. . . .

For all these reasons, then, when the pregnancy is carried on in the woman's absence, we intuitively feel that something creepy is taking place. The uniquely human elements of bringing a baby to term have all died away, leaving a mechanical and pharmacological mimicry of what the pregnancy should have been. This technological doppelgänger is in some instances arguably better than nothing—when the woman dies very late in pregnancy, perhaps, and an extra week inside her body offers the baby better care than an NICU can provide. But even then it is only the lesser of two evils. It is an imitation of pregnancy that should not be encouraged, much less insisted on in every case that stands a remote chance of success.

PERIODICAL BIBLIOGRAPHY

The following articles have been selected to supplement the diverse views presented in this chapter. Addresses are provided for periodicals not indexed in the *Readers' Guide to Periodical Literature*, the *Alternative Press Index*, the *Social Sciences Index*, or the *Index to Legal Periodicals and Books*.

Lisa Belkin	"Pregnant with Complications," *New York Times Magazine*, October 26, 1997.
Thomas W. Clark	"Thou Shalt Not Play God," *Humanist*, July/August 1995.
Cynthia B. Cohen	"'Give Me Children or I Shall Die!' New Reproductive Technologies and Harm to Children," *Hastings Center Report*, March/April 1996.
Geoffrey Cowley	"The Future of Birth," *Newsweek*, September 4, 1995.
Anne Taylor Fleming	"Sperm in a Jar," *New York Times Magazine*, June 12, 1994.
Norman Fost	"Case Study: The Baby in the Body," *Hastings Center Report*, January/February 1994.
Maggie Jones	"Donating Your Eggs," *Glamour*, July 1996.
Journal of Clinical Ethics	Special section on postmortem pregnancy, Winter 1993. Available from 107 E. Church St., Frederick, MD 21701.
Kelly Kershner	"In Vitro Fertilization: Is Conceiving a Child Worth the Cost?" *USA Today*, May 1996.
Gina Maranto	"Delayed Childbearing," *Atlantic Monthly*, June 1995.
Timothy E. Murphy	"Sperm Harvesting and Postmortem Fatherhood," *Bioethics*, October 1995. Available from 238 Main St., Cambridge, MA 02142.
Virginia Rutter	"Who Stole Fertility?" *Psychology Today*, March/April 1996.
Jean Seligmann and Karen Springen	"Fewer Bundles of Pain," *Newsweek*, March 4, 1996.

CHAPTER 4

WHAT ETHICS SHOULD GUIDE GENETIC RESEARCH?

Chapter Preface

Anthropologists have long theorized that Native Americans migrated to North and South America from Asia via a land bridge to Alaska thousands of years ago. Scientists soon may have proof of this theory when they are able to show that the Indians of the Amazon are closely related to the Inuit of Russia. This finding will come with the results of an international study known as the Human Genome Diversity Project (HGDP), an international effort that has been documenting the genetic variation of the human species since 1993.

While a similar project—the Human Genome Project (HGP)—will form a composite of the human genome from Europeans and Americans of primarily European ancestry, the HGDP will concentrate on collecting DNA samples from populations who do not trace their heritage to Europe. The HGDP estimates that between five hundred and seven hundred indigenous cultures will have their DNA collected, preserved, and studied. The cell lines (a group of cells that contain a person's entire genetic code) from isolated and remote indigenous peoples are desirable for research because they can contain genes found nowhere else in the world. HGDP researchers hope that cell lines from these little-studied populations will provide them with information they need to develop vaccines or to cure various diseases.

Critics of the Human Genome Diversity Project contend, however, that the researchers intend to exploit and patent DNA from native peoples, using it for commercial use. They also maintain that many tribes do not understand the purpose of the DNA collection or the value of their unique cell lines. For example, one scientist received a patent on the cell line of a tribal member from Papua New Guinea with a rare form of leukemia, but he did not seek the man's permission, nor give him a share of any profits that might be made from the cell line. Such actions are unethical and violate a person's right to his or her own body, these critics claim.

The controversy over the collection and patenting of human DNA are just two issues in the debate over genetic research. The authors in the following chapter also examine the ethics of genetic testing and genetic engineering.

| "Eliminating genetic diseases . . .
| could be accomplished in decades
| through genetic manipulation."

GENETIC ENGINEERING COULD BENEFIT SOCIETY

Joseph F. Coates, John B. Mahaffie, and Andy Hines

Biotechnology and genetic engineering will have a dramatic and beneficial impact on society in the twenty-first century, maintain Joseph F. Coates, John B. Mahaffie, and Andy Hines in the following viewpoint. Scientists working in the fields of genetics and genetic engineering will be able to create plants and animals that are better suited for their human use, they contend, and control or eliminate pests. The authors also assert that genetic engineering will make it possible to identify, treat, and prevent thousands of diseases, as well as positively influence human evolution. Coates, Mahaffie and Hines are the authors of *2025: Scenarios of U.S. and Global Society Reshaped by Science and Technology*, on which this article is based.

As you read, consider the following questions:

1. According to the authors, what percentage of the gross national product in 2025 will be the result of genetics?
2. In the authors' opinion, how might genetic engineering control pests in the future?
3. In the authors' opinion, how might people use genetics in the twenty-first century to enhance human evolution?

Reprinted from "The Promise of Genetics," by Joseph F. Coates, John B. Mahaffie, and Andy Hines, Futurist, September/October 1997, by permission of the World Future Society, 7910 Woodmont Ave., Suite 450, Bethesda, MD 20814; (301) 656-8274; fax: (301) 951-0394; http://www.wfs.org/wfs.

G enetics will be a key enabling technology of the twenty-first century, rivaling information technology, materials technology, and energy technology in importance.

The effects of all of these enabling technologies will be far-reaching across business and society, but advances in genetics in particular will be fundamental to many science and technology areas and societal functions, including health and medicine, food and agriculture, nanotechnology, and manufacturing.

One benefit of genetics that is already highly visible is in forensics. DNA identification will significantly enhance criminology. It may contribute to declines in violent crime, the identification of deadbeat parents, and the prevention of fraud. It may even deter rape and murder, as potential perpetrators fear leaving their DNA "fingerprints" on the scene.

Rising public interest in genetics is tied to the growing realization that humanity is capable of directly shaping its own and other species' evolution. We will no longer have to wait for nature's relatively slow natural selection. Genetics will bring the capability of speeding and redirecting evolution along paths of our choice. Eliminating genetic diseases, for instance, might take centuries through natural selection but could be accomplished in decades through genetic manipulation.

This power will doubtless inspire a profound global debate about how genetics should and should not be used.

THE GENETIC ECONOMY

On the economic front, genetics could reward those who invest in it for the long haul. It is an industry for patient capital. Its spread over many industries will make it an increasingly important factor in the global economy.

Genetics is not a typical industry, in that it is not measured as a separate entity. It will be a part of, or embedded in, so many industries that government statisticians will not attempt such a measure. A good guess is that genetics will account for about 20% of gross domestic product, or roughly $2 trillion in 2025.

The early emphasis on using genetics to improve human health and battle disease will be supplemented with more exotic applications, such as manufacturing and materials, human enhancement, energy, environmental engineering, and species restoration and management. The food and agriculture industries, for example, are steadily expanding their use of genetics. Advances will come from applying what seem like isolated breakthroughs into a systems framework. For example, researchers working on eradicating a species of locust may develop a microorganism useful in converting crop wastes into biomass energy.

SPECIES MANAGEMENT

The genomes of many animals, fish, insects, and microorganisms will be worked out, leading to more refined management, control, and manipulation of their health and propagation—or their elimination.

• *Designer animals.* Routine genetic programs will be used to enhance animals used for food production, recreation, and even pets. Goats, for example, are especially well suited to genetic manipulation. In affluent nations, goats will be used for producing pharmaceutical compounds; in less-developed nations, goats will produce high-protein milk.

Livestock will be customized to increase growth, shorten gestation, and enhance nutritional value. Farmers will be able to order the genes they want from gene banks for transmission to local biofactories, where the animals with the desired characteristics will then be produced and shipped.

Transgenic animals, sharing the genes of two or more species, may be created to withstand rough environments. Genes from the hardy llama in South America, for example, could be introduced into camels in the Middle East—and vice versa—to greatly expand the range of each. Some species will be introduced into entirely new areas. Parrots may be modified to withstand cold North American temperatures, becoming a boon to bird watchers in the United States.

Transgenic pets may become popular: Genes from mild-mannered Labrador retrievers could be put into pit bull terrier genomes.

• *Pest control.* Genetics will play a central role in pest management. The arms race between insects and pesticides has been marked by humans winning battles, but insects winning the war. Genetics will turn the tide.

One method is to breed pheromones into surrounding plants to lure pests away from their intended prey. Pests will also be sterilized through genetic engineering to disrupt their populations. Genetically engineered resistance to pests will be common through such techniques as inducing the plants to produce their own protective or repellent compounds.

Insects that carry disease will also be targeted through genetic engineering to control their populations. It is hoped that malaria will soon be eliminated this way.

• *Boosting plants.* Future farmers may have near total control over plant genetics. Plants will give higher yields and be more resistant to disease, frost, drought, and stress. They will have higher protein, lower oil, and more efficient photosynthesis rates than ever before. Natural processes such as ripening will be enhanced and controlled.

Genetics in 2025

Application	Genetics' Potential Impacts
Health	Eliminate almost 2,000 single gene diseases, such as Huntington's Chorea. Cut in half the diseases with genetic predispositions, including dozens of cancers.
Behavior	Substantial reduction of schizophrenia. Education overhauled to tailor learning to individual genetic/cognitive profiles.
Livestock	Revival of pork industry with custom-designed varieties, such as ultra-lean pork.
Fisheries	Overwhelmed natural fisheries supplemented by aquafarms specializing in transgenic specialty fish.
Pest management	Crop loss due to pests reduced by two-thirds in the United States; Lyme disease eliminated.
Crops	Intermittent blights eliminated, allowing record yields of Irish potatoes, Kansas wheat, and Japanese rice.
Food	The number of foods making up 90% of the typical human diet rises from six to 37; foods are customized according to consumers' taste, preparation, and storage needs.
Forestry	Superior strains of trees allow worldwide tree coverage to double.
Microorganisms	Specialty chemicals, medicines, and foods are produced in bioreactors, enhancing agriculture, mining, waste management, and other industries.

Joseph F. Coates, John B. Mahaffie, and Andy Hines, 2025: Scenarios of U.S. and Global Society Reshaped by Science and Technology, 1997.

Genetics will allow farmers to customize and fine-tune crops, building in flavor, sweeteners, and preservatives, while increasing nutritional value.

The first step in agrogenetics is to identify disease-resistant genes; the second step is to put them into plants. Eventually, plants will be genetically engineered to produce specific prevention factors against likely disease invaders.

Forestry will also benefit from genetics. Genetic manipulation will result in superior tree strains with disease resistance and improved productivity. Trees will be routinely engineered to allow nonchemical pulping for use in paper making. Genetic forests will also help in the global restoration of many denuded areas.

• *Engineering microorganisms.* Manufacturers will use engineered microorganisms to produce commodity and specialty chemicals, as well as medicines, vaccines, and drugs. Groups of microorganisms, often working in sequence as living factories, will produce useful compounds. They will also be widely used in agriculture, mining, resource upgrading, waste management, and environmental cleanup. Oil- and chemical-spill cleanups are a high-profile application.

The development of so-called suicidal microorganisms will be an important factor. Engineered microorganisms would self-destruct by expressing a suicide gene after their task is accomplished. These would be developed in response to fears of runaways—that is, harmful genetically engineered microorganisms that rapidly spread destructive power. They would be particularly useful in the bioremediation of solid and hazardous waste sites and in agricultural applications such as fertilizers.

GENETICS IN INDUSTRY

Genetics will first become a force in improving human health, food, and agriculture. But over the next few decades it will have a greater impact across many industries, such as chemical engineering, environmental engineering, manufacturing, energy, and information technology. It will even contribute to the burgeoning field of artificial life.

Chemical engineering, for example, has begun "biologizing"—i.e., incorporating an understanding of complex biological interactions. Genetics will help the chemical industry shift away from bulk chemicals to higher value–added products, such as food additives or industrial enzymes used as biocatalysts.

Genetic engineering will also help to clean the environment and may be used to create totally artificial environments, such as in space and seabed stations or even for terraforming Mars.

Manufacturing, too, will become "biologized" and more like breeding. Manufacturing applications of genetics will include molecular engineering for pharmaceuticals and other compounds, rudimentary DNA chips, biosensors, and nanotechnology based on biological principles such as self-assembly.

A key consideration in biologizing will be society's commitment to sustainability, which could drive a search for environmentally benign manufacturing strategies. Biological approaches, while slower than mechanistic ones, could prove more sustainable. In the future, all industrial enzymes may be produced by genetic engineering. Already, recombinant DNA is used in cheese making, wine making, textiles, and paper production. Bioreactors, in which engineered living cells are used as biocatalysts, will be used for new kinds of manufacturing, such as making new tree species.

GENETICS AND INFORMATION TECHNOLOGY

Linkages may be found between genetics and information technology: Researchers are striving for ways to take advantage of the fact that genes are pure information. A whole new discipline is evolving: "bioinformatics" to manage and interpret the flood of new biological and genomic data. A science of biological computing is also likely to evolve and compete successfully with silicon-based computing.

Genetics and information technology would work together in advanced computers. Biophotonic computers using biomolecules and photonic processors could be the fastest switching systems ever built.

GLOBAL DEVELOPMENT

Genetics could be a tool for igniting a second Green Revolution in agriculture. Synthetic soil supplements, crop strains that accommodate a land's existing conditions, and integrated pest management techniques could be a boon to developing countries, such as India, facing burgeoning population growth on increasingly tired and overworked cropland.

Another potential economic benefit of genetics may be in tourism. Kenya, for instance, could promote tourism associated with wildlife by strengthening its indigenous species. Genetics could be used to rescue lions and elephants from extinction by boosting their food supply or developing vaccines to prevent viral attacks.

Like Kenya, Brazil has an economic opportunity in protecting and enhancing its biodiversity. Brazil's niche would be in pharmaceuticals and other chemicals, and it could tap its lush tropical forest—storehouses of over half the world's plant and animal species. Genes that promote rapid growth could be engineered into the native rain-forest tree species, thus helping to save forests once thought to be lost forever.

GENETICS AND HUMAN HEALTH

Genetics will increasingly enable health professionals to identify, treat, and prevent the 4,000 or more genetic diseases and disorders that our species is heir to. Genetics will become central to diagnosis and treatment, especially in testing for predispositions and in therapies. By 2025, there will likely be thousands of diagnostic procedures and treatments for genetic conditions.

Genetic diagnostics can detect specific diseases, such as Down's syndrome, and behavioral predispositions, such as depression. Treatments include gene-based pharmaceuticals, such as those using antisense DNA to block the body's process of transmitting genetic instructions for a disease process. In future preventive therapies, harmful genes will be removed, turned off, or blocked. In some cases, healthy replacement genes will be directly inserted into fetuses or will be administered to people via injection, inhalation, retroviruses, or pills. These therapies will alter traits and prevent diseases.

Although genetics will be the greatest driver of advances in human health in the twenty-first century, it will not be a panacea for all human health problems. Health is a complex of interacting systems. The benefits of genetics will also be weighted more heavily to future generations, because prevention will be such an important component. Genetic therapies will ameliorate conditions in middle-aged and older people, but those conditions will not even exist in future generations. For example, psoriasis may be brought under control for many via gene therapy; if an effective prenatal diagnosis can be developed, then no future child would ever need be born with the condition.

HUMAN DESTINY

The greatest genetic challenge of the twenty-first century will be human enhancement. The human species is the first to influence its own evolution. Already, we have seen the use of human growth hormone for more than its original intent as a treatment for dwarfism. In many instances, use of HGH has been cosmetic rather than medically indicated.

In the future, genetics may also be used for mental enhancement. Parents lacking math skills, for example, may shop for genes that predispose their bearer to mathematical excellence and have these genes inserted prenatally or postnatally into their children. Other parents may select traits such as artistic ability, musical talent, charm, honesty, or athletic prowess for their children.

Of course, some challenging social questions are bound to arise as genetics leads to increasingly talented and intelligent children growing up in a society in which they are in many ways superior to their parents, teachers, and government authorities. Optimists may anticipate a more informed and enlightened society. Pessimists would worry about older people being warehoused in communities or homes for the genetically impaired.

2

"The cornucopia of prizes from
genetic engineering . . . is rapidly
becoming a mare's-nest of transgenic
creations that we neither need nor
want."

GENETIC ENGINEERING COULD BE DANGEROUS

Susan Wright

Susan Wright, a science historian who teaches at the University
of Michigan, is the author of *Molecular Politics*. In the following
viewpoint, she examines the history of genetic engineering and
how its lack of legislative regulations and oversight has led to an
industry that is out of control. While some of the products developed through genetic engineering are useful, Wright contends that many of them could be harmful to the environment,
plants, animals, and humans. Genetically engineered evolution
cannot easily be reversed, she asserts, so the only alternative is to
educate the public about the dangers of genetic technology.

As you read, consider the following questions:

1. What was the result of the U.S. Supreme Court's decision in
   Diamond v. Chakrabarty, according to Wright?
2. What does the Rural Advancement Fund International call
   "acts of biopiracy," as cited by the author?
3. In Wright's opinion, what is the danger of developing plants
   that are resistant to herbicides?

Reprinted, with permission, from "Down on the Animal Pharm," by Susan Wright,
Nation, March 11, 1996.

In the early 1970s, the first rather clumsy genetic engineering techniques were immediately recognized as aimed at the molecular basis of life. The human race had acquired the ability to wreak change on the "interior" as well as the "exterior" of earth's ecosystems. Doors began to open to designer bugs able to make a huge range of proteins for the pharmaceutical and chemical industries, and, further down the road, to genetic techniques capable of revolutionizing the slow-paced plant and animal breeding industries and the treatment of genetic diseases. Government, agribusiness, pharmaceutical and chemical capital has been moving through those doors ever since.

A quarter-century on, the brave new world of genetic engineering is populated by some remarkable and disturbing creations. The crassly utilitarian norms that are guiding innovations have so far produced animals to be used as factories for producing drugs; cows stuffed with bovine growth hormone; plants constructed to grow in soil drenched with herbicides that would normally kill them, as well as every other green thing in sight; bacteria that chew up materials used in weapons systems; and cross-eyed, arthritic pigs that yield more meat. What's most disturbing is that the genetic reconstruction of life is advancing on a global scale with almost no informed public discussion or effective oversight, and in the case of certain military uses, without even public knowledge.

At the outset, it was noticed that gene-splicing had a downside. Grave warnings were issued about its social misuse, about the health and environmental hazards of modified organisms, about the ethical problems of using our technical ingenuity on ourselves and other life-forms. In the course of the debates that followed, millions of pages flowed forth from committees, hearings, international bodies and the courts. And since all this happened in the heyday of the photocopying machine and the U.S. "sunshine" laws, both the controversy and the behind-the-scenes calculations by leaders of science and industry were captured in hard copy. Genetic engineering is perhaps the best-documented technology ever to emerge from a laboratory.

MOLECULAR POLITICS

In the early 1970s leaders of biomedical research quickly moved to contain the emerging ethical and social issues. A partial moratorium on research in 1974 was followed by the famous international conference at Asilomar, California, where scientists addressed the hazards of genetic engineering and agreed to impose controls on their own research. These events were celebrated as acts of scientific responsibility. But they were also pre-emptive strikes, demonstrating that control of genetic engineering was best left in the hands of experts, and defining the problem as one that only experts could address—that of "containing" possible biohazards. With that definition, genetic engineers were soon back at work under voluntary controls issued by the National Institutes of Health in 1976.

When intense controversy over these controls erupted shortly after their inception, however, biomedical researchers closed ranks, launching a sophisticated campaign against legislation designed to regulate genetic engineering and investigate its long-term effects. New evidence unavailable to the public at the time of these struggles shows that researchers closeted at the N.I.H. in 1976 decided to conduct a P.R. campaign aimed at persuading the public that hazards were exaggerated.

THE ANIMAL WORLD IS AT RISK

From the first, critics have raised fundamental ethical and moral concerns about humankind's right to use genetic engineering to redirect the evolutionary process of animals in the name of profit and efficiency. Critics have noted that genetic engineering not only causes great animal suffering but also puts the genetic integrity of many species of animals at risk. Unfortunately, too many scientists and corporations and the federal government continue to ignore the animal suffering and the ethical questions that surround the genetic engineering of animals.

Andrew Kimbrell, *The Animals' Agenda*, January/February 1995.

Claiming that science was under attack, they agreed to direct public attention to the inability of bacteria used for experiments to cause epidemics—an argument they knew was simplistic and misleading. In the words of one scientist: "In terms of P.R. you have to hit epidemics, because that is what people are afraid of, and if we can make a strong argument about epidemics and make it stick, then a lot of this public thing will go away. . . . It's molecular politics, not molecular biology."

The same group also agreed not to pursue experiments to test worst-case scenarios. Instead, they would do a "slick *New York Times* type of experiment"—one likely to produce negative results that would persuade reporters that the field was harmless.

Arguments for the safety of genetic engineering created many converts, just as commercial applications in the field began to loom on the horizon. In 1977 scientists demonstrated that bacteria could be persuaded to make a human protein. If this was possible, why not insulin, growth hormone and supercows making more milk? At this point, the president of the Pharmaceutical Manufacturers Association weighed in against regulation: "It is quite possible that legislation could be so restrictive, so much of a disincentive, that our people wouldn't lose interest . . . they would go overseas."

Stunned by the ferocity of the scientists' lobbying effort, soothed by the public relations campaign issuing from the N.I.H. and intimidated by the P.M.A.'s threat to move elsewhere, Congress retreated. Concern that the United States would lose out in the "genetic engineering race" became the new mantra. Rapid deregulation followed.

PLENTY OF LOOPHOLES

Now we are confronting the legacy of our failure to face the issues posed by genetic engineering. While the techniques have grown in power, precision and range of application, even the limited regulation that was put in place has been virtually dismantled. With one or two exceptions for genes encoding a few of the most dangerous toxins, pretty much any gene can be cloned in any organism. Most experiments and industrial processes involving genetic engineering are overseen only by local committees appointed by the institution doing the cloning.

Furthermore, the fundamental purpose of the original controls—containment—has been overturned. In the Reagan years, the N.I.H.'s prohibition on the release of genetically engineered organisms into the environment was replaced by a patchwork of existing regulatory law with plenty of loopholes. In theory, the Agriculture Department and the Environmental Protection Agency regulate releases of novel plants and microbes. In practice, these agencies have already allowed more than 2,000 experimental releases, indicating just how vigorously their "control" is exercised.

Moreover, changes in patent law are fueling aggressive efforts to monopolize novel gene combinations and the living things in which they are introduced. The landmark 1980 Supreme Court decision in Diamond v. Chakrabarty established patentability for any living thing "under the sun made by man." Over the past fifteen years, the Patent Office has taken this decision to cover cells, microbes, plants, animals—all living things except, presumably, ourselves. But who knows? Lawyer George Annas argues that there's nothing to prevent cloning enthusiasts from pursuing patents for genetically modified human embryos.

The once-unthinkable idea that a microbe, a plant variety or an animal breed could be owned has become accepted practice under the patent law of many industrialized countries. During the GATT [General Agreement on Tariffs and Trade] negotiations, the United States pressed hard for similar practices in the Third World. All genes are now seen as keys to new products. Not only the gene-rich ecosystems of Third World countries but also the cells and genes of indigenous peoples are now envisioned as lucrative targets. In the rush to stake claims on cell-lines and DNA samples, companies and scientists are committing what the Rural Advancement Fund International calls "acts of biopiracy," violating the rights of the people and countries from which the samples are taken. RAFI has launched a campaign to take the issue to the International Court of Justice at The Hague.

TRANSGENIC CREATIONS

A host of transgenic creatures is emerging from genetic engineering laboratories. Typically, these creatures are portrayed as benign additions to the natural world bringing "better, healthier lives to people," as Amgen regularly tells the listeners of National Public Radio. Few of biotechnology's critics would deny that the field will yield some useful products; Eli Lilly's human insulin and Merck's hepatitis B vaccine already help millions of people. Crops that can grow in the desert or resist major pests, and vaccines for diseases like AIDS and malaria, would be beneficial. Nevertheless, many of the applications prominent on corporate and military agendas pose explosive social, ethical and environmental problems. The following is a small sample:

• *Transgenic plants.* Agrichemical and seed corporations are well on the way to developing a wide range of transgenic crops and biopesticides. The most visible are those that will reach supermarkets. Calgene's Flavr Savr tomato, which can sit on store shelves for extended periods without turning into mush, made headlines in 1994. But the most lucrative products are emerging with much less fanfare. Over the past decade, corporations and the government have poured millions into developing plants and trees that tolerate the toxic effects of herbicides. According to the Union of Concerned Scientists, the Agriculture Department has received hundreds of applications for field trials of these crops. Two of them—a cotton resistant to bromoxynil and soybeans resistant to Monsanto's herbicide glyphosate, better known as Roundup—have already been approved. The E.P.A. must also approve any new use of a herbicide. Last year the agency cleared the way for full-scale commercialization by approving the sale of bromoxynil for a quarter-million acres of bromoxynil-resistant cotton. In the pipeline at the Agriculture Department are measures that will weaken the agency's oversight of trials of transgenic plants and expedite full-scale approvals.

The agrichemical industry claims that engineering herbicide tolerance will encourage the use of a new generation of "environmentally friendly" herbicides. The Biotechnology Working Group, a coalition of environmental, labor and other organizations, says there's no such thing: Herbicides have toxic effects on plants and animals; the more they are used, the greater the likelihood of producing herbicide-resistant weeds, contamination of water supplies and destruction of wildlife habitats. While producers claim that their present efforts are limited to resistance to less toxic herbicides, there is no guarantee they will accept this limitation in the future. Indeed, many research and development efforts have focused on crop resistance to high-toxicity herbicides such as 2,4-D and atrazine.

Environmentalists cite yet other worrisome scenarios for transgenic plants; the truth is, no one is able to predict what might happen in the long run. But if the past behavior of the National Institutes of Health is any guide, the Agriculture Department's risk-assessment program is unlikely to investigate worst-case scenarios or wait years for results before granting approval.

• *Animal pharms.* Meanwhile, back at the barn, bio-engineers are turning animals into factories to make drugs in their milk or blood. They're also making pigs and chickens with flesh that can be easily microwaved and bovine growth hormone (BGH) to increase milk production in dairy cows. The latter product has proved particularly controversial. Consumer organizations in the United States and elsewhere argue that injections of the hormone cause health problems in cattle, thereby increasing the use of antibiotics and in turn leaving antibiotic residues in milk. They also point to the risks of increasing the presence in milk of insulin growth factor, which stunts growth. And it's not as if there is a pressing need for milk. Michael Hansen of the Consumers Union points out that, because of the existing milk surplus, taxpayers have spent billions of dollars over the past decade keeping milk off the market. One may well ask, Who needs bovine growth hormone? The answer seems to be the four leading corporations—American Cyanamid, Eli Lilly, Monsanto and Upjohn—that are promoting BGH worldwide.

HUMAN GENE THERAPY

• *Genetically altered humans.* Applying genetic engineering to humans faces major technical hurdles. "Humans are not simply large mice," a recent scientific review states, and the introduction of novel genes to correct for genetic diseases or cancer is no simple mechanical matter. The human body tends to reject anything foreign, like a virus carrying a corrective gene into a diseased cell. Nevertheless, corporations are aggressively promoting human gene therapy even though no genetic cures are yet in sight. Researchers are moving quickly to clinical trials, 62 percent of which are funded by the private sector. The inserted gene, the protein it encodes and the drugs that make the gene function are all seen as likely commercial prospects. "Three for the price of one," was the way an editor of an industry newsletter recently acclaimed the approach.

So far, experimental human gene treatments have been limited to treating life-threatening diseases. They have also been confined to altering somatic cells, as opposed to the sex, or germline, cells that pass on altered genes to future generations. But expansion of these horizons is already foreseen. In 1994, the successful replacement of sperm-forming cells of a mouse with similar cells from another mouse at the University of Pennsylvania was hailed as potentially capable of "shaping future generations." Researchers already talk of treating non-life-threatening conditions like dwarfism or infertility.

We are approaching the time, perhaps ten or twenty years away, when gene alteration will be offered as a service. On whom should it be used? For what purposes? Where should the lines for human genetic interventions be drawn? No committee outside the N.I.H. has been established to address these questions. The research-dominated N.I.H., judging from its history, will insure that the boundaries change in tandem with researchers' shifting goals. But with so many of those doing research directly in the pay of the drug companies, who will insure that human needs, not profits, are foremost in the minds of those who decide priorities for human gene alteration?

MILITARY APPLICATIONS

• Military applications. After maintaining a low profile for use of the biological sciences throughout the turbulent 1970s, the Defense Department quietly initiated military applications of biotechnology in the 1980s. Citing a menacing Soviet biological warfare threat, the department embarked on efforts to use the new biotechnology to make therapeutic agents, detection devices and vaccines to protect against biological weapons.

Vaccines might sound like a viable form of protection, but in practice they present huge problems. There are about thirty known biological weapons agents, and genetic engineering may expand that number almost indefinitely. The long latency period between vaccination and the body's immune response and the logistical problems of manufacturing and deploying vaccines pose further obstacles. Undaunted by the prospect of multiple injections for U.S. soldiers in war zones and the risks such procedures carry [see Laura Flanders, "Mal de Guerre," *Nation*, March 7, 1994], the Pentagon aimed vaccines against more than forty different microbes.

SCARIER USES FOR BIOTECHNOLOGY

More recently, the military has launched scarier schemes for biotechnology. On the one hand, "anti-materiel" bacteria are being investigated for their capacity to degrade militarily significant substances like rubber, engine lubricants and other critical components of weapons systems. On the other, novel, opium-like substances whose minute presence induces sleep, euphoria, anxiety, submissiveness or temporary blindness are being pursued for their potential as incapacitants. Genetic engineering offers ways to refine both applications.

In principle, the Biological Weapons Convention and the Chemical Weapons Convention prohibit recourse to the use of such technologies. The biological treaty bans development, production and stockpiling of microbes and toxins made by living things for any weapons purpose. Pursuit of "anti-materiel" bacteria should therefore be taken as a violation. The Chemical Weapons Convention, however, allows development of "riot control agents" for "law enforcement." It is apparently through this loophole that the Pentagon is pursuing work on novel incapacitants. This year, Congress approved $36 million for a new, largely secret "non-lethal" weapons program.

AVOIDING A GENETIC CHERNOBYL

The cornucopia of prizes from genetic engineering projected in the optimistic 1970s is rapidly becoming a mare's-nest of transgenic creations that we neither need nor want. Can we reverse genetically engineered evolution? Not easily, and not without an educated and active public. But there are models for alternative responses. In pre-Thatcher Britain, a broadly composed committee that advised the government on genetic engineering policy moved much more cautiously than its U.S. counterpart, involving unions in policy-making at the local and national levels. In India, a well-informed public debate addressing the social impact of monopolizing life-forms continues. Despite their weaknesses, the treaties banning biological and chemical weapons show that harmful technology can be curbed when people all over the world press for restraints.

It's time for another Asilomar conference, this time led by those at the receiving end of genetic technology, to take a long look at the genetically reconstructed worlds being designed by corporations and the military. Or must we wait for a genetic Chernobyl?

| "The development of tests to detect genes ... opens the door for the invention of an unlimited number of new disabilities and diseases."

GENETIC TESTING THREATENS SOCIETY

Ruth Hubbard and Elijah Wald

Researchers have labeled many human diseases and disorders as genetic in origin, with specific genes responsible for each disease. In the following viewpoint, Ruth Hubbard and Elijah Ward maintain that such conclusions divert attention from social and economic factors that contribute to the disease. Furthermore, they contend, testing to detect the genes that are supposedly responsible for disease will lead to eugenics as people try to replace the "defective" gene with a "normal" gene. Hubbard, a professor of biology emerita at Harvard University and a director of the Council for Responsible Genetics, and Wald, a freelance writer, are the authors of Exploding the Gene Myth.

As you read, consider the following questions:

1. What is the hypothetical human, according to Richard Lewontin, as cited by the authors?
2. How does the development of tests to detect genes lead to the invention of new diseases or disorders, according to Hubbard and Wald?
3. In the authors' opinion, what will be the result when genetic tests become standard in schools and hospitals?

Reprinted from "The Eugenics of Normalcy," by Ruth Hubbard and Elijah Ward, Ecologist, September/October 1993, by permission of the Ecologist, Dorset, England. (Endnotes in the original version have been omitted.)

F ew people can have missed the growing flood of gene stories in the popular press. Within the last few years, genes have been announced "for" manic depression, schizophrenia, alcoholism and smoking-related lung cancer. These supposed identifications are invariably obtained with small samples of people, and much publicity accompanies every such "discovery." Like mirages, many of these genes disappear when one tries to look at them closely—the claims about manic depression and schizophrenia genes were withdrawn soon after their announcement and the gene for alcoholism has met a similar fate. However, there are so many gene stories that people are left with the impression that our genes control everything.

Indeed, a new industry is rapidly being built on hopes of "better living through genetics." Evoking images of the quest for the Holy Grail, molecular biologists—the scientists who study the structure and function of genes and DNA—have embarked on a project to map and sequence "the human genome." With a budget of $3 billion, the Human Genome Project has been described as "the most astonishing adventure of our time" and "today's most important scientific undertaking." Supporters claim that the project promises to reveal "what it is to be human" and to "illuminate the determinants of human disease"—even those diseases "that are at the root of many current societal problems."

THE HYPOTHETICAL HUMAN

This is reductionism at its most extreme: not only are such claims based on a flawed view of genes being "all powerful" in determining human disease and behaviour but, far from revealing "what it is to be human," the genome project and similar programmes will reduce the essence of humanity to a *hypothetical* sequence of sub-microscopic pieces of DNA molecules. As Richard Lewontin, Professor of Zoology at Harvard University, comments:

> While the talk is of sequencing the human genome, every human differs from every other. The DNA I got from my mother differs by about one tenth of one per cent from the DNA I got from my father, and I differ by about that much from any other human being. The final catalogue of "the" human DNA sequence will be a mosaic of some hypothetical average person corresponding to no one.

By magnifying the mythic importance our culture assigns to heredity—and by increasingly appropriating the right to define what is "normal" in human biology and behaviour—molecular biologists threaten to impose a new eugenics upon society. . . .

Despite the complexities revealed by current research, molecular biologists have been increasingly successful in persuading society at large that ill health should, and can, be viewed primarily as a genetic problem. One result is that, by focusing attention on what is happening inside us, attention has been distracted from environmental and social factors that need to be addressed.

Consider the search for a "gene for diabetes." Diabetes is a disturbance of carbohydrate metabolism. characterized by unusually high concentrations of the sugar glucose in the blood. Medical scientists recognize two forms of diabetes, Type 1 and Type 2. Type 1 diabetes usually appears during adolescence, though it can start earlier or later, and it begins quite suddenly. By contrast, Type 2 diabetes tends to come on gradually and not until people have passed their middle years.

"GREAT NEWS, MR. JONES... WE FOUND IN YOUR DNA THAT YOU WILL LIKELY HAVE STOMACH CANCER AT AGE 52... COLON CANCER AT AGE 58... AND IF YOU'RE STILL ALIVE, PROSTATE CANCER AT THE AGE OF 65!"

Ed Gamble. Reprinted with special permission of King Features Syndicate.

The metabolic patterns underlying the two forms of diabetes are quite different. Type 1 diabetes results from the destruction of cells in the pancreas that normally produce insulin, a hormone involved in glucose metabolism. Type 1 diabetes is thought to involve the immune system and be the result of an allergic response to toxic chemicals in the environment, a viral infection, or some other unidentified stimulus.

By contrast, people with Type 2 diabetes secrete normal or

above-normal amounts of insulin, but their tissues develop an insensitivity to it. Therefore the insulin loses its metabolic effectiveness. Type 2 diabetes, which is by far the more common of the two forms, can often be alleviated by a diet low in carbohydrates and fats, especially when coupled with moderate levels of exercise. Indeed a study of nearly 6,000 middle-aged men, published in the *New England Journal of Medicine*, showed that regular exercise, such as jogging, bicycling and swimming, markedly reduced the incidence of Type 2 diabetes. While this does not rule out the possibility that Type 2 diabetes has a genetic component, other factors clearly play an important role.

Molecular biologists believe that several proteins are involved in the development of Type 2 diabetes and the hunt is currently on to locate, identify and analyse the genes that specify the amino acid sequences of insulin and an "insulin receptor." Once enough is known about the structure and location of these two genes, scientists will be able to develop tests to detect differences in their base sequences. Such tests could then be used to predict a "predisposition" to develop Type 2 diabetes in healthy people who are members of families in which the condition occurs.

GENES AND ENVIRONMENT

All of this research is being done in the hope of finding a predictive test for a "predisposition" to develop a condition that many people could avoid by changing their diets and getting regular exercise. It would surely be better to educate everyone about the importance of diet and exercise and to work towards providing the economic and social conditions that could enable more people to live healthily, rather than spending time and money to try and find "aberrant" genes and to identify individuals whose genetic constitution may (but then again, may not) put them at special risk.

The susceptibility to Type 1 diabetes appears to cluster in families and in specific populations, for example, among people of northern European origin. If one child in a family has Type 1 diabetes, the probability of a sibling developing it is about 6 per cent, or twenty times the rate for the general population. While this might seem to indicate a genetic component, it turns out that an identical twin of someone who develops Type 1 diabetes has only a 36 per cent probability of developing the condition. This is higher than the probability for ordinary siblings, but proves that genes cannot be the sole determining factor. Indeed, since toxic environmental agents and viral infections are thought to provoke Type 1 diabetes, family correlations need not point to a genetic origin. Siblings who live together are often exposed to the same environmental agents.

Nonetheless, molecular biologists are trying to develop predictive genetic tests for this condition. This time they are not looking at the "insulin gene" but at genes that participate in the synthesis of proteins active in immune reactions. Whatever they find, we can be sure that predictive diagnoses will be tentative at best, both because of the complexities of the immune system and because no one knows what factors trigger this particular immune response. We can also be sure that the test will do nothing to reduce exposure to the toxic chemicals that have been linked to the condition. . . .

TESTING AND EUGENICS

Genetic research opens up new possibilities for reinforcing social control—and for legitimizing that control. Helen Rodriguez-Trias, former president of the American Public Health Association, cites a 1972 survey of obstetricians which found that "although only 6 per cent favoured sterilization for their private patients, 14 per cent favoured it for their welfare patients. For welfare mothers who had borne illegitimate children, 97 per cent . . . favoured sterilization."

This is classic eugenic thinking, but eugenics can appear in much subtler ways. Testing prospective parents to see if they are carriers of genetic "defects," for example, leads to labelling of large groups of people as "defective." Not only the people who manifest the condition but also the carriers are likely to be considered less than perfect. Such tests are often advertised as altogether helpful because they increase people's choices, but it would be a mistake to ignore the ideology that almost invariably accompanies their use.

In 1971, Bentley Glass, retiring as President of the American Association for the Advancement of Science, wrote:

> In a world where each pair must be limited, on the average, to two offspring and no more, the right that must become paramount is the right of every child to be born with a sound physical and mental constitution, based on a sound genotype. No parent will in that future time have a right to burden society with a malformed or mentally incompetent child.

INVENTING DISEASE

. . . The development of tests to detect genes, or substances whose metabolism they affect, opens the door for the invention of an unlimited number of new disabilities and diseases. For any trait that has a normal distribution in the population, some people can be defined as having "too much" and others "not enough."

Pharmaceutical companies and doctors stand to make a good deal of money from inventing new diseases—based on people not conforming to a "norm"—as fast as new diagnostic tools are developed that can be used to spot or predict their occurrence. Thus, Genentech, one of the first generation of biotechnology firms, markets a genetically engineered form of human growth hormone. This hormone previously could be obtained only in minute amounts, by isolating it from the pituitary glands of human cadavers. When the supply was limited, human growth hormone was only used to treat children with pituitary dwarfism, which results from the reduced secretion of this hormone by the pituitary gland. Once the hormone became available in quantity, doctors began to prescribe it to treat people who secrete normal amounts of growth hormone.

PITFALLS OF GENETIC TESTING

The fact that a woman from a "cancer-prone" family tests positive for one of the cancer-linked DNA variants does not mean that she will definitely have a tumor, even though her lifetime risk of breast cancer may be as high as 85 percent, and that of ovarian cancer as high as 45 percent. Clearly, other factors are also involved. If the woman tests negative for cancer-linked DNA variants, her risk of having a tumor is similar to that of any woman in the general population. Furthermore, it is not clear what a woman should do if she tests positive, whatever her family history, since there are no effective measures of prevention. "Early detection" is problematic because it is uncertain what is actually being detected, and even such extreme measures as "prophylactic" bilateral mastectomy and oophorectomy provide no assurance that a tumor will not develop in the residual tissue. Given the uncertainty of what being "susceptible" signifies, it is hard to know how to counsel women who are trying to decide whether to be tested for a cancer-associated variant. . . . It is also hard to know how to help women integrate the information they may receive from such a test into the context of their lives.

Ruth Hubbard and R.C. Lewontin, *New England Journal of Medicine*, May 2, 1996.

In one series of experiments, growth hormone was given to growing boys deemed "too short" for their age. A *New York Times Magazine* cover story on these experiments reports that Genentech scientists have suggested that it is proper to consider any child whose height falls within the lowest three per cent of the population as suitable for treatment.

But it is in the nature of characteristics like height that, no matter what their average distribution may be, there will always be a lowest—and highest—3, 5, or 10 percent. Dr. John Lantos and his colleagues point out that "of the three million children born in the US annually, 90,000 will, by definition, be below the third percentile for height." Since this "treatment" is not without risks, there is no telling how the health of the children will be affected by daily injections of growth hormone. However, since growth hormone treatment costs about $20,000 a year per child, if each of these children received a five-year course of treatment, this would constitute a potential market of about $9 billion a year for Genentech.

Researchers have also suggested that administering growth hormone to old people slows the aging process. A report on the use of synthetic human growth hormone for this purpose appeared in July 1990. The experiment involved twenty-one men aged between sixty-one and eighty-one years. Since all these men were healthy to begin with, the benefits of the treatment were measured by how far it brought a range of "symptoms" (from mass of fat tissue to skin thickness and bone density) into a more "youthful" range. In effect, the fact that human growth hormone can now be produced in quantity has opened the way for the medical establishment to turn the normal process of aging into a disease.

Genetic Discrimination

As genetic and other biologically based tests become part of the standard apparatus in hospitals, schools and other institutions, so their routine use "obscures the uncertainties inherent in [such] tests and [leaves] their underlying assumptions unquestioned."

The current love affair with predictive tests for "learning disabilities" sets up the potential for discrimination in the future as well as the present. Norms create deviance, and an "abnormal result" on a biological or genetic test, though it may not blame the child, stigmatizes her or him and projects that stigma into the future.

Diagnostic labels can affect a child's self-image and his or her relationships in school and at home. They also become part of that child's "file," the growing body of data that follow her or him from school to school and job to job. Dorothy Nelkin and Laurence Tancredi, two social scientists, put it this way:

The use of diagnostic techniques has substantial social force beyond the educational context. The school system has contact with most children in the society, and is traditionally responsible for assessing, categorizing and channelling them toward future roles. . . . School professionals . . . transmit their evaluations to other institutions to help identify who is genetically constituted to assume certain types of jobs. Thus, diagnostic technologies not only help schools meet their own internal needs, they also empower schools in their role as gatekeepers for the larger society.

Nelkin and Tancredi suggest that genetic testing in the schools could become mandatory if enough people come to believe that a specific genetic condition affects behaviour or the ability to learn. This is especially likely if people can be persuaded that such new information will help relieve behavioural problems and so benefit the affected children and their classmates.

It is all too easy for genes to take on a life of their own. Genetic "learning disabilities" are a stigma not only for the child who has them but for all the relatives and descendants of that child. They can be used to show why poor children do not do well in school and to explain why their families became poor in the first place, and will continue to be poor. The tests will serve as an explanation and an excuse, getting schools and society off the hook by placing the blame on the children's unchangeable genes.

PRESELECTING WORKERS

The dangers of genetic testing do not end there. In workplaces, genetic tests can be used to screen workers and to monitor them. One reason is to try to minimize health insurance claims by employees.

Another is that it is costly to keep workplaces uncontaminated by toxic chemicals used in the manufacturing process, and to take the various safety precautions that may be necessary to preserve workers' health and well-being. Employers therefore find it easier to use tests that promise to predict the future health of prospective employees, in order to weed out job applicants who might be unusually sensitive to hazards in the workplace. Already, employers have embraced the concept of genetic "hyper-susceptibility" to explain why some workers respond to lower levels of dusts or other contaminants than the "average worker" does. . . .

A BRAVE NEW WORLD

Here is a quotation from Daniel Koshland, a molecular biologist and editor-in-chief of Science magazine. Writing on the ethical questions posed by germ-line gene manipulations, Koshland muses about the possibility "that in the future, genetic therapy will help with certain types of IQ deficiencies." He asks: "If a child destined to have a permanently low IQ could be cured by replacing a gene, would anyone really argue against that?" (Note the use of the word "cured" for averting the "destiny" of a "child" who would, at the time of the "cure," be half a dozen cells in a petri dish). While voicing some misgivings, Koshland continues:

> It is a short step from that decision to improving a normal IQ. Is there an argument against making superior individuals? Not superior morally, and not superior philosophically, just superior in certain skills: better at computers, better as musicians, better physically. As society gets more complex, perhaps it must select for individuals more capable of coping with its complex problems.

Clearly, the eugenic implications of this technology are enormous. It brings us into a Brave New World in which scientists, or other self-appointed arbiters of human excellence, would be able to decide which are "bad" genes and when to replace them with "good" ones. Furthermore, the question of whether to identify the functions of particular genes or to tamper with them will not be decided only—or perhaps even primarily—on scientific or ethical grounds, but also for political and economic reasons. We need to pay attention to the experiments that will be proposed for germ-line genetic manipulations, and to oppose the rationales that will be put forward to advance their implementation, whenever and wherever they are discussed.

| "Genetic testing can give us the power to do everything we can to live a longer life."

GENETIC TESTING CAN SAVE LIVES

Carol Krause

Carol Krause is a former medical journalist and a two-time cancer survivor. In the following viewpoint, Krause testifies before the U.S. House of Representatives Subcommittee on Technology that genetic testing for predisposition to cancer can save lives. The results of genetic testing can help people make decisions that would reduce their risk of getting or dying from cancer, she argues. Furthermore, Krause maintains, the government should fund research to test the long-term accuracy of genetic testing and educate the public about genetics.

As you read, consider the following questions:

1. According to Krause, what agenda should drive the debate on genetic testing?
2. In the author's opinion, what is the worst argument against genetic testing?
3. What five steps can Congress take to help Americans continue to have access to genetic testing, in Krause's opinion?

Reprinted from Carol Krause's testimony before the U.S. House of Representatives Committee on Science, Subcommittee on Technology, September 17, 1996.

I congratulate the U.S. House of Representatives Committee on Science, Subcommittee on Technology for recognizing the historical impact that the new technology of genetic testing has on the world of medicine. But it also has an impact on lives of people I know and love, and an even greater impact on precious lives not yet born.

I sit before you as a two-timer in the cancer world—colon cancer at age 40 and breast cancer at age 43. How this unpleasant turn of events happened to me is still not fully understood, and it is still a mystery exactly what I'm going to do about it. Have I been tested for cancer susceptibility? Should I be at this point? Should my young son? Am I confident the tests are accurate? I will address these questions in a moment. . . .

A New Weapon

In the arsenal of tools for patient care, there is a new weapon: the genetic test. That means more choices for me as a patient, but more confusion as well. As we contemplate decisions about testing in my family I will tell you how I view my choices. Although I have been a health writer for years, the subject of genetic testing is new for everyone. There are few experts, and until we know more, common sense must guide us.

About a year ago I began to watch the debate about genetic testing and realized that common sense has not been driving the discussion. I have wanted to scream, "Will somebody please ask me?" So I am grateful for the opportunity to address the Subcommittee on this important issue.

But while I have offered myself as a consultant and speaker on the intellectual debate surrounding genetic testing, let me take a step back and reveal my more emotional response as a member of a cancer family. I have heard and read many interviews in the news on this subject of genetic testing, often with the same researchers interviewed over and over again, as if the issue belongs to them.

Not a Simple Issue

The media—in its sometimes well-intentioned ignorance—has treated the subject as a simple two-sided debate. As a former member of the media, I understand this temptation. But as you debate what role the government should take in regulating genetic testing, keep in mind that people are used to receiving their health information in this black-and-white context. And genetics is not an issue easily explained using the communication tools of our popular culture.

I have heard and seen interviews with women who are breast cancer survivors who argue against testing. There are the insurance and employment discrimination concerns, to be sure. But I hear something deeper, more emotional in their pleas. Their breast cancer was found a more traditional way, and for the time being they are O.K. So why shouldn't other women proceed that way? Why run around scaring people with tests that have no proven use? I have heard one breast cancer activist say her daughters will not be tested. And I want to say, "I wonder how they'll feel about that when they come of age?" As a breast- and colon-cancer survivor, I genuinely understand that tendency of caution. After all, dealing with a cancer diagnosis is frightening enough. Thinking that others in the family might be affected only escalates the emotional pain and adds a layer of guilt. I live in horror that I might have passed this curse on to my ten-year-old son.

I see the New York Times publish a front page article talking almost glowingly about a so-called "maverick lab" offering a genetic test for the breast cancer mutations associated with Ashkenazi Jewish women, virtually on demand.

And I hear people say "We don't know enough about the test," or "A positive result doesn't mean you will get cancer," or "There is nothing you can do to prevent it anyway."

From this mosaic of emotion and confusion, what stands out are people who seem more intent on preserving their own agenda than in helping families who are burdened with the horrible legacy of genetic disease. Of my 15 first- and second-degree relatives, excluding my children, 12 have been hit with cancer. We have an agenda too—to save the lives of the next generation. To reduce the risk of cancer, and if that is not possible, to reduce the risk of dying from cancer. That is the agenda that should drive the debate on genetic testing.

MY REACTION TO THE DEBATE

From where I stand, the best argument against genetic testing is the unknown impact it will have on my insurance coverage. The worst is "There's nothing you can do about it anyway."

Let me address the worst one first. This argument—"there's nothing you can do"—doesn't make sense to me. A woman who tests positive for an inherited breast cancer mutation [BRCA1 or BRCA2] does have choices. First of all, the risk for ovarian cancer with these mutations is often lost in the debate. Decisions can be made to have your children earlier in life, and then you can consider prophylactic removal of the ovaries. But then I hear, "But that's no guarantee you won't get ovarian cancer." But my questions are: "Will it reduce my risk of getting cancer," and if not, "Will it reduce my risk of death?" and "Will it give me extra years?"

Those immersed in the political battle, miss the most important point, so I want to repeat it: Will the information from a genetic test help me make decisions to reduce my risk of getting cancer? And, if not, will it reduce my risk of dying from cancer? Isn't that what it is all about? Patients who already have cancer don't think twice about undergoing treatment that shows promise but isn't 100 percent proven, or even 50 percent proven. In the fight against cancer, reducing the risk is a valid and powerful option. Six years ago, I had my ovaries prophylactically removed. It was not an easy or cavalier decision. I was trying to have another baby. And even though I knew the surgery might not prevent the cancer forever, I am convinced it has at least given me precious extra years. And the peace of mind that I have taken all the steps possible to increase the odds that I can see my son reach adulthood.

SOME WANT TO KNOW

Even when the onset of disease in presymptomatic individuals can be predicted with a high degree of reliability, what then? How many of us would really want to know, for example, that we carry the gene for ataxia, an incurable syndrome in which the brain cells controlling motor movement gradually waste away?

Actually, some people would. Darla Brockus, a 24-year-old mother from Yucaipa, California, who is at risk for ataxia explains: "it's good to be able to prepare your family both financially and emotionally. Also, I'd definitely have another child if I knew that I wasn't going to leave this terrible legacy behind."

Kathleen McAuliffe, *Glamour*, May 1994.

And, as more tests become available, patients can better evaluate their risk. For example, if BRCA2 mutations carry less of a risk for ovarian cancer than BRCA1, that could factor into a woman's choice for prophylactic removal of the ovaries.

What about breast cancer? I can't tell you the number of women I know who, despite family histories of breast cancer, find excuses not to have mammograms on a regular basis, and avoid self-exam. Denial is a powerful sedative. But a woman who tests positive for a mutation can no longer linger in denial. At least I wouldn't. Would you? Mammograms and self-exam could begin faithfully at a younger age. This is a particularly important issue to me because my cancer was first noted as a calcification in a mammogram that wasn't there a year earlier. I don't need to tell all of you about the importance of early detection. I had the mammograms because people in my generation had already been hit with cancer. But what about the woman . . . or man . . . who sees breast cancer in the previous generation and needs to know what to do? Should they have regular mammograms in their forties? There is much debate on the usefulness of this. A test could help people make healthcare decisions. I'm not worried about guarantees here. I'm worried about improving the odds.

"WE DON'T KNOW ENOUGH ABOUT THE TEST"

There is another argument against genetic testing: "We don't know enough about this test, so it should be kept in a research environment." I have heard this a great deal. I certainly agree that researchers need to pursue vigilant evaluation of these tests. But what about the man, woman, or family, who, for whatever reason, doesn't have access to a research project? It is arrogant for us to say, "Yes, you are high-risk, but no, you are not among the anointed 'testees'?"

Let's be realistic here. We don't know enough about many tests we take. As a colon cancer patient, I regularly take a CEA blood test. The results move up and down, mystifying my doctors, and giving me the jitters. We don't know enough about that test either, but do understand that a dramatic change could signal trouble, and that's why I continue to take the test. It is one weapon in an arsenal. And to fight cancer, you need an arsenal.

THE INSURANCE PROBLEM

The most powerful argument against genetic testing is the insurance problem. The optimistic side of me says that the more mutations we identify for cancer, other diseases or behavioral problems, it will be determined that everyone will eventually be at risk for something, and the insurance companies will either have to face that fact or go out of business. For the time being, though, insurance discrimination is obviously a real problem. You don't need to lecture a cancer survivor about that. . . .

MY FAMILY'S CHOICES

To me, the driving question is, "Will the knowledge from this test give me an opportunity to reduce my risk?" As for my family, my sisters and I are now being tested for the mutations that cause the Lynch II syndrome, which result in several cancers. We are especially interested to know if my oldest sister—the one who has not had cancer—carries the mutation. Then her four sons, young adults now, will consider testing.

I will encourage my one biological child, my 10-year-old son Zack, to undergo testing when he is a young adult. By the time he is in his mid-twenties—fifteen years from now—hopefully we will have some firm data on the accuracy and usefulness of the test. age. I have much faith in the technology, but we will not have the answers we need unless we move forward with testing.

Because of the strong history of ovarian cancer in my family and my own breast cancer, I am also a candidate for breast-cancer testing. I have recently learned that if I don't carry a mutation, I have a 15 percent chance of cancer in the other breast. With the mutation, I have a 60 percent chance. I cannot afford to put my head in the sand. I have been diagnosed with cancer twice. I know it does happen to me. I will soon decide, with the help of my doctors, if I should proceed with the BRCA1 test. If I do test positive for a mutation, I will not be afraid to consider a prophylactic mastectomy on the other side. I need to have the personal courage to do what I need to do to increase my odds of a long life. . . .

Those of us in a cancer family know that each moment of life is important. A thorough evaluation of family medical history followed by genetic testing if appropriate, can give us a chance to have more of those moments.

As for me, I remain disease-free. It was knowledge of my medical family history that saved my life not once but twice.

THE ROLE OF THE CONGRESS

There may well be many people who decide against genetic testing for a variety of personal reasons. The family dynamics might be shaky. The patient might have confidence in aggressive monitoring alone. Most likely it is the fear of insurance, social or employment discrimination. Health care professionals and counselors can help patients decide if they have the courage necessary to move forward, or the courage to say no to testing. But that decision for testing should be made only after a fair and commonsense evaluation of what you can do with the results. The politics behind how we get that information only gets in the way of our goal: which is the best chance at life.

Congress can help families like mine have access to these important tests, while taking these steps to safeguard the public:

1. It is my hope that genetic testing services be done only in appropriate laboratories. It is a complicated technology—complicated beyond belief—and I would not want to see it go the way of the Pap smear industry [which has] uncertain standards [and] sometimes unreliable results.

2. It is my hope that the Congress will encourage and fund research that will test the long-term accuracy of these tests. Although my ten-year-old son will be tested for our family's colon cancer syndrome in about fifteen years, if he tests negative, will we feel safe forgoing routine colonoscopies? Only if we move forward will we get the data we need to save the cost and personal burden of unnecessary tests.

3. It is my hope that genetic testing will be free to leave the research environment so all high risk people can have access to the tests. It has already been proven that commercial labs can handle these tests responsibly if they follow appropriate guidelines. These tests are not medical devices or drugs, and I would hate to see them bogged down in the regulatory framework of the FDA [Food and Drug Administration]. Instead, there are other appropriate government agencies that could set significant guidelines for accuracy while allowing this technology to move forward with prudent speed.

4. It is my hope that any government regulations that emerge from this discussion will include in-depth informed consent and counseling procedures on the benefits, risks and limitations of testing. At best, this could be mandated. At the very least, detailed counseling guidelines should be created.

5. It is my hope that government information and education programs will work to give the public a working vocabulary on the issues surrounding genetics. The science itself, and its implications for future medical care, are not well understood. In fact, the public, including the lay press, is abysmally ignorant on the subject. A person with a genetic predisposition to disease is often in a better health position that someone with a long history of environmentally caused high cholesterol, or the overweight smoker. Yet for some reason we have attached an explosive aura to being labeled "at risk." If knowledge about genetic information becomes more commonplace, the fear and misunderstanding will diminish.

With every new technology there are the naysayers and the potential for abuse. But I believe in the strength of the ethical fiber of our country. We are consistently debating and compromising on tricky questions of medicine, and we have a long tradition of finding a middle ground. I don't fear this new science,

I embrace it. Imagine that so many of the answers we seek about our health and longevity already exist within the tiny cells of our own bodies! Not knowing doesn't change the truth that lies beneath our skin. And knowing gives us power.

I don't pretend to understand the heartache of families who carry mutations for unpreventable or incurable disease, Huntington's Chorea being the classic example. And I humbly acknowledge that I am only one woman with one opinion. But to my family, genetic testing can give us the power to do everything we can to live a longer life. A certain kind of peace comes with that power. When my grandfather Ernst died at the age of 33, he did not know he was giving me a signal that would have been ignored only a decade ago. As families like mine give ourselves to research, don't let it be a useless endeavor. Don't let them be forgotten. Make their deaths mean something significant. Let the sadness we have suffered mean something to future generations.

> "There are, at present, no compelling reasons to prohibit the extension of current patent laws to the realm of human genetics."

SCIENTISTS SHOULD BE ALLOWED TO PATENT HUMAN GENES

David B. Resnik

In the following viewpoint, David B. Resnik contends that arguments against patenting human genes are unsound and that no moral reasons exist for forbidding patents on human genes. However, he cautions that because human gene patenting could have dramatic social implications, society must be willing to continually examine laws and policies and change them as necessary. Resnik is an associate professor of philosophy and the director of the Center for the Advancement of Ethics at the University of Wyoming.

As you read, consider the following questions:

1. What is a patent, according to Resnik?
2. In Resnik's opinion, why is the Kantian argument against human gene patenting unsound?
3. How does the dehumanizing argument against human gene patenting unravel when examined closely, according to the author?

Reprinted by permission of The Johns Hopkins University Press from "The Morality of Human Gene Patents," by David B. Resnik, *Kennedy Institute of Ethics Journal*, vol. 7, no. 1, pp. 43–61; ©1997 by The Johns Hopkins University Press.

S hould individuals or corporations be allowed to hold patents on human genes? This question has generated a great deal of moral, political, and legal controversy. A dispute over the ownership of human gene therapy technology erupted when the National Institutes of Health (NIH) and Genetic Therapy Incorporated were awarded patents on techniques for modifying cells outside a patient's body. Opponents of this patent argued that it was too broad and that it would prevent fair competition and slow research. The United States Patent and Trade Office (PTO) rejected NIH's bid to patent thousands of human gene fragments. Critics of this patent bid argued that human genes are not inventions and cannot, therefore, be patented. In 1996, the United States Congress considered a measure, the Ganske-Wyden Bill (HR1127), that would have prevented the PTO from awarding patents that do not involve a new machine or compound. [The bill did not pass.] In 1995, a group of 186 religious leaders called for a moratorium on patents on human and animal genes on the grounds that genes are creations of God rather than human inventions. As knowledge of human genetics and biotechnology continues to advance, the demand for patents will increase and more controversies about human gene patents will surface.

Although human genetics raises many important legal questions concerning the interpretation and application of patent laws, this viewpoint will discuss the morality of patenting human genes. The viewpoint will conclude that there are, at present, no compelling reasons to prohibit the extension of current patent laws to the realm of human genetics. However, since advances in genetics are likely to have profound social, political, and medical implications, the most prudent course of action demands a continual reexamination of genetics laws and policies in light of ongoing developments in science and technology. . . .

WHAT IS A PATENT?

According to the United States patent laws, a patent is a legal permission granted by the PTO that gives the patent holder the right to exclude others from making, using, or selling an invention within the United States, its territories, or possessions for a 20-year period. Patents cannot be renewed. To obtain a patent, one must "reduce the invention to practice," which involves making the invention or a model of it, and submit an application to the PTO. The invention must "work"—i.e. it must do what it is supposed to do. The patent application becomes public—people can study the invention—although rights to control the invention remain private. In most cases, the PTO will grant a patent if the inventor provides a specification of the invention that will allow someone skilled in the relevant technical field to make and use it. In the last 200 years, the courts and legislatures have refined and developed patent laws. A useful summary of these laws is that a patent is new, useful, and nonobvious invention. United States courts have ruled that some types of things cannot be patented, such as ideas, scientific principles or theories, or mere results. Things that are not useful or original also cannot be patented, nor can inventions designed for the sole purpose of violating the legal rights of others. . . .

PATENT LAWS

Given this thumbnail sketch of patent . . . laws in the United States, one can see that there is a legal basis for some forms of ownership pertaining to human genes, including (1) ownership of artificial human genes or artificial combinations of genes; (2) ownership of works describing human genes or scientific ideas or principles pertaining to human genetics; and (3) ownership of processes for analyzing, sequencing, copying, fabricating, or manipulating human genes.

As far as patent rights are concerned, there is a legal basis for patenting original—i.e., invented, non-naturally occurring—human genes, DNA sequences, parts of chromosomes, or combinations thereof; processes for manufacturing, analyzing, sequencing, or recombining human genes would also be patentable. However, patent laws would not allow anyone to own naturally occurring human genes or combinations thereof; nor would patent laws allow anyone to own scientific principles pertaining to human genetics, such as the central dogma of molecular biology. . . .

Thus, it would appear that there is a legal basis for extending intellectual property laws to the realm of human genetics and for allowing human gene patents on original (or artificial) human genes. Thus far, individuals and corporations have found patents to be the most profitable and advantageous form of protection for genetic discoveries and innovations, and most of the controversies relate to gene patents. But should current patent laws be applied to human genetics? Are human gene patents immoral even if they have a legal basis? . . .

HUMAN GENE PATENTS AND HUMAN DIGNITY

The remainder of the viewpoint will examine three nonutilitarian arguments against human gene patents. All of these arguments hold that the practice of patenting human genes is morally wrong, regardless of its benefits or harms for society. The first argument takes a Kantian perspective on human gene patents and proceeds something like this: (1) the practice of patenting human genes treats persons as property; (2) it is morally wrong to treat persons as property; thus, (3) the practice of patenting human genes is morally wrong. Gene patenting is wrong because it treats persons as things that can be bought, sold, traded, or modified. For the purpose of discussing this argument, this viewpoint will assume a Kantian perspective on personhood: a person is a rational, autonomous, moral agent. This perspective assumes that a human person is not the same thing as a human body, since there might be human beings that are not autonomous, moral agents—e.g., zygotes—and there might be autonomous, moral agents that are not human beings—e.g., dolphins. Human beings are members of the species *Homo sapiens*, but not all members of this species are persons.

Although this Kantian perspective merits consideration as an objection to the practice of patenting human genes, it does not offer a sound argument against this practice because the practice of patenting human genes does not treat persons as property. Gene patenting does not treat persons as property because it only allows individuals or corporations to own inventions for analyzing, sequencing, manipulating, or manufacturing human genes. Ownership of a process for making or manipulating a part of a human body does not (automatically) constitute ownership of a person. A human gene patent would be analogous to a patent for making or manipulating other kinds of human body parts, such as hair, bones, or hearts. If the patenting of technologies for transplanting, growing, analyzing, or modifying bone marrow is morally acceptable, then the patenting of human genetic technologies should also be morally acceptable.

PATENTS AND OWNERSHIP

So, this Kantian perspective would appear to regard the practice of patenting human gene processes as morally acceptable, since it would not violate the rights and dignities of persons. However, we can imagine extreme cases in which gene patenting might treat persons as property. Biotechnology companies now own patents on various kinds of genetically engineered mice, and these patents entail ownership of the whole animal. What if a biotechnology company attempted to patent a genetically engineered human? Would this kind of patent constitute ownership of a person?

One might argue that patents on genetically engineered humans would treat persons as property, since patenting a genetically engineered human being would be ownership of a process for making something that could become a person. If the biotechnology patents on genetically engineered mice extend to the whole animal, then patents on genetically engineered human beings should also extend to the whole (human) animal. Since patents give patent holders the right to control the buying, selling, and production of their inventions, a patent on a genetically engineered human being would be tantamount to slavery, since the patent holder could control the production and marketing of the body associated with the person.

Thus, I think the Kantian perspective on human genes patents provides us with good reasons for not allowing individuals or corporations to patent processes for making entire human beings, even though it would still allow more modest types of gene patents.

PATENTING HUMAN GENES AND OUR HUMANNESS

On the other hand, one might argue that the prospect of patenting human beings the way we patent mice raises issues that go beyond Kantian concerns about the ownership of persons, which brings up a second nonutilitarian argument against the practice of patenting human genes. One might challenge the metaphysical separation of human body and human person that has been assumed thus far and argue that humanity is closely connected to biological characteristics. One might argue that the practice of patenting human genes, though it does not violate the rights of persons in most cases, threatens our understanding of humanity itself and our notions of what makes a being human. The human body occupies a key role in how we conceive of ourselves. It is dehumanizing to think of bodies as property because who we are depends on our relationship to our bodies: if my body is property, then I am property. The practice of patenting human genes is dehumanizing in that it changes our view of humans from beings with dignity and respect into objects to be bought, sold, or modified. Our humanness is morally "sacred," and we should not allow anything to undermine it.

Though this argument has some popular appeal, it rests on some dubious scientific assumptions or questionable moral intuitions, depending upon how it is read. If read as an argument concerning the social/cultural consequences of certain practices, such as the practice of patenting human genes, then it is a kind of forward-looking, "slippery slope" argument that claims that these practices will lead us toward total disrespect for human beings and human dignity. But this argument rests on the dubious sociological/psychological assumption that we will go down this slippery slope. We have for many years treated bodies as objects or commodities in some fashion, yet we do not treat living humans, nor even dead human bodies, purely as objects or commodities. In the Western World, we champion human rights although we treat bodies as objects by modifying them, replacing body parts, studying bodies, selling body parts, and so on. Why should we think that the practice of patenting human genes will be any more "dehumanizing" than our present and past uses of the human body? Taken to its extreme, this reading of the argument would suggest that we should not even perform dissections of the human body on the grounds that this practice will take us down a slippery slope toward vivisection.

QUESTIONABLE ASSUMPTIONS

The argument can also be understood as a critique of specific ways of treating the human body. It is simply wrong, the argument asserts, to treat the body as an object that can be bought, sold, modified, and so on. It is wrong because the body is part of our humanity; it is part of what makes us human beings, and we should not tamper with our humanity. But this argument would seem to rest on some questionable moral intuitions about what constitutes "our humanness" and its moral sacredness. One might argue that "our humanness" depends more on psychological, intellectual, social, and other traits than on bodily features. "Our humanness" cannot be equated with the number of arms or legs we have, the shape of our eyes, the curvature of our spine, or even the number of chromosomes we have; "our humanness" is more closely related to our aspirations and dreams, our ideas and values, our personality and emotions, and our actions and attitudes.

Of course, there may indeed be no way to resolve this issue: who we are may depend on who we think we are. If I view my humanness as closely connected to my body, then my humanness is, for me, closely connected to having a specific kind of body, but another individual might view her humanness as closely connected to her mind, and another might view her humanness as closely connected to her clothing or her automobile. The question "what makes me a human being?" may have a different answer for every individual who asks it. We can now see how this argument begins to unravel. If the argument that views gene patenting as dehumanizing boils down to a purely subject-dependent answer about what constitutes humanness, then it cannot serve as a basis for a public policy banning gene patenting.

Having said that much against this argument, I should note that there may be some general consensus about properties of the human body that are intimately linked to humanness. For instance, most people might say that a being who is immortal is not human; or perhaps most people would agree that a being who has no feelings or emotions is not a human. But even if gene patenting allowed the creation of beings who we would not call human beings, this does not imply that it is dehumanizing. It would only be dehumanizing if it allows us to treat *ipso facto* human beings as nonhuman.

DELIBERATION, NOT DISMISSAL

The U.S. Patent and Trademark Office does not patent things that exist naturally, such as the human genome. It grants intellectual property rights on human ingenuity that meets three criteria: novelty, nonobviousness, and utility. What is invented is patentable. What already exists in nature is not. Nor, despite widespread propaganda to the contrary, does the PTO patent human beings or body parts. No persons get patented. This would violate the U.S. Constitution's proscription against slavery. Rather, the PTO grants patents for cell lines and even genomes of transgenic animals that are used in biological research for the purpose of developing medical therapies for genetically based diseases such as cancer, heart disease, cystic fibrosis, Alzheimer's, Huntington's, Wilson's Syndrome, and eventually perhaps four thousand other diseases. Such patents draw venture capital for this extremely risky and expensive process of research and development. This is an area of ethical concern, to be sure, and one that deserves careful and informed deliberation by our religious leaders. It does not deserve categorical dismissal.

Ted Peters, First Things, May 1996.

Finally, there is the question of why our humanness should be treated as morally sacred. Why should we refrain from changing human beings or directing human evolution? There are of course religious answers that can be given: tampering with the human genome is "playing God," usurps God's authority, and so on. However, for the purposes of this essay, I will only consider secular critiques of patent laws, since a discussion of the legitimacy of religious arguments in public policy debates would take us too far afield. The main reasons for not tampering with human evolution through genetic engineering have more to do with the possible bad consequences of the genetic revolution than with the erosion of our humanity.

HUMAN GENES AS COMMON PROPERTY

The final nonutilitarian critique of the practice of patenting human genes is the assertion that these resources should be viewed as common property, belonging to no single individual or corporation. Since human beings have so many genes in common, we can no more claim ownership of human genes than we can claim ownership of the air. However, this "common property" approach to human genes rests on a mistaken view of human gene patents. The practice of human gene patenting does not allow anyone to own naturally occurring human genes, since patents only apply to inventions. Individuals or corporations could attempt to patent a processes for copying, sequencing, modifying, and analyzing human genes, but ownership of these processes would not constitute ownership of our naturally occurring, common, human genes. Gene patents would apply to inventions that are not shared among all the people of the world and are not natural phenomena. As analogy, water cannot be patented but companies can patent inventions that make, analyze, or purify water.

PROCEED WITH CAUTION

Intellectual property rights for various forms of scientific and technical information relating to human genetics will undoubtedly occupy center stage in future legal, ethical, and political debates. It is important to give serious thought to any decisions to treat human genes as property, since these decisions will in all likelihood have a dramatic effect on the development of science, technology, and society. This viewpoint has considered several moral arguments for and against the practice of human gene patenting and has found no compelling moral reasons to forbid human gene patents at this time. Patents on genetically engineered humans should not be allowed, since these patents would amount to slavery, but this technology does not yet exist. If we want to obtain the potential benefits of the genetic revolution, then we need to be willing to take some risks, including those associated with the extension of patent rights to the realm of human genetics. However, this viewpoint should not be treated as an unabashed endorsement of the patenting of human genes, since this practice could have some very disturbing social, political, and medical consequences. The most reasonable position at this time is to proceed with caution, examine various applications for human gene patents as they arise, and be willing to change our laws and social policies in light of new evidence. We cannot close the Pandora's box of human genetics, nor should we attempt to run away from its curses and plagues. The best policy is to try to manage these potential evils as they enter our society.

"The patenting of human genetic material attempts to wrest ownership from God and commodifies human biological materials and, potentially, human beings themselves."

HUMAN GENES SHOULD NOT BE PATENTED

Richard D. Land and C. Ben Mitchell

In the following viewpoint, Richard D. Land and C. Ben Mitchell contend that patenting human genes amounts to the buying and selling of human life, a practice that dehumanizes its sanctity. Furthermore, patenting nonhuman genes is also problematic, they assert. What is needed, the authors maintain, is a careful investigation and examination of alternatives to gene patenting. Land is president of the Southern Baptist Convention's Christian Life Commission. Mitchell is a consultant on biomedical and ethical issues for the CLC.

As you read, consider the following questions:
1. What are some of the benefits of genetic technology, in the authors' opinion?
2. According to the authors, why is human life sacred?
3. Why is patenting nonhuman genes problematic, according to Land and Mitchell?

Reprinted from "Patenting Life: No," by Richard D. Land and C. Ben Mitchell, First Things, May 1996, by permission of the Institute on Religion and Public Life, New York.

Y ou do not have to be a religious zealot or a scientific Luddite to oppose the patenting of animal and human organisms and genes. In fact, as John Fletcher, ethicist at the University of Virginia, has said, "You don't have to be religious to realize that there ought to be a debate about patenting." It is true, however, that moral and theological concerns are at the heart of the debate.

We should be clear at the outset that we applaud and rejoice in many of the existing and potential uses of the new genetics. The treatment and cure of more than four thousand genetically linked illnesses are prima facie grounds for celebrating and endorsing some genetic technologies. Cures for diseases such as cystic fibrosis, breast cancer, Duchenne's muscular dystrophy, and colon cancer certainly merit both praise and the expenditure of significant financial resources.

A MIXED BLESSING

At the same time, genetic technology is not an unmixed blessing. The potential abuses of genetic technology warrant our careful and considered attention. Linkages between genetic screening and abortion, testing and discrimination, and the supposedly positive and negative aspects of the discredited pseudo-discipline of eugenics represent important subjects meriting wider public discussion. No less important are the implications of patenting human genes and genetically engineered animals. Unfortunately, due to the rapid expansion of the technology, we do not have the luxury of discussing these issues in a leisurely manner or one at a time. The breathtaking pace of technological advancement requires that the cultural discourse and the public policy with respect to genetics must develop simultaneously.

Unfortunately, some policies have been enacted imprudently. Consequently, some policy decisions in these areas will have to be replaced with policies that reflect more careful and mature moral examination, however embarrassing or disconcerting that may be. Bad decisions make bad policy and should not be defended just because they have been made.

In *Diamond v. Chakrabarty* (1980), the Supreme Court ruled in a five-to-four vote that a genetically engineered microbe could be patented. Less than a decade later, in April 1988, the first animal patent was issued to Harvard University for the so-called "onco-mouse." The patented mouse was genetically engineered to contain a cancer gene making it useful in human cancer research. E.I. du Pont de Nemours & Company was granted exclusive licensure "to practice the patent." According to the now defunded

Office of Technology Assessment (OTA), the patent specifically covers "a transgenic nonhuman eukaryotic animal (preferably a rodent such as a mouse) whose germ cells and somatic cells contain an activated oncogene sequence introduced into the animal." That is to say, the patent was granted not only on a mouse and its progeny, but on *any mammal that has cancer genes inserted into its genome at an embryonic stage.* The mouse now reportedly sells for about fifty dollars.

While whole human beings have not been patented yet, human genetic material is routinely patented. In July 1990, the California Supreme Court ruled that a patient whose diseased spleen had been used to produce patented cell lines had no right to the millions of dollars potentially resulting from the sale of pharmaceutical products derived from his spleen. By September 4, 1993, the National Institutes of Health had filed for patents on 6,122 gene fragments. Although patenting of "gene fragments of unknown biological function" is presently disallowed, who knows what the future holds? Most of this territory is uncharted. Boston University Professor of Health Law George Annas has asked, "Since cloned human embryos are not persons protected by the Constitution and theoretically at least could be as 'immortal' as cloned cell lines, could a particularly 'novel' and 'useful' human embryo be patented, cloned, and sold?"

HUMAN LIFE IS SACRED

Our candid presupposition is that both humans and animals are more than the sum of their genetic code. In our view, genetic patenting of *Homo sapiens* is, however, a separate issue in some respects from patenting other organisms. Both are problematic, but for slightly different reasons.

Opposition to patenting human beings and their genetic parts is grounded in the unique nature of *Homo sapiens*. Human beings, alone among living organisms, bear the *imago Dei*. "So God created man in His own image, in the image of God He created him" (Genesis 1:27). Human life is therefore sacred and possesses unique value derived from the Creator. Thus, as Philip Edgcumbe Hughes has said, "It is the image of God in which man was created, rather, which pervades his existence in its totality and is the cause of his transcendence over the rest of God's creation." The distinction between human life and animal life, as well as the prohibition against the unjustifiable taking of human life, is foundational to Jewish and Christian anthropology.

Human beings are pre-owned. We belong to the sovereign Creator. We are, therefore, not to be killed without adequate justification (e.g., in self-defense) nor are we, or our body parts, to be bought and sold in the marketplace. Yet the patenting of human genetic material attempts to wrest ownership from God and commodifies human biological materials and, potentially, human beings themselves. Admittedly, a single human gene or a cell line is not a human being; but a human gene or cell line *is* undeniably human and warrants different treatment than all nonhuman genes or cell lines. The image of God pervades human life in all of its parts. Furthermore, the right to own one part of a human being is [other things being equal], the right to own all the parts of a human being. This right must not be transferred from the Creator to the creature.

'SORRY, MR. GOD, WE ISSUE LICENCES FOR THE COMMERCIAL EXPLOITATION OF **NEW** LiFE FORMS HERE. IF YOU WISH TO **CHALLENGE** SOMEONE'S PATENT, THAT WOULD BE LEGAL SERViCES DOWN THE HALL......'

Imagine a society in which patented human cells, cell lines, and tissues are bought and sold in the scientific marketplace. If such a scenario seems impossible to conceive, consider that Nobel laureate Kary Mullis has bought the rights to extract a part of Elvis Presley's DNA from a lock of the rock idol's hair using a "genetic amplification" technique that Mullis himself invented. Mullis intends to make millions of copies of Presley's genes, according to a September 1995 *Washington Post* article, "and preserve these minuscule globs inside artificial gemstones, to be made into a line of necklaces, earrings, and other collectables." While Mullis' good sense may be questionable, the commodifi-

cation of human genes is not inconceivable with only a natural-
istic anthropology to guide genetic science.

POTENTIAL ABUSE

We argue that the current status of U.S. patent law is incapable of
dealing with the potential abuse of human genetic materials.
When the framers of the Constitution established congressional
power "to promote the progress of science and the useful arts,
by securing for limited times to authors and inventors the exclusive right to their respective writings and discoveries," it was
impossible to envisage the patenting of human genetic materials. Even in 1952, when Congress passed the Patent Act, intend-
ing patentable subject matter to include "anything under the
sun that is made by man," it is unlikely that they foresaw human
"biopatents." We, therefore, conclude that human genetic materials should not be patentable matter.

We further maintain that a moratorium should be placed on
animal patenting on slightly different grounds. In the case of animal patents, social justice issues rise to the fore. Animals, like human beings, are pre-owned entities. Every part of God's creation
is owned by the Sovereign. Most Jews and Christians would,
however, interpret the mandate of Genesis 1:28 to permit animal
ownership. "God blessed them and said to them, 'Be fruitful and
increase in number; fill the earth, and subdue it. Rule over the
fish of the sea and the birds of the air and over every living creature that moves on the ground.'" Responsible stewardship of the
created order is not only allowed, it is imperative.

Under U.S. patent law, patentable subject matter is defined as
"any new and useful process, machine, manufacture, or composition of matter, or any new and useful improvement thereof."
Rebecca S. Eisenberg, Professor of Law at the University of
Michigan, observes that "although products of nature may not
be patented as such, patents have been issued on such products
in human-altered form." This is exceedingly troublesome in our
view. Oncomice are, in fact, human-altered forms, but are they
really "compositions of matter"? Do they truly constitute an
"improvement thereof"?

NOT AN INVENTION

Philosopher Ned Hettinger has rightly said, "There is a substantial disanalogy between these biopatents and the traditional subject matter of patents. Edison really did *invent* the light bulb. The
Wright brothers *created* a flying machine. But Harvard did not in-
vent or create the oncomouse. Biotechnicians alter, modify, assist,

and manipulate nature. They are not inventors of novel organisms or genes that could be appropriate objects for patents."

In truth, the patent on the Harvard mouse constitutes a monopoly on an entire subclass of animal. Again, according to the OTA report, "The actual patent coverage is broad, embracing virtually any species of 'transgenic nonhuman mammal all of whose germ cells and somatic cells contain a recombinant activated oncogene sequence introduced into said mammal, or an ancestor of said mammal, at an embryonic stage.'" Since there are about forty known cancer-causing genes, the patent covers an inordinately wide variety of potentially patentable mammalian life.

AN ABUSE OF OWNERSHIP

While animal ownership per se is morally acceptable, patenting animals represents an abuse of the notion of ownership, and more importantly, of ownership rights. Patents presently protect the ownership rights of the patent holder. Changes in U.S. patent law were made under a new set of international trade rules, the General Agreement on Tariffs and Trade. After June 8, 1995, "the term of a patent begins on the date of issue and ends twenty years from the original filing date," according to an article appearing in the *Scientist*. Since animals are patentable, biotech companies, universities, or individuals may monopolize entire species or subclasses of animals and, as in the *Chakrabarty* decision, bacteria, for twenty years. In his superb discussion on this subject in *Toward a More Natural Science*, Leon Kass opines, "It is one thing to own *a* mule; it is another to own *mule*. Admittedly, bacteria are far away from mules. But the principles invoked, the reasoning, and the stance toward nature go all the way to mules, and beyond."

Bernard Rollin, professor of philosophy, physiology, and biophysics at Colorado State University, maintains that "the Patent Office rushed in where angels fear to tread. . . . The issuing of patents begs these questions or ignores them. It was a bureaucratic decision made in a value-free context (or value-ignoring context) by an agency that has notoriously avoided engaging the ethical and social issues raised by inventions like switchblades, assault rifles, shock collars, and devices for sadomasochists, an agency that judges applications only by the formal criteria of novelty, usefulness, and nonobviousness. It disavows concern with issues of safety; danger to humans, animals, or environment; or welfare of animals. The decision is, as it were, a punch line without a joke, an ending without a story. The decision to patent or not to patent should follow in the wake of a democratic social examination of the concerns discussed here, and in the wake of establishing a democratic regulatory mechanism for all aspects of genetic engineering of animals."

JUDGMENT AND RESTRAINT

The explosions of our capabilities without a concomitant expansion of ethical reflection demands that we resist the temptation to apply unthinkingly every technology the day it is conceived. We need careful investigation of alternatives to human and animal patenting. A blind frenzy of patenting is far more dangerous than a strict prohibition. We need to strive for and cultivate measured judgments and restraint with respect to the new genetics.

Recognizing that a moratorium on patenting genes may put some potential treatments and cures for genetically linked illnesses at risk, we advise that Congress and other policy-making bodies encourage the kind of democratic social examination and cultural discourse about biopatents for which Bernard Rollin calls.

There are, of course, social justice issues beyond these to be explored with respect to biopatents. The fact that on May 18, 1995, some 180 leaders from diverse religious perspectives gathered together to call for a moratorium on patenting is evidence that wider and deeper discussion must take place between science, law, and religion.

│ "Knowing thyself is not always a
│ comfortable process. But it is better
│ than ignorance."

STUDYING THE HUMAN GENOME WILL PROVIDE VALUABLE INFORMATION

The Economist

The Human Genome Project (HGP) is an international effort to decipher and map the entire human genetic code (genome). In the following viewpoint, the editors of the conservative British weekly magazine the Economist maintain that while some ethical questions may be raised concerning the use of the information learned from the project, the HGP will vastly increase the facts known about the workings of the human body. Therefore, they assert, the Human Genome Project is a necessary and important first step to understanding human life.

As you read, consider the following questions:

1. What is the formal goal of the Human Genome Project, according to the editors?
2. How is the human genome like a jigsaw puzzle, in the authors' opinion?
3. According to the Economist, why is destiny more than genetics?

B iologists are often accused by their colleagues in other disciplines of suffering from physics envy. Physicists, the jibe goes, work on more fundamental problems. Therefore they have bigger tools.

Until recently, the jibe was true. Subatomic-particle researchers have vast machines to pry into the building blocks of matter. Rocket scientists try to construct dwelling-places in space. Cosmologists plumb the origins of the universe with big, expensive telescopes. Now, however, biologists are matching their colleagues' ambition. Until recently, no project has sought to follow the Delphic Oracle's advice—"know thyself"—and disentangle what is, perhaps, the most intriguing fundamental problem of all: the nature of humanity.

THE HUMAN GENOME PROJECT

The Human Genome Project, though it will not do this by itself, will be a start. It will give biologists a toolkit with which to describe, and hence perhaps to explain, human life. The aim of the project is to catalogue and analyse all the genes whose collective instructions go to build, and then to run, a human body. This collection of genes is known as the human genome. The description of the human genome will be akin to the description earlier this century of atoms and the particles of which they are composed. Those are the basic units of matter. Genes are the basic units of life.

The implications of this project, like those of atomic physics, are enormous, and, for the moment, unpredictable. The project's protagonists hope to discover new medical insights, which should lead to new forms of diagnosis and treatment. Gene therapy—the introduction into the relevant tissue of working genes to replace faulty ones—may one day cure diseases. Biotechnologists may find ways to add tailored versions of newly discovered genes into existing human genomes. And, if it is possible to describe what makes up the simpler organs of the body, it should also be possible, one day, to analyse what happens in the brain and hence much of what determines human behaviour. So at the end of the process stands the goal of a new understanding of human life itself.

As happened with the description of atomic particles, all this opens up frightening possibilities and ethical dilemmas. Can new forms of life be created? If life can be mapped, can it be replicated? Might genetic weapons be made to spread diseases, either known or newly created? If a genetic basis can be described for criminal behaviour might criminals come to be seen as victims of their genes rather than violators of the law? Might individuals carrying such genes be persecuted even if they had done no wrong? If scientists can identify the genetic basis for height or brainpower, might parents be able to specify their children's height or intelligence? Can parents "choose" their children?

All those questions are for the future—some for a distant one. Meanwhile, there is one last thing that makes the Human Genome Project unlike any other big science project so far. It will lead to discoveries that will make some people a lot of money. And because of that, as well as because the thirst for knowledge seems unstoppable, the genome project seems certain to continue to its end—wherever that may be.

THE THREE BILLION NAMES OF GOD

Given the hopes and fears attached to it, the nuts and bolts of the project are surprisingly banal. The formal goal is to describe the sequence of all the DNA in the nucleus of a human cell— that is, to work out the order of the chemical "letters" that carry the genetic message. Working out this sequence is routine and rather dull. The technology for doing it was invented in 1975, by Frederick Sanger, of Cambridge University, and though it has been refined since, it has not been fundamentally improved upon. Most genomics laboratories consist of rows of quiet machines tended by a few technicians. The air of excitement is unpalpable.

Sequencing DNA, though, is the easy bit. The hard bit is making sense of the findings: this is what the project is really about. There appear, depending on whom you listen to and exactly what definition you use, to be anything between 50,000 and 80,000 genes hidden in the human genome. A few hundred were known about in general terms before the project started (they could be identified when they came in more than one variety or when they went wrong and affected the workings of the body). The rest remained to be discovered—and the complications were formidable.

The DNA amongst which the genes are scattered contains some 3 billion chemical letters. Only about 2% of these letters actually carry the message of the genes. Some of the rest help genes to function in various ways but most of them are either of unknown function or are parasitic junk.

Unfortunately, Dr Sanger's technique is only reliable for pieces of DNA less than about 500 letters long. Solving the human genome, therefore, means breaking the DNA up into 500-letter-long pieces, sequencing the pieces, sticking them together in the right order, and then tracking down the bits that actually constitute the genes. It is not just number crunching.

So imagine the genome project as a giant jigsaw puzzle. First, you have to assemble the pieces: 3 billion divided by 500—ie, 6 million of them. And 6 million is the minimum number. It does not allow for any overlaps (and it is by matching up overlaps that the pieces are put together), let alone for the errors and duplications that are the currency of scientific research.

EUGENICS IS UNLIKELY

It is doubtful that advances in genetic knowledge will lead to a revival of attempts to produce a super race. While the human genome project will undoubtedly accelerate the identification of genes for physical and medical traits, it is unlikely to reveal with any speed how genes contribute to the formation of those qualities—talent, behavior, personality—that the world admires. Equally important, the engineering of designer human genomes is not possible under current reproductive technologies and is not likely to grow much easier in the near future.

Daniel J. Kevles, "Eugenics and the Human Genome Project: Is the Past Prologue?" in *Justice and the Human Genome Project*, Timothy F. Murphy and Marc A. Lappé, eds., 1994.

So how can it be done at all? The answer is by taking advantage of two saving graces. First, there are several ways of breaking the puzzle up into sub-jigsaws. The individual pieces in the sub-jigsaws can be sequenced and assembled separately—and the sub-jigsaws fitted together again. The second saving grace is that lots of people can work on the jigsaw at the same time—the more the merrier, in fact. This is the main feature, other than its practical applications, which distinguishes the Human Genome Project from other big science. You do not need to build a particle accelerator or space shuttle to do it. Anyone who can afford a sequencer, a computer and a connection to the Internet can play. Thus, though the project started in American laboratories, it is now a global venture.

As a result, progress has been rapid. Both "physical maps" (linked sequences of sub-jigsaws) and "genetic-linkage maps" (which track the genes as they are mixed together from one generation to another) were completed in late 1995. The sequence will follow as night follows day (or as funding follows research). Completion is now predicted for 2000 or shortly thereafter.

So scientists have now reached the stage at which they have defined the questions, established a method for tackling them and produced early results. These results, however, suggest that the project is likely to disappoint those hoping for miraculous medical breakthroughs and may reassure those who fear the eventual worst. For good or ill, the genome project will, at least for a while, produce less dramatic consequences than most people think.

The Secret Labyrinth

Though the project was started largely because some top biologists realised it was technically feasible, it was sold on the back of its potential medical benefits. These will certainly come, but not as fast as politicians and the public have been led to believe nor, necessarily, in the way they might expect.

A genome project might be expected, mainly, to be about curing genetic disorders. Though hundreds of diseases—for example, Huntington's chorea and haemophilia—are indeed caused by single faulty genes, each one is rare. Natural selection has weeded them out. So even if they could all be eliminated by the project's discoveries, that would amount to less than 2% of the world's disease burden.

In most diseases the contribution of genes is fuzzier. A faulty gene may be a necessary but not a sufficient cause of a disease. Sometimes an environmental trigger may also be needed (some forms of schizophrenia are believed to fall into this category). Sometimes more than one gene may need to be faulty for an effect to show up (so-called polygenic diseases, such as colon cancer). Sometimes, a faulty gene may not be needed at all: some forms of breast cancer, for instance, are genetic (two genes that more-or-less guarantee its development have been isolated); other forms are not.

In short, the link between genes and disease is more complex than many people originally thought. . . .

Genetic Testing

[Genetic testing] makes it easy to check for known faults in genes once they have been identified. Far easier, in fact, than developing a treatment. Most genetic diseases are still incurable and gene therapy has been a dismal failure so far.

Genetic tests are useful early warning signals of susceptibility in cases where early surgery is desirable (as with breast and colon cancer). But where neither cure nor treatment exists (as for example, in Huntington's chorea), it is hard to see what purpose such a test can serve except to inform decisions about having children or perhaps, to alert insurance companies that you are a bad risk. Insurance companies want this information. Customers, understandably, are reluctant to give it.

The argument over genetic testing is symptomatic of what is—and is not—likely to emerge from the Human Genome Project. Fears of genetically engineered monsters look risible in the face of technology that cannot even put the genes needed to combat cystic fibrosis into the lungs of sufferers. And the flap caused whenever researchers think they have located a gene that influences behaviour is out of all proportion to the reality: most such claims have been withdrawn once further data have been collected.

ARE YOU THE PRISONER OF YOUR GENES?

There is a common misconception that genetics is destiny. The early results of the genome project suggest that this is not so. It appears extremely rare that there is a single gene for anything— not even for most diseases, let alone for complex forms of behaviour, such as aggression, or sexuality. The determinants of such behaviour are embedded in a jungle of genes which affect many different things at once. It will be a while before anyone can isolate any part of this jungle. It is possible that they will never be able to do so because the nature of organisms is that they are more than the sum of their parts.

What is certain, however, is that, though the project will not tell us everything about ourselves, it will hugely increase our knowledge. Some of that knowledge will be welcome (genetically engineered bacteria, once the bugaboo of those who oppose biotechnology, are now workaday tools in factories and laboratories across the world). Some, of course, will not be. But, once tried and tested, it will be presumed to be the truth and integrated into the way people think of themselves. Knowing thyself is not always a comfortable process. But it is better than ignorance.

"We would be deeply naive to believe that [the Human Genome Project] only exists for benign medical research."

STUDYING THE HUMAN GENOME VIOLATES THE SANCTITY OF LIFE

Julian Rose

In the following viewpoint, Julian Rose contends that the Human Genome Project, an international study of the human genetic code, is a foil for scientists and corporations to gain research on manipulating the genes of plants and animals. He argues that since these efforts are guided by profit, genetic engineering threatens the vast biodiversity of life and must be countered in any way possible. Rose is a farmer in England.

As you read, consider the following questions:

1. How will farmers suffer if genetically modified organisms are patented, according to Rose?
2. How many human genes have been located by Craig Venter, as cited by the author?
3. How many patent applications for DNA sequences have been filed by Human Genome Sciences, according to Rose?

Reprinted, by permission of the author, from "The Gene Industry," by Julian Rose, *Resurgence*, May/June 1995.

We now appear to have entered the "Brave New World" of which Aldous Huxley and George Orwell forewarned. And of its various manifestations, genetic engineering seems to occupy a central position. It is a strange territory. Academics, government officials and leading industrialists meet behind closed doors to decide what shape the industrialization of our common gene pool is going to take.

The goal which beckons at the end of such vision is nothing less than the complete reconstruction of our inherited genetic make-up. Any characteristic or trait which is perceived to be an obstacle to the established or desired lifestyle of our society will be a candidate for genetic manipulation, since it will be presupposed to be linked with a genetic disorder. It is not a pipe dream. Much of the technology is already in place and the momentum is gaining pace, under the title of the Human Genome Project.

Are we right to believe that we are more likely to realize our true potential in the form of a clinically assembled test-tube cocktail of designer genes? Or are we, by even entertaining the concept of genetic self-manipulation, playing Russian Roulette with our very raison d'être? And anyway: what is our raison d'être? It is probably our ability to answer this question which holds the clue to the future of the species.

AGRICULTURAL MANIPULATIONS

The current genetics race in biotechnology has a number of lines of development. The food- and agriculture-related one involves specific plants being given genes cloned from other species of flora in order, for example, to render them more capable of resisting herbicide sprays and attacks from indigenous predators. And in the livestock arena, farm animals are genetically manipulated to grow faster and leaner or to produce medical products such as haemaglobin. Also in this category is the now infamous FLVR SVR tomato, genetically engineered to have a longer shelf life and some flavour!

In another development genetically modified organisms (GMOs) have already been released into the environment at a number of UK [United Kingdom] locations. One such experiment involves hybrid rape seed which has been given a gene capable of resisting high pesticide applications. It is not known what happens if this rape escapes its field and breeds along road verges. Or cross-breeds with similar species, thus imparting its pesticide-resistant characteristics along the way.

Then there is BST, already legalized in the USA, the genetically engineered synthetic hormone which, when injected daily into the dairy cow, raises her milk production by up to 20%—as if she, or anyone else, needs it! There are plenty more such experiments. They are nearly all being conducted as private enterprise by powerful multinational corporations, and they are all heavily profit driven.

The organic farming movement has refused to allow the use of genetic engineering in organic foods.

Another desire of the genetic industry is to screen human foetuses for genetic diseases. If this is accepted, we are one step away from pressure for the modification or abortion of those foetuses.

All this is happening with almost no public debate. The British Department of the Environment has seen fit to allow an acceleration of GMO releases into the environment. We already have pigs injected with human growth-promoting genes as well as sheep with genes taken from bacteria. In other words, the race is on—but where is it going and where will it stop? No-one knows, of course, which is why the alarm bells should now be ringing in all of us. And it is not too late to act. Much can be done to contain and curtail these developments.

At the most manipulative end of the spectrum is the desire by those who consider themselves to have "created" these new life-forms to patent them. This is to ensure that nobody should get the benefit of using the new life-form or its offspring without paying royalties to the original inventor. Farmers, for instance, will have no right to save and re-use the seed from genetically altered cereal strains, because they cannot claim to own the parent seed. They will be forced to buy anew from the original company.

THE HUMAN GENOME PROJECT

The Human Genome Project (origins: California), to which I alluded earlier, is, on the surface, a seemingly benign attempt to produce a detailed mapping of all our genes (some 50,000 to 100,000). Within the human genome there exist some 3 billion pairs of DNA: "If all the 3 billion letters were written down, they would fill roughly two hundred 1,000 page telephone directories. The ultimate aim of the Human Genome Project is to determine the entire sequence of DNA pairs in the human genome" (*Gen Ethics News*).

Let me quote further from the same source: "The French Genethon team have published the most detailed map yet of the human genome. The map contains 3,300 markers spread over the twenty-three [pairs of] human chromosomes. At the current rate of progress, the target for the first stage of the Human Genome Project, 5,000 markers, will have been reached by the end of 1994.

| COMMERCIAL EXPLOITATION

Consider this: By the time today's offspring see their grandchildren . . . it is more than likely that every gene will be clinically decoded, fully programmed and made available for commercial exploitation. Multiplex genetic testing based upon a single blood or tissue sample would at that stage become routine medical procedure.

Jack Wandall, *Akwesasne Notes*, January 1996.

"Meanwhile, an American scientist, Craig Venter, who was earlier at the centre of an international row about patenting the human genome, is steaming ahead with the second stage of the Human Genome Project, DNA sequencing. Venter has moved to the private sector Institute for Genome Research, which is non-profit-making, but linked to the profit-making biotechnology company, Human Genome Sciences. The *Financial Times* reports that he has already found as many as 30,000 genes out of the 50,000–100,000 in the human genome and will probably have a virtually complete set in one or two years. Human Genome Sciences has filed twenty-five patent applications on the DNA sequences discovered so far. If the patents are granted (which is far from certain), a private company will have monopoly control over the human genome. The consequences of what Venter calls his 'giant business and social experiment' can only be guessed at."

We would be deeply naive to believe that such a project only exists for benign medical research. One does not have to look far to see the enormous commercial advantage which lies just under the surface and the immense power which could be wielded by any body or corporation owning the copyright of this awesome genetic map.

THE BIG QUESTION

The big question is: How do we overcome this latest bandwagon of technological terrorism and protect the sanctity of human life?

We must passionately counter these attempts to put life into a laboratory and engage in laboratory language to describe it, for it is as indefensible as any other form of repression of the living spirit. The gene pool is our common inheritance, our shared ancestry, it is the source of biodiversity and it enhances the very essence and mystery of life, which we have hardly begun to comprehend or express. Indeed, our ability to express the fullness of human potential which we each inherit is still largely an undeveloped art. Let it not be irrevocably altered by anyone or anything.

Our success in overcoming the gene industry hinges upon overcoming the fatalistic assumption that such issues are somehow outside us and beyond our control, for it is precisely this attitude upon which corporate giantism feeds. Protecting reverence for life is not a passive affair. Those who pride themselves in having a more conscious grasp of the way ahead have a special responsibility to act on their knowledge. If you never knew where to draw the line, let your genes finally make up your mind for you. For at the end of the day we all need to ask ourselves this question: do we want to retain responsibility for our destinies or allow others to decide them for us?

PERIODICAL BIBLIOGRAPHY

The following articles have been selected to supplement the diverse views presented in this chapter. Addresses are provided for periodicals not indexed in the *Readers' Guide to Periodical Literature*, the *Alternative Press Index*, the *Social Sciences Index*, or the *Index to Legal Periodicals and Books*.

Lori Andrews	"Body Science," *ABA Journal*, April 1997.
Maureen Dezell	"Genetic Testing: Do You Really Want to Know?" *American Health for Women*, March 1997.
Ted Gideonse	"Are We an Endangered Species?" *Advocate*, May 27, 1997.
Stephen Goode	"Questioning Rights to Life," *Insight*, June 26, 1995. Available from 3600 New York Ave. NE, Washington, DC 20002.
Elizabeth R. Hepburn	"Genetic Testing and Early Diagnosis and Intervention: Boon or Burden?" *Journal of Medical Ethics*, April 1996.
John Hodgson	"There's a Whole Lot of Nothing Going On," *Bio/Technology*, July 1995. Available from PO Box 1721, Riverton, NJ 08077-7321.
Leslie Alan Horvitz	"'Vampire Project' Raises Issue of Patents for Human Genes," *Insight*, July 22, 1996.
Michael Kinsley	"Oh, My Aching Genes!" *Time*, September 29, 1997.
Tony McGleenan	"Human Gene Therapy and Slippery Slope Arguments," *Journal of Medical Ethics*, December 1995.
George Poste	"Genomics," *Vital Speeches of the Day*, January 1, 1995.
Philip E. Ross	"Is DNA P.C.?" *Forbes*, October 9, 1995.
Charles Siebert	"The DNA We've Been Dealt," *New York Times Magazine*, September 17, 1995.
Gurney Williams III	"Altered States," *American Legion Magazine*, October 1997. Available from 5561 W. 74th St., Indianapolis, IN 46268.

GLOSSARY

AID   Artificial insemination by donor.

brain death   A legal condition of death in which a person's brain is no longer functioning. A person may be declared brain-dead even though his or her heart is still beating.

cell line   A group of cells containing the entire genetic code of an individual; these cells can be sustained and grown in laboratory culture media and are believed to be immortal.

chromosome   A chain of genetic material in the cell nucleus, consisting of **DNA**, **RNA**, and protein.

clone   A **gene**, cell, or other organism that is genetically identical to another gene, cell, or organism; also, to create such a genetically identical organism.

Diamond v. Chakrabarty   A 1980 case in which the U.S. Supreme Court ruled that an organism genetically altered by humans could be patented.

DNA   Deoxyribonucleic acid; the genetic material found in all living things; it exists in cells in the form of a double helix.

embryo   The developing human from about two weeks to about eight weeks after conception.

eugenics   The science of improving a race or breed through some form of genetic control, such as selective breeding.

fibroblast cell   A specialized cell, such as an organ cell.

gamete   A reproductive cell, such as an egg or sperm.

gene   A specialized segment of **DNA** whose sequence encodes the structure of a protein; genes are responsible for the inherited characteristics of all life forms.

gene therapy   The insertion of normal or altered **genes** into cells in an attempt to overcome the effects of defective genes.

genetic engineering   A technology used to alter the genetic material of living cells so that they will produce new substances or perform new functions.

genome   The complete set of **genes** in an organism.

genotype   An organism's genetic makeup.

germ cell   A reproductive cell.

Human Genome Diversity Project   An international project to document the genetic variation of humans around the world.

Human Genome Project   The federally funded initiative to map and sequence the entire human **genome**.

in vitro fertilization   A process in which an egg cell is fertilized with a sperm cell outside the woman's body.

ischemia   The deterioration of an organ due to the lack of blood flow.

IVF   **In vitro fertilization**.

marker gene   A **gene** used to help recognize and identify other genes or gene patterns.

OPO   Organ procurement organization.

pellucida zona   A natural shell that surrounds an **embryo**.

phenotype   The outward, physical appearance of an organism.

postmortem pregnancy   A pregnancy in which the mother is brain-dead but whose body is sustained on life-support equipment until her baby can be delivered.

RNA Ribonucleic acid; RNA molecules are made from and closely resemble **DNA**; these molecules carry genetic messages from DNA to the rest of the cell.

somatic cell A body cell not involved in reproduction.

surrogate mother A woman who bears a child for another couple.

transgenic A plant or animal into which has been inserted **DNA** from another species.

UAGA Uniform Anatomical Gift Act.

UNOS United Network for Organ Sharing.

xenotransplant An organ transplant in which an animal's organ is transplanted into a human.

zygote A fertilized egg.

For Further Discussion

Chapter 1

1. Andy H. Barnett, Roger D. Blair, and David L. Kaserman contend that the shortage of organs available for transplant would disappear if organs could be bought and sold on the open market. Alasdair Palmer asserts, however, that legalizing the sale of organs would encourage criminals to kidnap victims for their organs. Which author makes a stronger case? Support your answer with examples from the viewpoints.

2. Linda C. Fentiman advocates a policy called presumed consent to ease the shortage of organs available for transplant. In your opinion, should consent from the potential donor be presumed or required? Explain. Should the next-of-kin be able to override the donor's wishes? Why or why not?

3. The organization People for the Ethical Treatment of Animals contends that animal-to-human organ transplants should be banned since none have been successful. Jennifer Cunningham argues that if the transplant will save a human life, it should be permitted. Based on the viewpoints in this chapter, do you think animal-to-human organ transplants should be performed? Explain your answer.

4. Harry Wu is a Chinese-American human rights advocate who maintains that executions of Chinese prisoners are timed to coincide with the need for organ transplants. Robert Wright is a journalist who argues that using condemned prisoners as organ donors is a practical way of easing the shortage of organ donors. Which argument is more convincing and why? Do the authors' backgrounds influence your assessment of their arguments? Explain.

Chapter 2

1. Richard T. Hull, George Johnson, and *Nature Genetics* all maintain that cloning research could benefit humans. The National Bioethics Advisory Commission, Allen Verhey, and Kevin T. Fitzgerald contend, however, that the risks involved in cloning outweigh the benefits. In your opinion, would cloning humans violate the sanctity of human life? Use examples from the viewpoints to support your answer. Which of the arguments is more convincing, and why?

2. Some critics of cloning argue that people have a right to an open future, in which they are free to choose their own future based on their wants and desires and not on the expecta-

tions of their parent/genetic twin. Do you think a clone would be able to grow up without trying to fulfill the expectations of his or her parent/genetic twin? Why or why not?

CHAPTER 3

1. Both Janice G. Raymond and Rickie Solinger identify themselves as feminists, yet they hold opposing views on reproductive technologies. How does Solinger respond to Raymond's argument that these technologies are a form of violence against women? Whose argument is more convincing, and why?

2. Scott B. Rae contends that surrogate mothering is nothing more than legalized baby selling. Wendy McElroy maintains that such criticisms are invalid. Based on your reading of the viewpoints, which author makes a stronger case? How might the author's gender influence his or her assessment? Explain your answer.

3. The reasons a doctor may give to sustain the pregnancy of a dead pregnant woman are invalid, according to Hilde Lindemann Nelson. Christoph Anstötz maintains, however, that keeping a woman alive until her baby is born does not deprive her of her dignity. Using examples from the viewpoints, do you think postmortem pregnancies are ethical? Why or why not?

4. Barbara Ehrenreich argues that pregnancy and childrearing are activities that are too difficult for postmenopausal women. How does Lawrence M. Hinman respond to her concerns? In your opinion, should postmenopausal women bear children? Support your answer using examples from the viewpoints.

CHAPTER 4

1. Carol Krause tells how genetic testing is just one weapon in an arsenal to fight the cancer that runs in her family. Ruth Hubbard and Elijah Wald argue that genes alone are not responsible for many diseases. Would you undergo genetic testing to determine if you were predisposed to a specific disease? Explain your answer.

2. Richard D. Land and C. Ben Mitchell contend that patenting human genetic material treats people as property and is therefore morally wrong. How does David B. Resnick respond to this argument? Which viewpoint is more convincing, and why?

ORGANIZATIONS TO CONTACT

The editors have compiled the following list of organizations concerned with the issues debated in this book. The descriptions are derived from materials provided by the organizations. All have publications or information available for interested readers. The list was compiled on the date of publication of the present volume; the information provided here may change. Be aware that many organizations take several weeks or longer to respond to inquiries, so allow as much time as possible.

Ag Bioethics Forum
c/o Professor Gary Comstock, Bioethics Program Coordinator
402 Catt Hall, Iowa State University, Ames, IA 50011-1306
(515) 294-0054 • e-mail: comstock@iastate.edu
web address: http://www.grad-college.iastate.edu/bioethics
The forum examines bioethical issues concerning agriculture, food, animals, and the environment. It publishes *Ag Bioethics Forum*, a biannual newsletter that explores the ethical dilemmas that arise when genetic engineering is applied to agriculture.

American Anti-Vivisection Society
801 Old York Rd., Suite 204, Jenkintown, PA 19046-1685
(215) 887-0816 • fax: (215) 887-2088
e-mail: aavsonline@aol.com • web address: http://www.aavs.org
The oldest animal rights group in America, the society opposes all animal experimentation. It publishes educational pamphlets and the quarterly *AV* magazine.

American Civil Liberties Union (ACLU)
125 Broad St., 18th Fl., New York, NY 10004-2400
(212) 549-2500 • publications: (800) 775-ACLU (2258)
e-mail: aclu@aclu.org • web address: http://www.aclu.org
The ACLU champions the civil rights provided by the U.S. Constitution. The union is concerned that genetic testing may lead to genetic discrimination in the workplace, including the refusal to hire and the termination of employees who are at risk for developing genetic conditions. The ACLU publishes a variety of handbooks, pamphlets, reports, and newsletters, including the quarterly *Civil Liberties* and the monthly *Civil Liberties Alert*.

American Medical Association (AMA)
515 N. State St., Chicago, IL 60610
(312) 464-5000
web address: http://www.ama-assn.org
The AMA is the largest professional association for medical doctors. It helps set standards for medical education and practices, and it is a powerful lobby in Washington for physicians' interests. The association

publishes journals for many medical fields, including the monthly *Archives of Surgery* and the weekly *JAMA*.

American Society of Law, Medicine, and Ethics (ASLME)

765 Commonwealth Ave., 16th Fl., Boston, MA 02215
(617) 262-4990 • fax: (617) 437-7596
e-mail: aslme@bu.edu • web address: http://www.aslme.org

The society's members include physicians, attorneys, health care administrators, and others interested in the relationship between law, medicine, and ethics. It takes no positions but acts as a forum for discussion of issues such as genetic engineering. The organization has an information clearinghouse and a library. It publishes the quarterlies *American Journal of Law & Medicine* and the *Journal of Law, Medicine & Ethics*; the periodic *ASLME Briefings*; and various books.

BC Biotechnology Alliance (BCBA)

1122 Mainland St., #450, Vancouver, BC V6B 5L1, CANADA
(604) 689-5602 • fax: (604) 689-4198
web address: http://www.biotech.bc.ca

The BCBA is an association for producers and users of biotechnology. The alliance works to increase public awareness and understanding of biotechnology, including the awareness of its potential contributions to society. The alliance's publications include the bimonthly newsletter *Biofax* and the annual magazine *Biotechnology in BC*.

Biotechnology Industry Organization (BIO)

1625 K St. NW, #1100, Washington, DC 20006
(202) 857-0244 • fax: (202) 857-0237
e-mail: info@bio.org • web address: http://www.bio.org

BIO is composed of companies engaged in industrial biotechnology. It monitors government actions that affect biotechnology and promotes increased public understanding of biotechnology through its educational activities and workshops. BIO is committed to the socially responsible use of biotechnology to save or improve lives, improve the quality and abundance of food, and clean up hazardous waste. It publishes on-line bulletins and the bimonthly newsletter *BIO News*.

Childbirth By Choice Trust

344 Bloor St. West, #306, Toronto, ON M5S 3A7, CANADA
(416) 961-7812 • fax: (416) 961-3473
e-mail: cbctrust@idirect.com
web address: http://web.idirect.com/~cbctrust

The trust aims to educate the public on fertility control issues, such as contraceptive use, abortion, and unintended pregnancy. It hopes to make all options available to women who are unhappily pregnant, including abortion, childbirth, and adoption. The trust provides educational pamphlets that provide information about fertility control issues, such as *Abortion: The Medical Procedure*, *Contraceptive Use in Canada*, and

Economics of Unintended Pregnancy. These pamphlets can be ordered through their website or by mail.

Council for Responsible Genetics
5 Upland Rd., Suite 3, Cambridge, MA 02140
(617) 868-0870 • fax: (617) 491-5344
e-mail: crg@essential.org • web address: http://www.essential.org/crg
The council is a national organization of scientists, health professionals, trade unionists, women's health activists, and others who work to ensure that biotechnology is developed safely and in the public interest. The council publishes the bimonthly newsletter *GeneWatch* and position papers on the Human Genome Project, genetic discrimination, germ-line modifications, and DNA-based identification systems.

Foundation for Biomedical Research
818 Connecticut Ave. NW, Suite 303, Washington, DC 20006
(202) 457-0654 • fax: (202) 457-0659
e-mail: info@fbresearch.org • web address: http://www.fbresearch.org
The foundation supports humane animal research and serves to inform and educate the public about the necessity and importance of laboratory animals in biomedical research and testing. It publishes a bimonthly newsletter, videos, films, and numerous background papers, including *The Use of Animals in Biomedical Research and Testing* and *Caring for Laboratory Animals.*

The Hastings Center
Garrison, NY 10524-5555
(914) 424-4040 • fax: (914) 424-4545
e-mail: mail@thehastingscenter.org
Since its founding in 1969, the center has played a central role in responding to advances in medicine, the biological sciences, and the social sciences by raising ethical questions related to such advances. It conducts research on ethical issues and provides consultations. The center publishes books, papers, guidelines, and the bimonthly *Hastings Center Report.*

Living Bank
PO Box 6725, Houston, TX 77265
(713) 528-2971 • fax: (713) 961-0979 • hot line: (800) 528-2971
e-mail: jeiche@livingbank.org
web address: http://www.livingbank.org
The bank is an international registry and referral service for people wishing to donate organs and/or tissue for transplantation, therapy, or research. Its volunteers speak to civic organizations about the benefits of organ donation, and its 350,000 donor population spreads through fifty states and sixty-three foreign countries. It provides educational materials on organ donation and publishes a bimonthly newsletter, the *Living Banker.*

People for the Ethical Treatment of Animals (PETA)
501 Front St., Norfolk, VA 23510
(757) 622-PETA (7382) • fax: (757) 622-0457
web address: http://envirolink.org/arrs/peta

PETA is an educational, activist group that opposes all forms of animal exploitation. It conducts rallies and demonstrations to focus attention on animal experimentation, the fur fashion industry, and the killing of animals for human consumption—three issues it considers institutionalized cruelty. Through the use of films, slides, and pictures, PETA hopes to educate the public about human chauvinist attitudes toward animals and about the conditions in slaughterhouses and research laboratories. It publishes reports on animal experimentation and animal farming and the periodic *People for the Ethical Treatment of Animals—Action Alerts*.

United Network for Organ Sharing (UNOS)
1100 Boulders Pkwy., Suite 500, Richmond, VA 23225
(804) 330-8500 • fax: (804) 330-8507
web address: http://www.unos.org

UNOS is a system of transplant and organ procurement centers, tissue-typing labs, and transplant surgical teams. It was formed to match organ donors with people in need of organs. By law, organs used for transplants must be cleared through UNOS. The network also formulates and implements national policies on equal access to organs and organ allocation, organ procurement, and AIDS testing. It publishes the quarterly *UNOS Update*.

BIBLIOGRAPHY OF BOOKS

Robert M. Arnold et al., eds.	Procuring Organs for Transplant: The Debate over Non-Heart-Beating Cadaver Protocols. Baltimore, MD: Johns Hopkins University Press, 1995.
Patricia Boling, ed.	Expecting Trouble: Surrogacy, Fetal Abuse, and New Reproductive Technologies. Boulder, CO: Westview Press, 1995.
Ed Brassard	Body for Sale: An Inside Look at Medical Research, Drug Testing, and Organ Transplants and How You Can Profit from Them. Boulder, CO: Paladin Press, 1996.
Arthur Caplan	Due Consideration: Controversy in the Age of Medical Miracles. New York: Wiley, 1997.
Arthur Caplan	Moral Matters: Ethical Issues in Medicine and the Life Sciences. New York: Wiley, 1995.
Ron Cole-Turner, ed.	Human Cloning: Religious Responses. Louisville, KY: Westminster John Knox, 1997.
Gail Dutton	A Matter of Trust: The Guide to Gestational Surrogacy. Irvine, CA: Clouds, 1997.
Dion Farquhar	The Other Machine: Discourse and Reproductive Technologies. New York: Routledge, 1996.
John Harris	Clones, Genes, and Immortality: Ethics and the Genetic Revolution. New York: Oxford University Press, 1998.
Andrew Kimbrell	The Human Body Shop: The Engineering and Marketing of Life. Washington, DC: Regnery, 1998.
Philip Kitcher	The Lives to Come: The Genetic Revolution and Human Possibilities. New York: Simon & Schuster, 1996.
Mary Kittredge	Organ Transplants. New York: Chelsea House, 1995.
David Lamb	Organ Transplants and Ethics. Brookfield, VT: Avebury, 1996.
Gina Maranto	Quest for Perfection: The Drive to Breed Better Human Beings. New York: Lisa Drew Books, 1996.
Elizabeth L. Marshall	Conquering Infertility: Medical Challenges and Moral Dilemmas. New York: Watts, 1997.
Scott McCartney	Defying the Gods: Inside the New Frontiers of Organ Transplants. New York: Lisa Drew Books, 1994.
Peter McCullagh	Brain Dead, Brain Absent, Brain Donors: Human Subjects or Human Objects? New York: Wiley, 1993.
Gilbert C. Meilaender	Body, Soul, and Bioethics. Notre Dame, IN: University of Notre Dame Press, 1995.

Cheryl L. Meyer

The Wandering Uterus: Politics and the Reproductive Rights of Women. New York: New York University Press, 1997.

Derel Morgan

Surrogacy and the Moral Economy. Brookfield, VT: Ashgate, 1997.

Timothy F. Murphy and Marc A. Lappé, eds.

Justice and the Human Genome Project. Berkeley and Los Angeles: University of California Press, 1994.

National Bioethics Advisory Commission

Cloning Human Beings: Report and Recommendations of the National Bioethics Advisory Commission. Rockville, MD: GPO, 1997.

Gregory E. Pence

Who's Afraid of Human Cloning? Lanham, MD: Rowman & Littlefield, 1998.

Jeffrey Prottas

The Most Useful Gift: Altruism and the Public Policy of Organ Transplants. San Francisco: Jossey-Bass, 1994.

Janice G. Raymond

Women as Wombs: Reproductive Technologies and the Battle over Women's Freedom. San Francisco: HarperSanFrancisco, 1996.

Bernard E. Rollin

The Frankenstein Syndrome: Ethical and Social Issues in the Genetic Engineering of Animals. New York: Cambridge University Press, 1995.

Marine Rothblatt

Unzipped Genes: Taking Charge of Baby-Making in the New Millennium. Philadelphia: Temple University Press, 1997.

Frederick B. Rudolph and Larry B. McIntire, eds.

Biotechnology: Science, Engineering, and Ethical Challenges for the Twenty-First Century. Washington, DC: Joseph Henry Press, 1996.

Lee M. Silver

Remaking Eden: Cloning and Beyond in a Brave New World. New York: Avon Books, 1997.

David C. Thomasma and Thomasine Kushner, eds.

Birth to Death: Science and Bioethics. New York: Cambridge University Press, 1996.

LeRoy Walters and Julie Gage Palmer

The Ethics of Human Gene Therapy. New York: Oxford University Press, 1997.

INDEX